Making Manhood

Making Manhood

Growing Up Male in
Colonial New England

Anne S. Lombard

HARVARD UNIVERSITY PRESS
Cambridge, Massachusetts
London, England
2003

Library of Congress Cataloging-in-Publication Data

Lombard, Anne S.
   Making manhood : growing up male in colonial New England /
  Anne S. Lombard
     p. cm.
   Includes bibliographical references and index.
   ISBN 0-674-01058-2 (alk. paper)
   1. Men—New England—Social conditions. 2. New England—History—
Colonial period, ca. 1600–1775. 3. Sex role—New England—History.
4. Masculinity—New England—History. I. Title.

HQ1090.5.N36L66 2003
305.31'0974—dc21   2002191336

To Mark

Contents

Preface

This book began when I was a graduate student at the University of California, Los Angeles, in the 1990s. I think it will help the reader to understand what it is trying to say if I also explain that my path to graduate school was not the usual path of a history student straight out of college. Instead, it meandered and wound about, for I first spent almost a decade getting a legal education and then working as a lawyer before deciding that to live the kind of life I wanted, I needed to return to school to learn more about the past.

When I returned to graduate school in history in 1990, I was sure that I knew what I wanted to write about. During the 1980s, while working in the male-dominated world of corporate litigation and surrounded by friends who liked to get together and argue about constitutional law, I had sometimes thought about the ways in which Americans' often admirable commitment to egalitarian principles is limited by assumptions about status categories such as gender and race. For example, it seemed to me that basic assumptions about things like what it means to be a productive worker or how we expect citizens to behave were inextricably bound up with the unstated assumptions that workers and citizens are white men, and that white men behave in particular ways. When I began my graduate work at UCLA I told my professors that I wanted to think about how struggles over gender had been implicated in the larger history of American political conflict and political ideology ever since this country's colonial origins. The three American historians whom I asked to be on my dissertation committee were supportive, perhaps because all three are women who had entered the profession when it was mostly male and had thought about similar issues.

But as I became more involved with my course work, and in discussions with various professors, I found myself becoming fascinated by a different set of intellectual concerns, which grew out of feminism but also out of my personal experience at that particular stage in my life. By 1990, when I entered graduate school, I was the mother of two small children. Like many other idealistic couples of our generation, my husband and I were committed to the idea of equal parenting, so we took turns with everything: feeding babies, working on papers, going to the library, going to the park. I wondered how our children's experience growing up in this newfangled family would affect the way they imagined the world and their own roles in it, and I became increasingly interested in thinking about parenting and gender.

Luckily for me, my advisors in the history department remained supportive as I began to develop a study of gender and parenting in early New England. They not only shared ideas about how the experience of raising children might have been shaped by the religious, economic, and social environment of colonial New England but also offered empathetic insights gleaned from their own experiences raising children in the twentieth century. My dissertation advisor, Ruth Bloch, who has herself written about such subjects as gender and the history of motherhood, got me thinking about how historical variations in parenting arrangements might affect not only gender ideologies but also the entire cultural imagination of particular societies. Her own theorizing about gender and culture, in fact, offered a whole new intellectual perspective from which I began to think about history. Joyce Appleby listened hour after hour as my thinking about the Puritans meandered, evolved, and, finally, through her trenchant questions, became focused on the subject of masculinity. And Regina Morantz-Sanchez responded to my ideas with her characteristic enthusiasm and sharp wit, and reminded me when my confidence flagged that this was a worthwhile subject on which to focus such a large part of my life.

This study of masculinity in early American history was born, then, out of a set of interests raised by contemporary life. While it is based on a close reading of sources left by people who lived two and three hundred years ago, whatever insights it contains have been based on my attempt to imagine how their experiences were both different from and similar to my own experiences as a late-twentieth-century American parent. My own attempt to understand what manhood meant for early New England men is, of course, limited by the fact that they were male and I am not, but trying to imagine what it was like to be an eighteenth-century man has been an engaging project for me, and I hope it will be equally so for readers.

In addition to the teachers mentioned here, a number of colleagues and friends have been influential in helping me to frame the issues and refine the conclusions I have reached. My thanks to Holly Brewer, Jim Drake, Tony Iaccarino, Lisa Jacobson, John Majewski, Richard Olivas, Jim Pearson, Jonathan Sassi, Paula Scott, and Barbara Wallace for reading drafts, asking important questions, and providing me with a community that made the project seem worthwhile. As the manuscript evolved into a book, Sharon Block, Holly Brewer, Trevor Burnard, Nina Dayton, Kenneth Lockridge, Tony Rotundo, and Danny Vickers provided careful readings and astute comments on various versions, for which I am very grateful. Joyce Seltzer at Harvard University Press has been an astute and supportive editor throughout the revising process. I would also like to thank Jeff Kehoe for his help with the manuscript at an earlier stage.

Because my career path has not been a traditional one, I have also accumulated debts of gratitude to a number of teachers and mentors who have supported my efforts to become a historian, including all of my professors at UCLA as well as Richard Bushman and Eben Moglen at Columbia University. In addition, I would like to express my gratitude to the three historians who set me on this path in the first place: Allan L. Damon and the late Michael Jimenez, two of the most inspiring teachers any young person could have asked for, and Shirley S. Abrahamson, who enabled me to imagine for the first time how a life of the mind might be lived in the real world.

This book was completed with assistance from a UCLA History Department Dissertation Fellowship and research grants from the UCLA Center for the Study of Women and Gender and the Mellon Foundation. My thanks to the staffs at the Massachusetts Historical Society, the American Antiquarian Society, the Peabody Essex Museum, the Boston Public Library, the Huntington Library, the Connecticut Historical Society, the New England Historic Genealogical Society, and the Yale University Library for help with research and for their permission to quote material from their collections in this book. I would also like to thank the history department at California State University, San Marcos, for giving me the time to complete this book.

Finally, I wish to thank all those who have provided moral and intellectual support throughout this project: Jennifer Brand, Danny Kessler,

Susan Elsen, Charlie Rooney, Alice Thurston, Alice Reynolds, Scott Williams, Larry Young, Anne Haskins, Jenny Oderkirk, Lisa Chapman, Janet Lent, Eunice Ahn, Tom Millar, Jim and Tamoe Lombard, Claire and Elwin Cammack, my mother, Arlene Lombard, and above all my father, Richard Lombard, without whom this book would never have been written. My children, Jessie and Jimmy Cammack, have willingly shared their lives with their mom's book for as long as they can remember. Finally, my deepest gratitude goes to Mark Cammack, whose love, patience, and belief in me have given my life its center.

Introduction:
The Ideal of Rational Manhood

Toward the end of the 1600s, the place we now call New England was an isolated stretch of territory on the far northern and western edge of the English-speaking Atlantic world. It was an austere place, with its gray skies, rocky seacoast, and little villages, each dominated by the spire of its plain, stern congregational church. Let us picture it in the early summer, full of activity. Here and there along the coast were towns crowded with houses and shops, the streets full of seamen and merchants, craftsmen's apprentices on errands, children playing, housewives on their way to call on their neighbors. Inland, on farms hewn from the woods, cattle grazed and corn was beginning to grow. Fathers and sons worked outside, on land bounded by walls built of the stones they had wrested from the rocky soil. Mothers and their older daughters worked within differently bounded spaces, inside spare wooden houses and in gardens that lay just beyond kitchen doors, younger children playing nearby.

The men of early Anglo-American New England have been the stuff of Americans' earliest history lessons; from the first dawning of American national consciousness, they have populated our literature and our myths. Many a scholar has tried to understand and come to terms with their complex theology, their patriarchal, anti-individualistic social values, and their distinctively religious outlook on life. Many have also been critical of them, for they clearly did not aspire to such modern democratic ideals as tolerance, respect for individual rights, and social equality. Recently, some have tried to move them from the center of our historical consciousness by telling instead stories about the white women, Native Americans, and other marginalized people who lived in

1

their society and in the larger English colonial world. But the early Puritan "founding fathers" continue to intrigue us, with their sober visages gazing down from those old portraits, their complex ideas about predestination and original sin, their harsh judgments of people who were different.

Every generation has to face the past in its own way, and for us, some of the most interesting questions about these stern, austere early New Englanders have concerned their ideas about gender—that is, the culturally and historically constructed distinctions that they ascribed to women and men. Women's historians have for the first time brought to life for us the women who inhabited the houses, gardens, and streets of these early New England farms and towns.[1] It has become clear that struggles over gender, and in particular over the proper place of women, were central to the colonists' experiences in North America from the earliest years.[2] In turn, our new appreciation that the colonial enterprise involved both women and men has thrown the subject of manhood into new perspective. We have become more conscious than any generation before us that experiences of manhood and ideas about masculinity are as culturally and historically constructed as those of womanhood. But we still have little sense of what this actually signified for Anglo-Americans in early New England.[3]

What did it mean to be a man in early New England? To what ideals of masculinity or manhood did Anglo-American colonists there aspire? What were the social, cultural, and emotional imperatives that shaped those ideals, and in particular, how did women affect the ways that manhood was imagined? How did men think and feel about their bodies and their sexuality? What kinds of husbands and fathers were they? Did their sons love them and want to be like them, or did they secretly resent them and long to get away? How were their ideals of manhood related to attempts by the Puritan founders of the New England colonies to reform early modern English society and culture? And how did those ideals ultimately become obsolete, to be replaced by others more like those with which we are now familiar? Finding the answers may tell us something interesting not only about these people, who are part of our past, but also about the historical process that has made us who we are.

To answer these questions, we will need to begin by placing colonial New Englanders and their families in the larger context of both English and North American history. Their story begins in England, sometime in the latter part of the sixteenth century, where society was in the throes of a transition from aristocratic feudalism to agrarian capitalism. The commercialization of the economy and the growth of a market in land had produced a growing group of what I will call middling people, shopkeepers, tradesmen, and prosperous yeomen whose material prosperity made it possible for them to lead a particular kind of family life. Their moderate wealth both enhanced their ability to provide for their children and strengthened the authority of male household heads, for a man's legal ownership of his family's productive property gave him considerable economic control over his dependents. In turn, a new sectarian Protestant ideology added a religious dimension to the man's familial role. Puritan preachers and moral writers spiritualized the household and suggested that husbands and fathers should assume greater responsibilities as the spiritual and moral guides for their families—as little priests within the home. These writers also suggested that fathers were the centerpiece of the social order, not only because they protected their families from want but also because they could exercise control over their dependents and create an orderly, disciplined society.[4]

The ideology of the English Protestant Reformation found its greatest resonance among people who lived in England's southeastern region, an area of relatively advanced commercial development. Most of the converts to the new dissenting sects, whom their critics called Puritans, were shopkeepers, craftsmen, or prosperous yeomen, and their families: people who had benefited from economic development. They were the kinds of people whose family lives had most come to resemble the patriarchal nuclear family that Puritan ministers portrayed as vital to social and moral order.

But as they looked around them, many of these middling people saw a society that seemed increasingly in disarray. The same economic transition that had allowed them to prosper had produced a time of great dislocation for the poor. The decline of manorial tenures and the privatization of land were forcing many former tenants off land they had inhabited for generations, and they had to subsist instead through a variety of economic strategies, from working for low wages as agricultural laborers, to working at by-employments, to begging. Middling people viewed the social results of these strategies with horror: the increased independence and visibility of poor women, who often fended for themselves by taking advantage of opportunities to sell domestic produce or to work for wages; the youths whose parents could not provide for them and who wandered the roads in search of work; the apparent increase in open hostility by the poor against the rich. Their dismay over these changes in traditional forms of community life made the Puritans want to create a purer, ostensibly more Christian way of life.[5]

During the years between 1630 and 1642, a period of increasing political instability and religious conflict in England, thousands of these English Puritans migrated to the Massachusetts Bay Colony, Connecticut, and New Haven to create new, more godly societies there. A smaller number from another group of dissenters had already settled in Plymouth, beginning in 1620. Most of the migrants were middling people: shopkeepers and craftsmen and their families. While they came hoping to create a new world in New England organized around biblically sanctioned communities, they also carried with them a set of expectations very similar to those of other middling English people about the kinds of lives they would lead.[6] Among these, two expectations would be particularly important in shaping the family strategies they adopted. The first concerned their economic aspirations, and the second concerned their attitudes about women.

Most middling Englishmen in the sixteenth and seventeenth centuries hoped that they would live out their adult lives in economic independence. While the economic transition of the sixteenth century had made England into a more commercialized society, the people who experienced it continued to aspire to an ideal of property ownership and self-employment that hearkened back to an earlier period, an ideal that they called "competence." To be competent or independent was described in masculine terms; it referred to a man's ability to support himself and his family without becoming permanently dependent on wage earning, debt, or other forms of outside control. Specifically, it meant freedom from dependence on feudal lords—once the fate of English peasants—and being able to avoid the dislocations that were driving so many English men into a low-paid proletarian workforce. The best source of independence, or competence, was owning land, which gave men not only a livelihood but also political privileges such as the right to vote and to serve in local offices. But a man could also become competent by acquiring the skills and capital that would allow him, with the assistance of a wife and other helpers, to provide a comfortable level of economic independence for himself and his family.[7]

This ideal of male independence was in some sense built on a fiction, because a substantial part of men's fortunes (and the authority that flowed from them) rested on the hard work, frugality, and trustworthiness of their wives. In part, it may have been middling men's awareness of their dependence on women that provoked a lively discussion among English pamphlet writers during the late sixteenth century about the nature of women, a discussion that depicted women in contradictory ways. Writers defending women tended to celebrate marriage and praise women in their role as wives. Advice books reminded men that their economic well-being depended on the industry of their wives and "help-meets." But other writers articulated a number of traditional stereotypes that suggested women's potential unreliability, portraying them as being by nature unstable, changeable, and dangerous. Women were inherently more lustful and emotional than men, they said, for they had a weaker rational capacity, and hence were more subject than men to corruption.[8] At the same time that this debate was taking place, a growing number of prosecutions against witches, scolds, and adulterous wives gave expression to a subterranean hostility toward widows and other women who would not be governed by men, perhaps expressing men's antipathy toward the kinds of independent women who failed to conform to their image of the ideal wife.[9]

But in important ways, the ideal of competence was probably shared by members of both sexes, with men and women alike expecting to work together to achieve an economic competence if they could. The Puritan men and women who migrated to New England shared these same aspirations, a fact that is illustrated by an incident from the early history of the Plymouth colony. According to the colony's governor and first historian, William Bradford, early attempts by Plymouth's leaders to have settlers farm the land communally, as they believed the apostles would have done, were met with bitter complaints from the people. Young men "did repine that they should spend their time and strength to work for other men's wives and children without any recompense," while strong men complained that they "had no more in division of victuals and clothes" than weaker men. Older and "graver men" resented having to do the same kind of work as "the meaner and younger sort." And for women, "to be commanded to do service for other men, as dressing their meat, washing their clothes, etc., they deemed it a kind of slavery, neither could many husbands well brook it." These men and women expected to spend their time doing work defined by their roles in a nuclear family economy, on privately owned land. These expectations proved too powerful to be swept away, and in 1623 the colony's leaders gave in to popular pressure and began the process of privatizing land ownership, allocating separate parcels to individual families to farm for their own support.[10]

The public policies of most of the colonial governments helped a large percentage of those who went to New England to realize their wish to live in an independent, property-owning family group after they arrived. Most of the migrants became farmers, regardless of what their occupation had been back in England. And the governments were committed to helping them obtain plenty of farmland. Most colonies distributed land very widely to the male heads of settler families, meaning that New England became a society dominated by politically enfranchised yeoman farmers. Although Native American peoples already lived on the land, the colonial governments never fully acknowledged their presence or their right to remain. In 1675, a long-simmering conflict over appropriate land use boiled over into a full-blown war between various factions of Indians and Englishmen, out of which the English colonial governments emerged the victors. Their military triumph ensured that Anglo-American land use patterns prevailed in the region and, by driving away many of the Native Americans, made the land available for succeeding generations of Englishmen.[11]

Just as significant for the settlers' economic future was the particular set of demographic and geographic conditions they found in New England. Unlike most other European colonizers in the Americas, among whom single young men predominated, the English people who settled New England came mostly in family groups.[12] Although the land in New England was rocky and hard to farm, with work it could afford them an independent living. But lacking ready access to any other labor source, to survive and prosper the settlers had to rely on their family members much more heavily than farmers in England had done. Male householders would be far more dependent on their wives and on their sons in New England than they had been before.[13]

As of about 1676, when this study begins, Anglo-American colonists in Massachusetts, Connecticut, and Rhode Island were no longer newcomers to North America. Most of them were descended from immigrants who had come over in the Great Migration. By this time, with their economy slowly emerging from a long recession and recently shaken by the destructive war with the Indians, a small number of Anglo-American New Englanders were becoming involved in commerce or working in the seafaring and shipbuilding trades in towns like Boston, Salem, and New Haven. Over the next century this commercial and maritime sector would grow, but most families would continue to make their living through farming until the end of the eighteenth century. Their commitment to the ideal of competence and to the nuclear family as the center of economic life had produced an unusual set of family dynamics. Widespread land ownership and the absence of a labor market gave male household heads even more power over family members than their English counterparts had. The role of reformed Protestant thought in enhancing their authority as fathers was probably greater in a society so dominated by the Puritans. Fathers made decisions about production and work, influenced their children's decisions about when and whom to marry, and controlled their sons' access to productive property. These were patriarchal families.[14]

The extensive powers of fathers in seventeenth century New England, however, did not mean that these patriarchal families were "traditional," as many historians once assumed.[15] Patriarchal authority within early modern English and Anglo-American New England families was bound up with an emerging commitment to increasing economic productivity, expanding private property rights, and reforming an unruly traditional culture. These were modern commitments, not traditional ones. They entailed both an increased level of interdependence between family members and a heightened level of investment in the future economic as well as spiritual well-being of children. New England parents were determined that sons, like their fathers, would be able to enjoy the privileges of patriarchal status and a "competence," and would grow up to live in a godly society.[16]

How did the members of this society, with its heightened focus on the patriarchal family as the center of work and spiritual life, imagine the ideal man? Before we can answer this question, the first issue is how to address it using available sources. Where does a historian look to find evidence about ideals of manhood in a place as remote in time as New England in the seventeenth and eighteenth centuries? Today it is easy to find explicit statements of how modern Americans think about masculinity. Not only can we turn to survey data or sources from popular culture, such as movies and novels, for evidence about our ideals of manhood, but we also have access to scholarly debates about the hormonal, psychological, social, and cultural sources of manhood. A recent article from a widely read magazine, for example, claims that testosterone levels in men "correlat[e] with energy, self-confidence, competitiveness, tenacity, strength and sexual drive."[17] Such a source provides a good catalogue of the qualities that most modern Americans would identify as masculine, as well as our assumption that these masculine traits are created by hormones.

But evidence of early modern English assumptions about manhood is not so easy to find, for people rarely spoke or wrote explicitly about them. One could not walk into a bookstore in Boston in 1690 and find a dozen books giving advice on how to raise a boy, or pick up a newspaper to read an article debating whether masculinity is more influenced by hormones or socialization. In fact, a perusal of books read by seventeenth- and eighteenth-century New Englanders will rarely yield even a reference to the term *masculine,* which we use to describe characteristically male as opposed to female traits, for the words *masculine* and *masculinity* were not yet really a part of the English language.[18] The absence of such familiar words provides an important clue about early modern categories for classifying men and non-men, for manhood in the early modern era was not defined as the opposite or the complement of womanhood, as it is today.

The clearest, most explicit articulations of early New Englanders' assumptions about manhood come from prescriptive literature: letters from fathers instructing their sons in how to behave, sermons or obituaries describing men who led an exemplary life, books of advice for boys, descriptions of ideal family life, medical books explaining ideas about procreation and contraception. Such books were probably the most popular type of literature in the bookstores and libraries of seventeenth- and eighteenth-century New England. We will find no references here to "masculine" traits, but there are references to people, or qualities, that are described as "manly."[19] The manly traits, it appears, were not generally physical; they were moral and psychological. Sermons and obituaries describing admirable men, for example, most commonly listed maturity, rationality, responsibility, self-control, and courage as the qualities men should strive for.[20] Similarly, the writers of secular books advising boys in how to succeed in life emphasized the same virtues of rationality, moderation, and self-control.[21] Other seventeenth-century English sources, too, suggest that manliness was the opposite of sensual indulgence or "effeminate" longings for pleasure.[22]

Manly qualities were moral virtues, not physical characteristics. This tells us something important about the conceptualization of manhood in this culture. Manly characteristics were not attributes that a male person would have been born with; they had to be acquired. Certain anthropologists have observed that manhood in most cultures has to be made or earned—that it is not simply a physical fact.[23] Early New Englanders' concepts of manliness expressed such an understanding of manhood. Our modern perception that adult male gender identity is simply a function of a natural essence like testosterone would, to early modern English people, have seemed not only strange but inaccurate. They *did* believe that certain types of behavior were rooted in the male body. But the source of this behavior, the "passions" (the rough equivalent of what we would call hormones), could endanger manhood and had to be mastered before manhood status could be claimed.

The source of manhood, then, was not inside the individual but without, in the attribution of virtues that signified a community's agreement that a man had fulfilled its expectations for the male role. Concepts of self in early modern Europe were often understood more as a function of social convention than in terms of the modern notion that people's true selves are defined by some inner essence.[24] As this book will argue, claims to manhood in early New England were based less on having a male body than on having attained rationality, self-control, and mastery over whatever was passionate, sensual, and natural in the male self. Thus, ministers in seventeenth- and eighteenth-century Massachusetts often exhorted their male listeners to "play the man," which meant to act responsibly and virtuously instead of being selfish or childish.[25] Manhood was a role, not a physical essence, achieved by an act of will.

Early New Englanders also understood ideal manhood very differently than European Americans in the nineteenth century would come to do. The manly Puritan was no rugged individualist, no self-made entrepreneur, pursuing his own dreams of success on the frontier or in the marketplace, like the men who populated nineteenth-century American dime novels and folklore. He was a sober, conservative father, responsible for a household full of dependents. His "sphere" was not separate from the sphere of women and family life but bound up with it: as a recent study of colonial New England men put it, "a man demonstrated his worth in the domestic context of service to his family and community."[26]

Also, unlike nineteenth-century Americans, early New Englanders did not imagine manhood as simply the opposite of womanhood. Instead, they conceptualized gender in hierarchical terms. A hierarchical way of thinking about gender can be found in the medical literature of the period, which depicts the male body not as the opposite or complement of the female, but as superior to it.[27] The idea of manhood articulated in prescriptive literature similarly placed manly men in a hierarchy, but there they were being compared with less manly or unmanly men as much as to women. Moreover, the relevant distinction between manly men and others appears to have been age. It is notable that the qualities of manly men were the kinds of traits that are more likely to be displayed by mature, middle-aged men than by youths: rationality, moderation, self-control. Early New Englanders assumed that mature men were more capable of rational control over their passions than the young, who were still ruled by their appetites. They commonly voiced such aphorisms as, "At the flower of youth . . . the blood still boils," and believed that adultery and fornication were "particularly called Youthful Lusts."[28] They associated manliness with mature, rational household heads, property owners, and fathers.[29] So while we define masculinity in comparison to femininity, early New Englanders defined manhood at least partly in comparison with boyhood or dependence. A man who had achieved the status of an independent household head, responsible for his family, was more likely to be considered "manly" than a man who was still dependent on others (father, master, or employer).[30] Thus, a distinctive characteristic of manhood in colonial New England was that it was a category of age as well as gender. "Manliness" in seventeenth- and early eighteenth-century New England distinguished men (rational, responsible, mature) from sensual women, but it also distinguished them from rash, volatile, and vulnerable boys.[31]

Bifurcating the category of male persons into two subcategories (independent and dependent, rational and lustful) produced a way of thinking about gender that was not so much binary as triangulated. Males were thought to be more capable than females of reason, self-control, and courage, the virtues on which society depended for its stability. But not all men could act reasonably, and men who failed to control their passions were described, in certain settings, as effeminate. Manhood was defined not only in terms of difference from womanhood but also by a comparison between independent, manly men and dependent, implicitly less manly men. Instead of the modern opposition of masculine and feminine, the comparison was a hierarchical one that could be made between two men as easily as between a man and a woman: manly versus effeminate, rational versus sensual, virtuous versus corrupt. This conceptualization gave manhood a certain instability. Not only did every adult man remember having had to play the feminine role in relation to a superior adult male for much of his younger life, but his failure to act reasonably and responsibly could cause him to slip back into it again.

The idea of manliness had a particular ideological importance for Puritans in early New England because it was bound up with their vision of the orderly Christian society they hoped to create in the New World. When they imagined a stable, peaceful social order, they saw mature, rational, manly men at its center. The Puritan merchant John Hull observed in the mid-seventeenth century that New England had been blessed, largely because its male settlers and magistrates "were no babes nor windy-headed men."[32] Boston Puritan John Saffin, when he was the middle-aged father of three children in their teens and midtwenties during the 1680s or early 1690s, copied out a passage in his commonplace book that nicely captured the relationship he imagined between manhood and a stable society:

> The whole world is upheld by moderation, from the highest to the
>   lowest
> without moderation affection conquers reason . . .
> without moderation the soul submits to the body . . .
> It makes Courage valour, that without which would be anger and then
>   turn to fury.
> It separates justice from cruelty, providence from feare, power from
>   tyranny . . .
> no man is wise or virtuous without Moderation.
> Thus age has preeminence over youth.[33]

Both Hull's and Saffin's statements evoke an imagined political community made up not of all men, free and equal, but of fathers only. Sons, daughters, wives, and other dependents were represented by household heads, but did not take part in the rational, deliberative process that would guide the community, because they were not sufficiently rational. Unlike a later American society whose political rhetoric and ritual would constantly affirm the solidarity of all white men, the society founded by Puritans in early New England was based on a hierarchical world in which fathers ruled, by virtue of their ability to rationally govern a passionate, uncontrolled, and sensual majority of dependent women, youths, children, servants, and enslaved Africans. Also unlike that later American society, the Puritans did not picture society in terms of an all-male civil order differentiated from the "separate sphere" of womanhood and family, but in terms of a series of hierarchical relationships, in which fathers' authority within the polity and their authority within the family were homologous. The ideology of patriarchal manhood provided the foundation for one form of seventeenth-century patriarchalism.[34]

Having identified a structure of ideas about manhood and gender in early New England, a number of questions remain. How far reaching was it? We need to keep in mind that no conception of manhood is universal. This one was the ideological construction of the middling Protestant men who dominated colonial New England society, and was the product of particular historical developments. In some ways, New Englanders' definition of manhood was part of a seventeenth-century attempt to remake men into responsible and self-controlled members of society, and to eradicate certain violent, unruly variants of manhood traditionally found in England. Undoubtedly members of other classes, religious denominations, and racial groups elsewhere in England and its colonies defined manhood somewhat differently. In the southern colonies, where white men's identities depended in large part on their ability to master or to demonstrate their superiority to African slaves, manhood was probably defined in more overtly physical and demonstrative ways, although claims that real men were more rational than the members of various other groups may have been a constant.[35] Among propertyless working men in England and the colonies, manhood may have been defined less in terms of maturity, self-control, and economic independence than in terms of physical strength or the ability to fight. Age, too, may have been a factor in how men in various groups proved their manhood to themselves and each other. In England as well as its colonies, many young men defined their manhood in ways very different from older men, although this was certainly less true in New England, because the exaggerated interdependence of fathers and sons in these colonies gave young men less room to develop a distinctive subculture of their own.[36] But certainly the construction of manhood we have been discussing *was* the dominant one in colonial New England, not only during the seventeenth century but also well into the eighteenth century, long after Puritan control over colonial governments had ended.

What is most surprising about this concept of manhood is that it was defined in terms of two sets of relationships, between men and women and also between men and boys. Where this set of ideas about manhood originated is a methodological question of great importance. Before now, most historians' thinking about early Anglo-American gender ideologies imagined them primarily as a technology deployed by men to maintain power over assertive or economically independent women. Such an understanding has often very fruitfully allowed us to see how men's and women's power struggles have been related to other historical conflicts.[37] But a framework that understands gender entirely as a technology of power or a pretext for suppressing female independence ignores other aspects of gender that may be equally important to the historical process and may obscure some important ways in which women have shaped historical change.

The social purpose of gender categories is not just to rationalize men's power over women, but also to explain experiences such as procreation, parenthood, and mutual dependence.[38] Gender categories are learned in infancy, through experiences of bonding with and differentiation from parents, and they become the building blocks that human beings use to define themselves as well as their relationships. They shape the ways in which people imagine themselves not only as sexual beings but also as family members, friends, members of communities. To understand how people in different societies have conceptualized the gendered self, we need to start with these relationships. Especially in studying a group like Anglo-Americans in colonial New England, among whom the most significant development in family relationships was not an increase in the economic independence of women or children but rather an increase in the level of economic *inter*dependence between men, women, and children, an approach to the study of gender that looks at these relationships seems appropriate.

In our inquiry into early New Englanders' ideology of manhood, then, we will begin not by asking how men used notions of manhood to gain power over women, but how ideas about manhood were conveyed to children within the family. Historical sources, including letters between parents and children, diaries, and memoirs, reveal patterns of behavior among parents who raised sons, as well as the assumptions about gender that underlay that behavior. Although it is likely that most preindustrial agricultural societies relied to some extent on the paternal socialization of sons, these sources show that early New Englanders consciously sought to limit the role of mothers in raising boys and placed a particularly strong emphasis on the father's role as parent. Their system of child rearing was organized around a desire to wean boys of their "effeminate" dependence on sensual, irrational women and to replace it with an identification with rational adult men. There were various reasons for this: the exaggerated level of economic interdependence between fathers and sons, the Protestant emphasis on fathers' responsibility to inculcate rationality in their children, and the characteristically Protestant suspicion of motherhood and the emotionality associated with women. The result was that the most central relationships in a man's life were not with women (his mother, his wife) but with men (his father, his sons).

Out of these patrilineal relationships emerged a distinct way of imagining the male self, far different from the masculine selves that men would construct in the nineteenth century, in reaction to the emotionally intense bonds with mothers, lovers, and wives that would by then have become the norm for middle-class males. Men learned how to be men not so much by differentiating themselves from their mothers and becoming conscious of their autonomy as by learning to identify with their fathers. Because learning to be a man was a gradual process, masculine gender was conceptualized in progressive terms. Boys had to evolve through various stages of maturation—weaning from dependence—to become fully manly. Early modern writers often referred to the "ages of man": infancy, boyhood, youth, manhood. These were not only a way of understanding maturation but also a way of understanding masculinity. As boys progressed through each stage, they came closer and closer to real manhood, which was finally achieved only when they established their own household and became a father.[39]

Understanding the centrality of the father-son bond in the socialization of boys leads to questions about a variety of experiences beyond childhood: the kinds of bonds that boys form during youth, the social meaning of those bonds, and the experiences of sexual maturation and marriage. We will look at how ideas about manhood, conveyed in childhood, shaped the social meaning of relationships between youths and their friends, young men and their lovers, husbands and their wives. Both the patterns of these relationships and how they were understood can be discerned from diaries, autobiographies, memoirs, letters, and even court records. We will also be able to see how changes in these relationship patterns were beginning to be forged by the eighteenth century, changes that would eventually reconfigure the emotional experience of Anglo-American manhood.

While the major focus of this book will be on the ways in which men's intimate relationships in early New England shaped their conceptions of manhood, a subsidiary question concerns the effectiveness of early New Englanders' attempts to reform male behavior. The ideal of responsible, rational manhood was formulated as part of a conscious attempt to suppress the rowdy, disorderly, sometimes violent behavior endemic to the popular culture of early modern England.[40] How successful was this effort to remake manhood? Using court records as our main source, we will examine the nature of aggressive behavior between adult males and the mechanisms that early New Englanders devised for controlling it. Not surprisingly perhaps, family heads took most of the responsibility for restraining aggressive youths, leaving the legal system with the more limited task of controlling violence by adult men. But a system of patriarchal rule had certain built-in contradictions as a system for regulating violent male behavior, for it still gave adult men substantial leeway to use force in asserting their authority as householders. A certain amount of violence was an inevitable byproduct of the same human relationships that were supposed to prevent it.

A final question this book raises is how New Englanders' patriarchal ideals of manhood changed. A conventional narrative of American history tells us that in eighteenth-century New England, economic and social changes eroded the power of patriarchal household heads over their sons, sons became more individualistic, and a politics of deference gave way during the American Revolution to a politics of self-assertion. This book raises questions about that narrative. Patriarchal ideals of manhood, it will be suggested here, emerged not primarily to justify fathers' assertion of power over their sons, but out of a complex relationship between older and younger men that allowed them *both* to maintain a safe emotional distance from women. The decline of fathers' economic power over sons did not, in fact, produce a dramatically new set of manhood ideals. Instead, changes in Anglo-American gender ideology emerged several generations after fathers had effectively lost their economic leverage with sons, once *women* began to assume new roles vis-à-vis men in courtship, marriage, and parenting.

To take a relational approach to the study of gender is not to suggest that we examine it in isolation from the rest of the historical process; rather, it is to make visible other important ways in which gender relationships have influenced history. Lessons about the meaning of gender, conveyed in childhood, become the building blocks of language and of deep structures of meaning or symbolic systems. These cultural structures affect much more than relationships between men and women; they pervade the ways in which people imagine their world and think about change.[41]

Nor does it preclude an examination of how gender influences struggles over power. In forging imagined communities that include some people and exclude others, gender categories provide ways of rationalizing various forms of domination or legitimating political conflict. But if we want to understand the full range of ways in which gender is a dynamic in the historical process, we need to think about the ways in which it shapes relationships and not just the ways in which it is employed in conflicts over power. We shall look in a final chapter at one of the ways in which the idea of manhood, and the idealized father-son relationship that lay beneath it, permeated New Englanders' collective political imagination from the seventeenth through the eighteenth century. Although the interdependence that had characterized father-son relationships at the beginning of the colonial period was weakening by the 1760s, the idea of manliness remained part of a deep structure of ideas about political obligation until the American Revolution. This structure of ideas may help to explain why New Englanders were so receptive to classical republican political theory, another philosophical system that privileges age over youth and reason over passion, and that assumes that political authority should be exercised by mature, independent, rational men rather than by the dependent or the sensual.[42]

And finally, although this study will not attempt to explore the implications, the relational approach may suggest some other ways in which this thinking about manhood influenced struggles over power. Anglo-Americans in early New England thought of manly people as those who exercised reason and nonmanly people as those whose passion or sensuality got the better of their reason. We will look at some of the ways in which a manly man was defined as a nonwoman and a nonboy. Further research might show how categories of gender and age also shaped the language used to describe categories of class and race, for it seems likely that a manly man was also a non-servant, a non-Indian, a non-African, a non-Anglican, a non-fop, and (during the American Revolution) a non-aristocrat. Persons who fit into these various other categories tended to be portrayed as being in thrall to their passions or addicted to sensuality, whereas "manly" men had achieved a level of self-mastery that placed them morally above these others.[43] The idea of manliness may thus have helped to give property-owning white men a collective sense of righteous superiority on which they could draw during political and military conflicts with a range of foes, from the "savage" Indians, against whom they fought in various wars in the seventeenth and eighteenth centuries, to the "sensual, effeminate" English gentlemen in Parliament whose policies provoked such outrage during the American revolutionary crisis.

Our narrative begins with a close look at how men experienced manhood in early New England, beginning in 1676, one hundred years before the beginning of the American Revolution. The terrible war known as King Philip's War, which had pitted New England's English colonists against a coalition of Native American tribes, was just ending. Though for a time the English would remain wounded and psychologically shaken, they had emerged the victors in the contest and would thereafter play the dominant role in defining New England's culture and institutions. An intensely religious early period, during which New England's colonial leaders had been able to claim that their society was set apart by God, was drawing to a close, and the sons and grandsons of New England's earliest settlers were beginning to have to think about themselves as Englishmen within an English empire. Let us look at the ways in which they learned the meaning of manhood, starting with the birth of a boy.

Fathers and Sons from Infancy through Boyhood

At about two in the morning on April 1, 1677, a young Boston Puritan merchant named Samuel Sewall woke up and realized that his wife, Hannah, was in labor. He asked her if he should call her mother, who lived with the couple. "She said I should go to prayer, then she would tell me." Sewall got up, lit a fire, and prayed. Then, he wrote, "after 5 when our folks up, went and gave Mother warning. She came and bad me call the Midwife . . . which I did . . . [M]y Wives pains went away in a great measure after she was up . . . toward night came on again." That night at a quarter past ten, as he sat waiting with his father-in-law outside his wife's chamber "in the great Hall," he "heard the child cry." The baby was a son, Sewall's first; he was subsequently named John. At two in the morning, Sewall escorted the midwife home, carrying her birthing stool in a bag. Along the way they "met with the Watch at Mr. Rocks Brew house, who bad us stand, enquired what we were. I told the Woman's occupation, so they bad God bless our labours, and let us pass."[1]

Becoming a new father was an event of great significance for an Anglo-American man in seventeenth-century New England. In the eyes of the world, his ascension to fatherhood gave him a new status and made him for the first time a full member in the community of adult males. Partly, of course, the special status was the same accorded to all fathers as a traditional marker of manhood in early modern English society. This was still a universe in which the fate of dynasties rested on a man's proof of his ability to sire an heir. But to the Puritans who had settled in New England over the past forty years, fatherhood conferred a special moral stature and a set of heightened moral obligations to protect community order and ready their children for membership in the church. Full manhood status was limited to men who had become homeowners and heads of families, responsible for the governance as well as the care of their dependents. Marriage alone did not confer that status. According to William Perkins, "A Family is a natural and simple Societie of certaine persons . . . under the private government of one. These persons must be at least three, because two cannot make a societie."[2]

A few weeks after the birth of his son, Samuel Sewall celebrated his entry into the community of household heads on an overnight trip to Dorchester with his father-in-law, John Hull. While staying in a local tavern there, they met William Adams, a minister from the town of Dedham, who "at Supper told of his wife being brought to bed of a Son about three weeks before, whom he named Eliphelet."[3] Probably the men around the table drank to the health of the two new fathers, perhaps to the health of their infant sons. For Sewall, it was a notable event, and he memorialized it in his diary.

Fathers in seventeenth- and eighteenth-century New England typically greeted the arrival of children with joy and hope for the future, especially the birth of sons. In personal writings, new fathers often described their expectations for their sons, though they rarely did so for their daughters.[4] John Saffin predicted that his newborn sons would take after him, and copied into his commonplace book the maxim, "Strong men from strong, their native Strength doe Gather, Both Bull and Horse, take spirit from their father."[5] Joseph Green hoped that his first son would grow up to have an experience of saving grace and own the covenant of the church.[6] Ebenezer Parkman, a minister in Westborough, Massachusetts, a half century later, prayed to God to make his newborn son, Breck, "a blessing in his Generation."[7] Like Joseph Green, fathers often noted who their children were named after, suggesting that fatherhood gave them also a sense of connection with their forebears.[8] Still, the absence of details in men's personal writings about their infants as individuals suggests that, at least until babies were weaned, fathers did not become very involved with them. This lack of involvement might suggest an emotional distancing, perhaps to guard against the very real possibility that the new baby would die in infancy. But a better explanation for fathers' seeming distance from their infants may simply be that taking care of small children was women's work.

Thus Samuel Sewall's baby would be cared for entirely by women for the first six weeks after his birth, while his mother recovered from her lying-in. Because the family could afford it, there was a wet-nurse to provide for the baby until Hannah Sewall's milk came in, then a nurse to help Hannah care for the infant. On the fifth day after the birth, Sewall reported, "my Wife set up, and he sucked the right Breast bravely."[9] So the newborn was initially surrounded by women, holding him, warming him, offering the breast when he cried, encouraging him to suck. Sewall watched with interest but remained mostly on the margins.

Two features of parenting in early New England would affect the kinds of relationships that children formed with their parents and the way that they learned about gender roles. First, a traditional division of labor between the sexes would determine with whom the child spent his time at various stages while growing up. Second, concerns about children's moral development got Puritan fathers more involved with childhood education than tradition dictated, and strengthened cultural associations between manhood and rationality. The Puritans sought to reform what they thought of as a disordered society by remaking human personality, and their formula for creating self-controlled, sober, disciplined individuals included an expanded role for fathers in child rearing.

A child's primary parent in the early years was always the mother, who had the major day-to-day responsibility for the care of infants and toddlers. Thus, babies inevitably bonded first, and most deeply, with women. In Puritan families, that bond was doubtless strengthened by an almost exclusive reliance on maternal breast-feeding.[10] The first year or more of a child's life would have been defined by an intense, enveloping experience of maternal nurturing, in which the child had little sense of a separate identity from his or her female parent.

But for the earliest New Englanders, that maternal bond was morally suspect if prolonged for too long. Reformed Protestantism advocated an ascetic rationality and attempted to eradicate irrational and sensual influences on behavior.[11] This emphasis on rationality in some ways increased both parents' moral responsibilities for children, who had to be trained in rationality and self-discipline to prepare for God's grace. But it also exacerbated a traditional critique of women as more emotional and less rational than men, and promoted the opinion that maternal indulgence was harmful to a child's moral development.[12] Mothers who showed too much tenderness to children risked being criticized as weak.

Various child rearing techniques worked to help separate babies from their mothers, beginning with a fairly rapid weaning at around one year to eighteen months of age. Relatives seem to have assisted in the weaning process, to help mothers suppress any ambivalence they might have felt about this separation. In the Sewall household, for example, both Hannah Sewall's mother and "Nurse Hill" helped by babysitting infants during weaning, in order to keep them physically away from their mother.[13] In some households, women took weaning journeys to remove themselves from the temptation of giving in to children's demands for the breast.[14] Once the child was weaned, such implements as standing stools and leading strings encouraged toddlers to stand upright and learn to walk as quickly as possible.[15] We do not know whether women longed to keep on babying their little ones, but practicality argued against it, for they had meals to cook, gardens to tend, soap to make, laundry to boil, and most likely other children to tend to as well. Admonished by ministers to teach their toddlers absolute obedience, mothers must have felt pressure to avoid indulging clingy children.[16] Husbands, too, may have urged women not to coddle their children, perhaps spurred by uncomfortable feelings of resentment toward the infants with whom their wives enjoyed such a prolonged period of intimacy.[17] Toddlers would have soon learned to avoid making too many demands.

Still, mothers remained the primary parent for all children up to at least age six or seven. Small children required close supervision, and women's work, centered as it was in the house and garden, kept mothers close enough at hand to keep watch over their little ones. So for the next five or six years, a child would spend most of his time around the house, supervised by his mother or older sisters, playing with siblings. Early New Englanders perceived childhood as an irresponsible and unproductive stage, and acknowledged that children before the age of six or seven were too young to assume much responsibility. Minister John Cotton, for example, believed it no sin for young children to "spend much time in pastime and play, for their bodies are too weak to labour, and the minds to study are too shallow . . . even the first seven years are spent in pastime, and God looks not much at it."[18] The legal practice of requiring the fathers of illegitimate children to pay child support until six or seven also rested on the common assumption that young children would remain dependent and unproductive until that age.[19]

The perception that little children were dependent and nonproductive was visually reinforced by their clothing. Both boys and girls wore long gowns and petticoats from the end of infancy until approximately age seven—gowns that resembled women's dresses and made all little children look like girls.[20] As little boys grew out of the toddler stage, parents made very tiny changes in their garments, for example allowing them to abandon the head coverings that their sisters still wore. But all children continued to wear skirts or gowns, a sartorial reminder of their dependence on and identification with women.

Though surrounded by women and older girls, children growing gradually aware of their world would also before long have become aware of the presence of their fathers. Puritans taught that fathers had the primary responsibility of providing spiritual instruction and guidance to their family members, as well as maintaining order in their household. One consequence of this emphasis on paternal spiritual responsibility was to pull Puritan men out of the tavern-centered subculture of male conviviality that was central to other Englishmen's gender identity (and remained so in other parts of the British Atlantic world, such as in colonial Virginia).[21] In Puritan New England, adult men were often at home, and children of both sexes would likely have had more contact with fathers during early childhood than many other English children.

It was generally the father, for example, who presided over family prayers, led the singing of psalms, and conducted the Scripture readings that were supposed to take place in every household twice a day. Josiah Cotton, the son of the minister whose family lived in Plymouth from 1667 to 1697, recalled that his father's "Way in his Family was to read a Chapter morn And Evening and to make a short (yet profitable) Exposition upon it, before Prayer."[22] Fathers also led prayers before and after meals, and before sleep.[23] Even very young children, as they gained consciousness of themselves and their surroundings, must have been aware of the powerful man at the head of the table every morning and evening who called for everybody in the house to be quiet while he read from a big book.

In addition to leading family devotions, fathers also had special moral responsibilities toward children, even when the children were still fairly young. Fathers were to pay close attention to their children's spiritual development, for it was the father who would have the primary responsibility for his children's salvation. The proper antidote to excessive maternal indulgence, urged ministers, was paternal instruction and reason.[24] By 1676, fathers in the colonies of Massachusetts, Connecticut (which after 1665 had come to include New Haven), and Plymouth were legally obligated to provide religious instruction to the children and servants in their home.[25] Ministers urged parents to "endeavour to infuse good principles, great truths" into their children "while you lay them in your bosoms, and dandle them on your knees."[26]

The evidence would suggest that fathers often did invest high levels of attention and care in their religious duties. Because the doctrine of predestination gave them no assurance that their children would be saved, fathers (and probably many mothers, as well) threw themselves into their children's spiritual education with an energy that parents who could take God's grace for granted did not. Some men undertook this obligation in partnership with their wives, as did the father of John Barnard, who joined with John's mother in teaching the boy how to pray when he was five or six years old in the 1680s.[27] Others, like the father of Joseph Green, who grew up around the same time, undertook this duty personally. The great principles infused by his father were too much for little Joseph to handle, although they made a lifelong impression. He later recalled: "In my Infancy (it may be w[he]n I was about 4 or 5 years old at most) my father used to tell me I must be a good boy and must serve God, and used to ask me whether I went alone and prayed to God to bless me & to pardon my sins and save my soul from hell; and I sadly remember how my corrupt heart used to hate such motions; I loathed to hear of such things."[28]

Fathers also assumed at least some of the duty of disciplining young children during their "infancy," before age six or seven.[29] As the Puritan theologian William Perkins suggested, one of the main duties of the father and master of the house was to "keep order and . . . exercise discipline . . . sometimes by admonition, otherwhiles by correction and chastisement according to the quality of the offense."[30] "Correction" could certainly include corporal punishment. Samuel Sewall, for example, recorded punishing his son Joseph when the boy was four.

> Nov. 6, 1692. Joseph threw a knob of Brass and hit his Sister Betty on the forehead so as to make it bleed and swell; upon which, and for his playing at Prayer-time, and eating when Return Thanks, I whipped him pretty smartly.[31]

Those of us with modern sensibilities cringe at the thought of these stern patriarchs "correcting" their children. Undoubtedly parental discipline in many Puritan households was much more repressive than it is in modern ones. Some Puritans even urged parents to "break the wills" of their children before age two, to beat down their children's strivings for autonomy, so as to begin as early as possible to control children's aggressive and assertive drives.[32]

But to emphasize the disciplinary, educational role of fathers too much may prevent us from seeing another, affective side of the relationship between fathers and children, which was ultimately what gave it so much power. Fathers had many opportunities to form emotional bonds with their small children from the toddler stage on, although the existence of these relationships is sometimes hard to locate beneath the somber rhetoric of pious diarists. Diaries show that farmers, tradesmen, and ministers were often at home, especially during the winter months.[33] The concern fathers expressed when their children were ill suggests that many, perhaps most, formed deep and meaningful attachments with their children after infancy.[34]

"Nursing Fathers"

Minister Joseph Green, writing in the early 1700s, seemed to worry constantly about his third son, Edward, who was seriously ill at least three times during his first seven years. About a month after Edward's seventh birthday, Green related an incident that shook him profoundly. Edward, playing with his two older brothers, had fallen off a wall. His brothers saw him lying in the snow and thought he was dead.

> So John stayed with him & Jose[ph] came in & told us Nedde was dead & we all ran crying, & when I came I perceived life in him but no sense, & so I brought him home, & after he had vomited, & we had put him to bed and he had lain awhile he revived & after his fall it was almost an hour before he could take any thing.

"I doe not remember that I ever was in greater distress than at this time," Green wrote.[35]

Fathers often played a major role in the care of children when they were sick or injured. Certainly this was true in the family of autobiographer John Barnard, who grew up in the 1680s and 1690s in Boston. In Barnard's most vivid memories of childhood, his father figured prominently in a nurturing role during illnesses and mishaps. Once, when he was ten years old, Barnard remembered, he fell from an eighteen-foot scaffold inside a church. "I lay upon the ground until somebody ran to my father's house, about two hundred feet off, and acquainted him with my fall; who came and took me up, without any apparent signs of life in me, and carried me home; where, by the blessing of God upon the means used, in some hours I recovered breath and sensation."[36] When Barnard was eleven and contracted scarlet fever, it was again his "tender father" who came into his bedchamber early in the morning after a feverish night, to check on his symptoms.[37]

Records of fathers taking major responsibility for child care alongside mothers during children's illnesses are common.[38] For example, in March 1755 during an illness of his three-year-old son John, New Hampshire farmer Matthew Patten wrote, "Our son John was taken very bad in ye forenoon so that we almost Dispaired of his life." During the afternoon, the child "was easier" after his father had medicated him with "Chamber Lie and Molassess, sweet oyl and neatsfoot oyl." The following morning "he was easy . . . but was taken bad again about Nine or Ten of the Clock in the forenoon and Complained of his being like to Choak." (Perhaps this had something to do with the chamber lye, molasses, and oil!) Patten's record of his vigil continued in enough detail to suggest that he was very actively involved in the boy's care: the child "continued very bad till the moon rising which was 30 minutes after 10 at night and then he got easyer and slept till morning." Significantly, Patten noted, "I had to get up after the moon rising but once till morning."[39]

It makes some sense in terms of the division of household labor in early modern families that fathers should have assumed a substantial role in parenting during children's illnesses. A seriously ill child requires intense and concentrated care around the clock, care that a mother could not provide alone, especially if there were more than one sick child in the house. Allocating to fathers the responsibilities of diagnosing and medicating children also reflected the reality that men tended to be better educated than women (and thus were thought to know about medicine and illness), and that fathers had the ultimate legal and moral responsibility for their children's well-being.[40]

When they compared their rulers and religious leaders with fathers, early New England ministers often described them as tender and compassionate "nursing fathers."[41] As Thomas Shepard urged in 1672, "Moses must remember that he is a Nursing father, and Paul as a Nurse must be gentle."[42] Or, as Joseph Belcher explained, God promised his chosen

people that their rulers would be "Nursing Fathers . . . as careful in providing for them, in dealing compassionately and tenderly with them,
and in extending comforts and consolations to them, as Nurses are with
respect to their Children."[43] Such descriptions seem anomalous when
we emphasize only the authoritarian side of patriarchal fathering. But
the act of nursing sick children, side by side with mothers, attests to another, more affectionate side of fathering. Perhaps the ministers who invoked the image of "nursing fathers" remembered the actual experience
of having their own father at their side during childhood illnesses, providing for their physical needs and offering comfort.

Fathers' affections were perhaps most fully expressed when they faced
the prospect of a child's death, which was a ubiquitous event in early
modern families and perhaps all the more difficult for parents who were
uncertain whether God had chosen to bestow his grace on their own little one. Nicholas Gilman may have thought of fatherhood in terms of
teaching his little boys to avoid the "vanities of childhood," but he had a
hard time mastering his own feelings when Bartholomew, at ten years
old, died during a diphtheria epidemic in 1741. It comforted the elder
Gilman that Bartholomew had expressed faith and trust in God during his illness. He "underwent his affliction with Admirable Patience
and Sweet Composure of mind, tho' Breathing with great difficulty yet
mostly answering with a pleasant Smile." Perhaps it helped the struggling boy to have his father sitting constantly next to his bed, reading
and praying; certainly it helped the father. Gilman wrote that he "desird
me to pray with him frequently—& read to him in the Bible—which
seemed to be more & more to his delight."[44]

Within three weeks, Bartholomew's eight-year-old brother, Nicholas,
succumbed to the same illness. Gilman stoically prayed to God that his
bereavements might "be for my purifying—may they wean me from this
World and quicken Me in My preparations for a Better." This was not a
man who indulged his feelings; in reformed Protestant culture, excessive
sadness was a sign that a person's affections were too far engaged with
the world and not sufficiently fixed on God. But it is hard not to sense
the grief of this man, who recorded, on the fifteenth of January 1742, after Nicholas's funeral, "The remains of My Little Son laid in the Silent
grave." Returning home, he wrote in his diary, "Blessed be God I find the
three remaining children pretty well—Oh! that they may be spared Lord
if it may be thy Will."[45]

The feelings of these fathers for their children were as strong as the feelings of parents for their children anywhere. An entry in the journal of John Pike, a minister in Dover, New Hampshire, in 1702, leaves no doubt about his affection for his small son: "My Dear son Samuel was born 1695, Ap. 1, betwixt two & 3 of the clock afternoon Monday. Lived seven years, seven months, twenty eight days. Died Nov. 29 1702, sab-morning, after two days Relapsed into a fever his principal malady was sore throat and caput-dolor The joy of my heart."[46]

The images of anxious, attentive, and grieving fathers belie stereotypes of early New England fathers as unfeeling or emotionally distant. But though early New England fathers were capable of deep love for their children, in an unsentimental age they would have found it unnecessary and even perhaps unwise to speak of that love very often. Families existed not for their members to indulge in their feelings for one another but to produce what their members needed to live on, to teach children to overcome their passions, and to pass on to children the skills they would need to be productive adults.

Reaching Boyhood

The roles of the parents in fulfilling these responsibilities would shift as a child's moral capacities developed. The growing involvement of fathers coincided with the expectation that, as children grew older, they would become increasingly capable of self-control. While maternal parenting was indulgent and affectionate, fathering signified moral responsibility and reason.[47] The task of parents was to teach children to overcome their dependence on mothers and to become responsible and productive. For girls, this meant assuming a greater share of women's work, alongside their mothers. For boys, it meant not only responsibility but also a dramatic shift in their social status.

At the age of seven, when they reached the "age of reason," boys ceased to be treated as infants and became boys. The turning point was recognized symbolically by a change in their clothing, which was now to consist of the breeches and other clothing worn by adult men. "Breeching," as it was called, conveyed a significance beyond convenience, for in early modern Europe, dress was an important signifier of status. Sumptuary laws in seventeenth-century New England, as elsewhere, prohibited ordinary people from wearing clothes appropriate only to gentlemen and ladies, and even in the eighteenth century etiquette books still suggested that it was important to wear clothes appropriate to one's rank in society. So it is highly likely that a boy would have seen his shift from the feminine clothing of childhood to the masculine clothing of adult manhood as a meaningful rite of passage.

What did boys' new costume of breeches and a jacket signify? Surely it suggested, above all, that maleness was a ticket to the wider world outside the family. Breeches allowed a boy to travel: to run, to climb onto wagons and over fences, and to ride horses. His sisters remained confined in dresses, which inhibited their movements and kept them closer to the house. What is more, a boy's new costume emphasized not only his difference from his sisters and his mother but also his similarity to men, perhaps suggesting his entry into a world of relationships with other men, especially his father.[48] Boys' transition to a new stage of childhood at age six or seven coincides with what Freudian psychoanalytic theorists have suggested is the age at which boys normally undertake a repression of their Oedipal desires for the mother and begin to consciously identify with and imitate the father.[49] The reward for giving up the mother would have been a more meaningful relationship with the father or another adult male.

The ideological currents of the Protestant Reformation suggest a further valence to the ritual of breeching in Puritan New England. In earlier centuries, children had simply worn a robe, an item of clothing not associated with either gender. But it was at the height of the Reformation in the sixteenth century that western Europeans commonly began to put both little boys and little girls in female dress. The new costume suggested a new consciousness that childhood was a special stage in life, qualitatively different from adulthood.[50] But perhaps it also suggests a new consciousness about gender. At the very time when moralists were paying so much attention to the need for reason and rationality in adult men, little boys' clothing was made to reinforce their initial similarity with women and girls. Perhaps the growing association between rationality and manhood produced a heightened awareness of its absence in women *and* children.[51]

Breeching, then, would have suggested that becoming a man meant becoming rational and giving up the passions and feelings of childhood.[52] The custom reinforced the classical notion that men's ability to reason and master their emotions was what made them men.[53] Especially for Puritans, "reason, logic, and order . . . expressed masculinity and a masculine God. Feeling . . . connoted femininity, sin, excess."[54] Part of what made a boy a man in Anglo-American families in early New England was his achievement of rational control over his feelings, which were associated with his childhood, his mother, and his sisters. His progress toward maleness was connected with his growth into adulthood, whereas femininity remained static, permanently childlike.

Not only customs surrounding children's dress but also certain medical ideas about gender seem to have reflected a larger cultural sense or belief that little boys in infancy had perhaps not yet *become* masculine in some vital sense, that specifically manly characteristics were still inchoate and undeveloped.[55] Early modern English medical beliefs about conception understood gender difference as relatively fluid, rather than as the product of fixed or innate characteristics. The predominance of male or female seed in the womb was rarely absolute and was thought to become established only as an infant developed.[56] Thus males underwent a gradual transition from an initial "effeminate" state in childhood to manhood—some more successfully than others. Females, on the other hand, simply remained female throughout their lives.

To suggest that early New Englanders thought of masculinity as developmental should not suggest that Anglo-American families in early New England lacked a perception that there were "natural" differences between boys and girls. Early modern medical theory suggested, for example, that males were more ruled by aggressive passions, females by sexual ones.[57] But these "natural" qualities were neither celebrated nor encouraged. Especially in Puritan families (and in the eighteenth century in evangelical families), whatever incipient tendencies little boys might have for aggressive, rowdy behavior were viewed with disapproval. The daughter of Jonathan Edwards, Esther Edwards Burr, described her own son as "a little dirty Noisy Boy" very different from his more placid older sister.[58] Desirable male traits such as rationality and moderation—those that justified giving legal and political privileges to adult men but not to women—were not yet visible in early childhood.

Besides a change in clothing, boys experienced other changes in their lives around age seven. It was at about this time that Puritan and evangelical fathers began to provide spiritual counseling for their children, both sons and daughters. Seven marked the age when boys and girls were seen to have a developed enough rational capacity to understand their own sinfulness and the necessity of God's grace.[59] Cotton Mather, in his diary, resolved to take "more of Care . . . to educate my little Daughter, for the Lord" about a month before his daughter Katy's seventh birthday. He had a serious and lengthy conversation with her about the need to pray constantly for salvation when she was eight years and two months old.[60] Exeter, New Hampshire, minister Nicholas Gilman began a diary at the time his eldest son, Bartholomew, was eight and a half, by which time he was teaching his son not only in the group sessions of family prayer but also in periodic individual sessions in which he talked to him about the state of his soul.[61] Fathers provided spiritual counseling to children of both genders, suggesting that both were thought capable of rational moral understanding. But for girls this contact would have been occasional, while for boys it added intensity to a relationship that from now until adulthood would dominate their lives.

As boys gradually grew old enough to do men's work, their relationships with their fathers would become more regular and sustained. This was as true in non-Puritan as in Puritan families, especially if they were farming families (the vast majority of the population in early New England). A valuable record of the developing relationships between an early New England farm father and his growing sons is a work diary, such as the diary of Matthew Patten, a Scots-Irish farmer who settled in Bedford, New Hampshire, during the eighteenth century. Patten's diary was mostly a record of his labors in the field, and then, as his children grew old enough to help him, a selective record of theirs. He first mentioned assigning his eldest son, John, a job when he had the boy rake hay for several days in August 1760, at the age of eight. For the next few years, Patten sporadically recorded giving John tasks like digging potatoes, raking hay, or running errands, but did not perceive himself to be relying regularly on John's labor until the summer of 1763, when John was eleven. Patten began receiving help from his next two boys, James and Robert, during the harvest in the summer of 1766, when they were eleven and nine, respectively.[62]

Work records like Matthew Patten's provide evidence that New England farm fathers with boys reaching the age of seven or eight began to become the primary parents and mentors for their sons as the boys were increasingly involved in male work under their supervision. Although fathers might assign tasks to some boys as early as the age of five, most boys probably were first given specifically male work assignments

around seven: age-appropriate tasks like watching livestock and check-
ing fences, or fetching water and kindling. Fathers valued a boy's work
differently, depending on his age. Their records of young children's work
tended not to indicate children as individuals, referring merely to "children" or "little boys."[63] But once boys began working in the fields, first
helping with harvests and then, as they grew older, doing the heavier
work of plowing and planting, men paid more attention to what their
sons could do. In Patten's records, each record of an older boy's work
was an acknowledgment of that boy's growing capacity for the thing the
father respected most: economically productive work.

Giving a boy specifically male work began the process of integrating
him into the male world outside the house. A nine- or ten-year-old boy
who was trusted by his father to carry messages to neighboring farmers
or to drive the family's wagon into town would have been brought more
and more into contact with adult men and the male world outside his
home. He would also have been brought into a new sort of relationship
with his father. To be given an errand must have been a source of considerable pride for a little boy, as it was an acknowledgment that he was
growing big and smart and worthy of trust.

Developmental theory has shown that infants establish their primary
identity in the experience of near-merger with female caregivers—in
most societies, the mothers. As children mature and begin to develop an
identity separate from their mothers, they must also choose a gender
identity that will bring them social acceptance. For a girl, according to
this theory, this separation is not problematic, since her early identification with her mother reinforces a developing sense of femininity. But
boys must establish a sense of male gender identification apart from this
primary bond. A boy's successful negotiation of a masculine identity de-
pends on his ability to separate himself from his mother and construct
a sense of self that is distinctively male.[64] Early New England culture
recognized that this acquisition of manhood could be difficult, and
imagined it as progressive. Boys were expected gradually to distinguish
themselves from women by learning to master their emotionality and
dependency, and to identify with rational adult men.

Aside from its special emphasis on mastering emotion, the pattern of
male socialization found in early New England would have been fairly
typical for western European societies in the early modern period. In
these preindustrial societies, the frequent presence of fathers around the

house and an expectation that boys would soon follow their fathers into the fields or shops to do men's work produced cultural mechanisms for easing mother-son separation in early childhood. Boys would learn how to be male not by learning to think of themselves as independent from their mothers but by establishing relationships with adult males, either their fathers or other older male mentors. They would work their way into manhood in stages. As they grew older, they would begin to assume responsibility for men's work, their contact with older males would progressively increase, and they would be integrated into the male social role through relationships with these older men. This progressive integration into relationships with men also meant that boys would increasingly spend time in a realm without women, where they would distance themselves from childhood dependencies and feelings.

Meanwhile, their sisters' coming of age would be more continuous with their early childhood experience. Girls around the age of seven or eight would begin to do women's work, learning to knit and sew and spin and care for small children. They would become further integrated into the female social role by intensifying their identifications with their mothers, identifications that they had been developing since early childhood. Few special markers would be needed to coax girls into adulthood, since the process of growing up did not require them to repudiate childhood relationships. Unless girls were bound out, sent out to live and work in other families, their role would keep them close to home until they married, and only at that point, when they moved out of their mothers' household, would they truly have to become adults.

Early New England society also provided a second way in which boys became identified with other males during their younger years: schooling. In communities that had schools, and during those months of the fall and winter when they could be spared by their families, boys were sent to school. Although in New England girls and boys often were both taught to read at home (or in dame schools if their families were well-to-do), learning the skills of writing, doing sums, and keeping accounts was limited primarily to boys.[65] Unlike the dame schools of early childhood, writing and grammar schools tended to be all-male environments, in which boys were generally taught by young men who planned to become ministers.[66] Here again, boys could form bonds of enduring significance with male mentors, as Peter Thacher did when he formed a lifelong friendship with his schoolmaster, Jeremy Belknap, in the early

1760s.[67] The experience of being in a mostly male world encouraged boys to continue distancing themselves from their mothers and sisters. Through identification with other boys and men, as well as through their classroom activities, boys could feel that they had special abilities that girls did not. For those few boys who remained in school to prepare for college, Latin gave them a language in which they could even communicate privately with other men.[68]

Fathers tended to become more involved with their sons' education around ages eight to eleven, beginning to make decisions about the boys' formal training or schooling outside the family, as well as teaching boys themselves. Ideally, fathers looked for special capacities or interests, and headed those sons who displayed them out of farming and into trades or the ministry.[69] John Barnard's father, for example, directed him toward the ministry and decided where John would be schooled beginning in his eighth year, in 1689.[70] If a school was unavailable, fathers were supposed to educate their sons at home. Josiah Cotton remembered his father's role in educating him and his brothers in the 1690s: "My Father never aimed at laying up for or Leaving a great Estate to his Children. But yet Took special care of, and was at great Charge About their Education, which is better than an Estate without it—He did as his Father and Brother before him had done, bring up all his Four Sons (that grew up) to the College—and that without the advantage of a School in the Town."[71]

Generally, only the wealthiest early New England fathers had the financial or the educational resources to train their sons for entry into the ministry. But even in ordinary families, fathers singled out their sons for training in whatever basic skills in writing and cyphering they themselves possessed. For example, the eighteenth-century Massachusetts farmer William Stickney taught his son John to sign his name and to write, with John practicing his cursive writing in the back of the family's 1766 almanac. Stickney also taught his daughters Jane and Polly to sign their names, and they used the backs of the 1767 and 1768 almanacs, but Jane and Polly got no handwriting practice beyond the basic skill of signing.[72]

Gradually, as they matured, boys' contact with their fathers deepened into sustained involvement. It would be impossible to fix with precision the age at which this occurred, since in this society neither consciousness of age nor the correlation between age and life stage was very precise.[73] But between the ages of about ten and perhaps fourteen or fifteen, most farm boys could be expected to assume genuine responsibilities for work and to have regular contact with their fathers. Records of sons' labor found in the account books of early New England farmers like Patten are in effect records of boys' physical and emotional growth and of the growing attentiveness of their fathers. By their midteens boys were generally both strong enough and emotionally mature enough to be regarded as genuinely productive workers. By recording their work, fathers were not only keeping track of their sons' labors but also manifesting their growing respect for them: a respect founded on their ability to work.

Nonfarming families followed a similar pattern of boyhood socialization, though often the older male mentor was someone other than the father. Those families that had the necessary funds often placed boys with a master beginning at age ten to fourteen, a master who could provide them with training in the "mysteries" of an artisan's craft, or the art of trading and merchandising. They might seek a scholar to teach Latin, if they hoped to direct a boy into the ministry. The fact that families had to pay the master for these apprenticeships indicates that they were thought of primarily as benefiting the boys and not their employers.[74] Boys whose fathers were too poor to support them, were unable to educate them, or, worst of all, were dead or had abandoned the family, were often bound out to masters until age twenty-one.[75] Before young John Patten had started working for his father, for example, Matthew Patten had employed the labors of an older boy, Jonas Cutting, who had been indentured to him since childhood. Although Jonas Cutting's mother was still alive, she could not give him what Patten could, a long-lasting relationship with an older man who trained him to do productive work. From time to time during his teens, Jonas Cutting was allowed to hire out his own labor, and when he reached twenty-one the family gave him a party and a payment of "freedom dues" to mark his coming of age.[76]

The expectation of male socialization, in whatever form, was that by the time a boy reached the age of fourteen or fifteen, he would be involved in productive work with an older male mentor, learning the skills he would eventually need to support a family of his own. In the case of indenture, expectations were not always met, as cases in the record books testify; it was well known that masters often exploited their young charges instead of training them. Widow Hannah Crockett of Kittery, Maine, petitioned for her son's release from an indenture made to John

Jypson, a tailor. Widow Crocket complained that Jypson had moved too far away for her to visit her son. Moreover, the boy "has Learnt Nothing But Drudgery work and his Time wholly thrown away."[77] The mother's complaint about her son's master revealed what she believed was the most important feature of an education: to teach boys to become responsible, skilled, and socially useful male members of society. If it did not do that, it was a waste of time.

Here, in the acknowledgment of a boy's productive capacity, lies a second aspect of the ideal of manhood in early New England, closely related to the emphasis on rationality. Pietist Christian moral thinkers in seventeenth- and eighteenth-century England and America suggested that the source of true fulfillment in life was not to pursue selfish passions but to discipline the self in order to live productively within society. They demanded that individuals work at some useful and productive calling in order to serve God and the public.[78] Human beings had been created to be active, to direct their energies into useful activity. Some even suggested that industrious activity provided the best way to maintain bodily health, since it would keep the blood and other humours circulating.[79] It was in adolescence that a boy became a genuinely productive member of society. His identity as a man would be constructed around his capacity to work, the property that he was able to build up through his work, and the family it would enable him to support. Independence or "competence," in the sense of heading a household that was sufficiently productive of land and sustenance to avoid wage work or tenancy, was the goal.

A boy would not, however, expect to achieve this capacity alone. The "self-made man" was not yet a cultural ideal—these men acknowledged their interdependence with their families.[80] Most important, they did not think of themselves as having achieved independence without the aid and support of their fathers. Their fathers would make the career choices, provide the training, and even, in most cases, provide the property on which a man's ability to become a competent householder would depend. New England farmers found it necessary to rely on their sons as a labor source to a far greater extent, and for a longer period in their sons' lives, than either England or the southern American colonies. While the abundance of available frontier land gave all Anglo-American sons the opportunity to move away from home as they reached adulthood, sons in Puritan New England were more likely to remain close by.

Until recently, most historians have interpreted the prolonged interde-

pendence of fathers and sons in terms of the coercive power it gave to fathers. They have argued that the abundant supply of land available to
the original proprietors of the towns and the absence of legal restrictions
on testation, which left the proprietors free to distribute their land as
they chose, gave fathers a powerful source of leverage to induce each of
their sons to stay at home and work for them. Fathers could offer future
bequests of land as an incentive for their sons' obedience. It has been argued that the widespread use of partible inheritance to provide parcels
to each of the family's sons, diverging from the English pattern of primogeniture, in which the bulk of the family estate went to the oldest son
only, enabled fathers to maximize their leverage by offering the incentive
of property to every son in the family. In other words, fathers offered the
carrot of land if their sons would remain on the family farm and work
for them, and wielded the stick of disinheritance if sons failed in their
duty or were disobedient. It has been assumed that New England youths
succumbed to paternal control because the harsh child rearing methods
of their parents prevented them from acknowledging resentment of their
fathers and from forging out on their own.[81]

The most recent scholarship, however, emphasizes the reciprocality of
the relationship between fathers and sons in early New England rather
than its coercive elements. Fathers needed their sons' labors and earn-
ings as much as their sons needed paternal inheritances. New England's
farms were small and incapable of producing the profitable commodities
that would have made it possible to obtain alternative sources of labor
through a market. Sons may well have had other options—for example,
tenant farming on the land of large landlords in other colonies, such as
New York and New Jersey.[82] But the cultural value placed on competency, or self-employment, made sons willing to sacrifice their desires
for autonomy from parents for the greater economic payoff that would
come from staying on the family farm. They stayed not because they
feared leaving but because they understood that their partnerships with
their fathers and brothers were ultimately devoted to the goal of providing an independent landholding, a competence, for each of them.[83]

There was a considerable difference between what New England fathers had to offer and what fathers in other parts of the English Atlantic
world could offer their sons during the seventeenth and eighteenth centuries. In England, middling fathers could rarely hope to give their sons
farms. Instead, their sons were encouraged to enter the labor market,

which emerged early in England as the supply of labor surpassed the supply of land. Sons in England could hope to better their situations early in their productive lives by finding trades, seeking paid employment, and befriending potential sponsors.[84] Aspiring gentlemen in eighteenth-century Virginia did not expect to give farms to all their sons. Recent findings show that by the middle of the eighteenth century, as much as 80 percent of all land in that region was entailed and passed according to the rules of primogeniture.[85] But seventeenth-century New England fathers could offer their sons farms of their own—inheritances that, from the point of view of the rest of the English-speaking world, must have seemed very appealing, especially for men who were second, third, and fourth sons.[86]

Certainly such arrangements required sons to give up a considerable degree of independence. Especially in the earliest generations, most sons had to devote at least a part of their labor to the family enterprise for a prolonged period, because fathers generally retained title to family lands until they died. This remained true even after a young man had cleared and begun working the share of family land he expected eventually to inherit. But the ultimate goal of this prolonged deferral of autonomy was to provide a farm for *each* son. It was not enough simply to allow one or two heirs to continue working the same piece of land that had been in the family for generations, as in a traditional patriarchal arrangement. In New England, a family's collective goal was to improve enough new land so that every son would have enough to support his *own* family.

As the leaders of these family enterprises, early New England fathers had great power and bore a tremendous responsibility, for it was clear that their sons were supposed to be the ultimate beneficiaries of their decisions. In farming families, this meant finding economic strategies to obtain land for all the sons, and it usually required them to stop their sons' schooling around the age of twelve. Merchants, ministers, and wealthier farmers might decide to provide sons with further education, in the form of continued schooling or placement outside the household as tradesmen's apprentices. Patriarchal expectations dictated that the father, not the boy, would make the decision about his son's calling, an inherently coercive situation for the boy. Still, the father had a moral obligation to make a decision that would benefit the boy, weighing his own ambitions and the family's needs and interests against his son's individual psychological and material needs. Reformed Protestant teachings emphasized that fathers must choose callings to suit their children's "in-clinations and . . . natural gifts of both body and mind."[87] "Parents," they were warned, "cannot do greater wrong to their children and the societie of men, then to apply them to unfit callings, as when a child is fit for learning, to apply him to a trade."[88] When a father decided to settle a son in a calling, his skill as a father was put to the test.

Although sons could not openly challenge their fathers or directly assert their own desires, the moral responsibilities of fathers did give wealthier sons, at least, a potential source of leverage in getting to do what they wanted. The experience of Sam Sewall, the second son of Boston merchant Samuel Sewall, is a good example. Though the elder Samuel Sewall initially placed his son Sam with a tutor to prepare him for college, the placement proved unsuccessful, as Sam turned out to be a mediocre scholar. His father brought him home again after two years, and when he reached sixteen sent him to Michael Perry, a shopkeeper, "to live with him upon Trial." After three months of winter, however, Sam was complaining about the poor living conditions and lack of heat in his new master's house. "I go to Mr. Perry," wrote Sewall, "and speak to him to send home Sam. from the Shop, that so his sore and swollen feet might be cured; which standing in the cold shop would prevent. He sent him home. Had no Coals."[89] Sam came home, reassured for the mo-ment that his father would look out for his interests.

The elder Sewall continued for the next six months to try to find an appropriate placement for Sam, becoming increasingly worried and discouraged. What is striking about his account of this period is the amount of pressure he felt himself under to make a decision. In March Sewall recorded a dream: "that all my Children were dead except Sarah; which did distress me sorely with Reflexions on my Omission of Duty toward them, as well as Breaking off the Hopes I had of them." In June he "Kept a Day of Prayer in secret" regarding, along with a death in the family, "Sam's being to be place[d] out." His seeming inability to settle Sam in a trajectory toward successful adulthood seemed to indicate that he was failing as a father. The death of his wife's mother, who had lived with the family and helped to raise all of his children, seems to have heightened his anxiety about his children. At church one Lord's Day in August, Sewall was overcome with tears. "I appointed this day to ask God's Blessing after the death of my dear Mother [Hull], and in particu-lar to bless Sam with a Master and Calling."[90]

Soon Sam began to work for Captain Samuel Checkly, another shop-keeper, but this situation was not satisfactory either. Sewall's brother spoke to Sam about "removing to some other place, mentioning Mr. Usher's." No doubt sensing his father's frustration, the boy became up-set. He could not sleep. Sent by his father to fetch some wood, he fainted. Was his father sharp with him? Perhaps. Curiously, though, the adult males who surrounded Sam do not seem to have blamed the boy for these repeated failures and instead urged the father to continue his search for the right master. Sam's uncle suggested the boy be removed "forthwith and place[d] . . . somewhere else," or else brought to live with him in Salem.

The process of finding an appropriate situation for Sam was his fa-ther's responsibility, not Sam's, an indication of the tremendous author-ity possessed by Puritan fathers. Still, in performing his duty Sewall was subject to considerable scrutiny. Relatives, neighbors, and other men ac-quainted with teenaged boys seem to have been willing to intervene in their negotiations with fathers over the choice of master or calling, just as Sam's uncle did in his case.[91] Moreover, Sewall felt a good deal of pres-sure from Sam. Their minister had preached against idleness, so Sam made the argument to his father that the calling of a shopkeeper "was an idle Calling, and . . . he did more at home than there, take one day with another." He had a hard time remembering the prices of all the goods, since they were not marked. But selling books would be easier, he hinted, since "the price of them was set down." Finally, Sam tried a more direct approach. He broke down and cried, saying that he did not want to go back to Captain Checkly's shop, convincing his father once and for all that Checkly was the wrong master for his son. The elder Samuel prayed, "The good Lord give me Truth in the inward parts, and finally give Rest unto my dear Son, and put him into some Calling wherein He will accept of him to Serve Him."[92] A year later, he found a situation for Sam with Richard Wilkins, a Boston bookseller. The placement took; Sam had gotten what he wanted.

What made this decision difficult for both father and son was that the *father* had the responsibility for finding the calling upon which the *son's* adult identity would be founded. By no means was their relationship egalitarian. Sam could not directly assert his desires but had to influence the outcome without making it appear as though he was challenging his father's authority. At the same time, the relationship was clearly reciprocal. Sam depended on his father's approval and patronage in finding a placement, but his father's self-esteem, as well as his standing with his own kin, depended on his providing a situation in which the son could succeed. The responsibility for directing a boy on the route to manhood belonged to the father. The blame, if the boy regressed and failed to assume manhood's responsibilities, was the father's as well. Sewall thus felt himself to be under considerable pressure to find a solution that would confirm his love and commitment to his son, to prove that he was a "tender father" who would reward the boy's loyalty by providing him with the property or skills that were his entree into manhood.

John Adams's account of his negotiation with his father over the choice of a calling during the mid to late 1740s is quite similar to the story of the Sewalls. The elder Adams was a prosperous Braintree, Massachusetts, farmer who aspired to upward social mobility for his children. The father sent John during his childhood to school with the local schoolmaster, evidently designing him for a career in the ministry. John, meanwhile, felt utter disdain for the schoolmaster, whom he later described as "the most indolent Man I ever knew," and instead of studying spent his time playing. His inattention to school "alarmed my Father, and he frequently entered into conversation with me upon the Subject." Two key conversations have been left to us. John told his father that he did not "love Books and wished he would lay aside the thoughts of sending me to College." "What would you do Child?" queried the elder Adams. "Be a Farmer," the boy answered. "A Farmer?" said his father, "Well I will shew you what it is to be a Farmer. You shall go with me to Penny ferry tomorrow Morning and help me get Thatch." For the moment the matter was settled, and "accordingly next morning he took me with him, and with great good humour kept me all day with him at Work."

On the basis of this interaction it might seem that family mores had changed, and that John Adams was being permitted greater freedom to assert his wishes than young Sam Sewall had been fifty years earlier. But in fact the elder Adams was only humoring his son: "At night at home he said Well John are you satisfied with being a Farmer. Though the Labour had been very hard and very muddy I answered I like it very well Sir. Aye but I don't like it so well: so you shall go to School to day."[93] John went back to school, evidently swallowing his feelings. He continued to be an indifferent scholar, however, and wrote, "In this idle Way I passed on till fourteen and upwards, when I said to my Father very seriously I wished he would take me from School and let me go to work upon the Farm." His father replied, "You know . . . I have set my heart upon your Education at College and why will you not comply with my desire."

At this point, fourteen-year-old John adopted a tactic similar to Sam Sewall's in his negotiation with his father. Rather than risk a direct confrontation, he took a compromise position, saying "Sir I don't like my Schoolmaster." With the wrong master, he pointed out, he was unable to thrive and do credit to his family. With another, his own inclinations would lead him to fulfill his duty. "If you will be so good as to persuade Mr. Marsh to take me, I will apply myself to my Studies as closely as my nature will admit, and go to College as soon as I can be prepared." At this point, Adams's father agreed to send him to Mr. Marsh, and he "began to study in earnest."[94]

In both the Sewall and the Adams episodes, an enormous importance was attached to finding the right master, so that a mentoring relationship could work. A boy's master had to be capable of governing the boy but also worthy of the boy's respect and emulation, never slipping into selfishness or tyranny or otherwise failing as a role model. If the boy felt respect and admiration for the mentor (father, master, or teacher), he would want to identify with the man, and would try to be as responsible and strong as he believed the older man to be. Adams later recalled his own early successes as the product of a desire to please his father and his schoolmaster, his two older male mentors, rather than of his own self-confidence or strength. His early sense of self grew out of a sense of identification with these models of manhood.

Even the well-known attempt by the father of Benjamin Franklin to choose the right master for his son, famous because of its failure, illustrates the ways in which the moral expectations placed on fathers could limit the exercise of paternal power. Benjamin Franklin's father was a Puritan convert who had migrated to New England in 1682, and he supported his family as a tallow chandler. Ben, the youngest son in a family of thirteen children, was sent to school beginning at eight because his father hoped to make him a minister. But his father could not afford to keep him there, so when Benjamin was ten he was taken out of school to work in his father's shop, which he disliked. The elder Franklin set about finding a trade that both he and Ben could agree on. "[H]e sometimes took me to walk with him and see joiners, bricklayers, turners, braziers, etc., at their work that he might observe my inclination and endeavour to fix it on some trade that would keep me on land." By turns his father decided to make him a cutler, then a printer, finally binding him out to his elder brother James, a Boston printer. In his autobiography, written in 1771, Franklin appears to have been a good bit more assertive and direct than either Sam Sewall or John Adams, recalling that he refused to sign the indenture for some time. Living in the seaport of Boston in the early eighteenth century, and having had an older brother who had run away to sea, he was of course aware of the option of becoming a sailor, and so was his father. Like Sewall and Adams, Franklin relied on his father to find him a trade in which he could succeed, though ultimately his dislike of his master provoked Franklin to run off to Philadelphia.[95]

Reconsidering the History of the Family in Early New England

Much of the historiography of childhood and parenting in early New England and elsewhere in the early modern world has been focused on the issues of early autonomy and ego development. It is argued that Puritan and other early modern beliefs in the need to control children's passionate, animal natures, and parents' attempts to "break" or "beat down" the stubborn and sinful wills of their children, had the effect of repressing children's development into autonomous individuals.[96] Some have gone so far as to portray the suppression of boys' autonomy in early New England as dysfunctional and neurotic.[97] But if we can put aside the assumption that males can achieve a healthy masculine role identification only by asserting their independence from their parents, we can understand why the Puritans' method of socializing boys made sense to them.[98] The main goal of Puritan child rearing was to teach children, especially boys, to become productive, morally responsible adults. They feared that children might become willful and selfish if not taught to obey their parents. But at least as important in child rearing was guarding children from the temptation to regress into childish feelings of narcissism and dependence on the mother. It was important for boys to find older males to identify with so they did not slip back into the narcissism of early childhood. As a young man proved his manliness through acts of loyalty and devotion to a powerful older man, he constructed a masculine self "based on devotion to the father," a "filially defined masculine self," which functioned to keep the boy from slipping into a world of fantasy and self-absorbtion.[99]

To suggest that boys in early New England defined themselves in relationship to older male mentors is not to say there were not emotional costs to this system of male socialization. One of the most significant was the attenuation of the bonds between mothers and sons. Mothers and sisters apparently figured little in the mentoring relationship, except perhaps as reminders of the emotionality and dependency that boys had outgrown. It is rare to find memoirs by seventeenth- or eighteenth-century men that even mention a mother's influence after early childhood. The emotional focus was all on the father.

To some extent, paternal socialization of boys was traditional, predating the Puritans by hundreds if not thousands of years. Parental supervision of the transition from childhood to adulthood had been the norm in England at least since the Middle Ages.[100] But what appears to have been different about early New England was the level of commitment that was expected from fathers, as well as the suspicion of maternal parenting. The Puritans who settled early New England increased expectations for the father's role in raising children.

It has been common for historians to contrast the parenting style of Puritan fathers (supposedly harsh and controlling, systematically directed toward stifling children's strivings for autonomy) to that of a later generation of parents, who supposedly took to heart the injunctions of John Locke's psychology and nurtured their children as individuals. But if we examine what Puritan and evangelical Protestant parents thought they were trying to achieve in the education of boys, the differences between Puritan and Lockean ideas dissolve. Locke's suggestions for the socialization of sons directly parallel Puritan child rearing practices, which is perhaps not surprising, since Locke had had a Puritan education. The aim of Puritan fathering was to keep children from being indulged or spoiled by their mothers, and to wean children, particularly boys, from what was considered an emotional, frivolous infancy and turn them into rational men. Similarly Locke, in his clearest statement on child rearing, *Some Thoughts concerning Education* (1693), began with the premise that children's constitutions would become spoiled by too much maternal "cockering and tenderness." The core principle of his educational system was that the child must learn in early childhood to deny his desires for luxuries and "soft and effeminate" things so he can "hearken or submit to his own Reason, when he is of an Age to make use of it."[101]

The Puritans are often compared unfavorably with Locke for their advocacy of beating down the will of children, but Locke was very much a Puritan in his insistence that parents should master their children's will absolutely, especially when the children were still toddlers. He said that "the younger they are . . . and the less Reason they have of their own, the more they are to be under the Absolute Power and Restraint of those in whose Hands they are." And although it has often been assumed that Puritan fathers were such tyrants that they sought absolute control over their children throughout their youth, in fact both the Puritans and Locke believed that boys should be brought up by adult male role models whose rational faculties they could learn to emulate, and who would offer them increasing levels of recognition and responsibility as they grew.[102]

New England minister Nicholas Gilman, when his fifth son was born in 1740, made an entry in his diary that articulated the goals that had been attached to paternal education in evangelical families since the seventeenth century. Gilman prayed to God to "[s]ave [the boy] from the Vanities of Childhood, Let his Youth be Wisely Spent [and] grant that his whole life may be pious and Usefull."[103] His role in rearing his own boys was primarily (as contemporaries understood it) a matter of teaching them to master the regressive impulses of childhood, grow in rationality, and gradually assume adult responsibilities. Whether Gilman should be seen as the intellectual descendant of the Puritans or of John Locke is a meaningless question. Both Puritan *and* Lockean ideas express the rationalist philosophy of child rearing that typified middleclass English Protestant culture in the seventeenth and early eighteenth centuries.[104]

Child rearing in early New England, then, was aimed at weaning young children, especially boys, from their infantile dependence on their mothers and teaching them to master their "effeminate" desire to be babied or coddled. The father took an active part in the child rearing process. By the time a boy reached puberty, the most central relationship in his life was with his father or some other adult male mentor. Although the boy was clearly subordinate to the authority of his father or master, the relationship was based on a mutual understanding that the older man would provide the boy with the training and usually the property that would allow him to become an economically productive, independent man.

Once a boy in early New England reached the age of fourteen or so, he would be considered a child no longer, but a youth. This new stage of life would last until a boy married, typically at around age twenty-five. And just as they had shaped his childhood, concerns about rationality and the passions, as well as manliness and effeminacy, would shape the course of a New England boy's youth as well as his ideas about friendship, sex, and love.

2
_____

Youth and the Passions:
Friendship and Love before 1700

On March 1, 1697, John Marshall, a thirty-three-year-old Braintree, Massachusetts, blacksmith, noted in his diary that he "went to town meeting to choose town officers and other needfull business." On other days in the month of March he borrowed money, attended two funerals, took grain to the mill for his father, participated in a militia training day, and traded work with neighbors. Except for the funerals, these events involved male-only interactions. During the course of the month Marshall received or provided labor, goods, or money to one Mr. Allen, Mr. Walker, his father, John Nucum, Eb Spear, James Puffer, and Samuel Penimon. Rarely did John Marshall refer in his diary to a woman; the reader learns that he was married and had children only when he mentions, on March 17, "I went to Cambridge about my son John to Mr. Bowers", on September 28, that his wife had a baby, and on September 29, that he "[w]ent to Boston to fetch Sister Fairfield to nurse wife."[1]

A relational approach to the study of gender ideologies among colonial Anglo-American New Englanders should logically require us to examine not only the relationships of fathers and sons but also those lateral relationships that produced what we now call male bonding. In our own culture, male friendships are among men's most important relationships, especially during adolescence but to some extent also at later stages in life. Largely because of the self-portrayals of men like John Marshall, we have imagined Anglo-American society in early New England as a society of men securely grounded in harmonious communities of male neighbors. But while such relationships existed, and were important in the lives of adult men, historians have sometimes overlooked the familial context that structured most Anglo-American men's experiences of community in early New England. Both the meaning of such lateral relationships, or friendships between men, and their availability were determined by a man's stage in the life cycle and his status within his own family.

In early New England, there were two socioeconomic frameworks for legitimate male companionship. The first was family labor and property distribution. Young men typically worked for their fathers and in the company of their brothers, cousins, and other male kin until the age of twenty-five or more.[2] As Marshall's references to his father attest, family land was often distributed so as to allow men to remain near their fathers and brothers in adulthood, creating a patrifocal world in which fathers, sons, and grandsons often lived side by side throughout their lifetime.[3]

The second framework was the system of labor exchange, credit, and trade that bound household heads into networks of mutual dependence. Exchanges of work and goods created mutual debts, which were tallied up every so often to ensure parity. On April 29, 1712, New London, Connecticut, farmer and ship's carpenter Joshua Hempstead wrote: "I was in town all day. in ye forepart I was Reckening with Brother Plumbe Mr. Christophers &c." Mutual obligation in turn bred goodwill and encouraged familiarity and bonds of camaraderie. Over the next two days Hempstead sent a couple of cows to pasture at James Rogers's, paid Daniel Lester for pasturing another, and went to visit his friend Roland Rogers, who was sick.[4] Within this world, companionability went hand in hand with trade and mutual indebtedness.[5]

We need to understand, though, that when it came to teenagers, male friendship and companionship did not have the same positive valences in this culture as they do in ours. Male companionship was judged according to its context. The companionship of fathers, brothers, and cousins was of course consistent with virtue and household order. Male companionship emerging out of neighborly labor exchange among mature, independent men was also viewed as socially useful, since trade, labor exchange, and friendship between household heads enabled them to better use their productive resources to provide for their families.[6] But parents looked askance at friendship and camaraderie among young, dependent males and did what they could to discourage it. The peer group relationships that are so important to teenagers' coming of age experience in modern Western society were viewed as obstacles to successful maturation in this world, and boys were instead encouraged to define themselves in relation to older, more virtuous adult males.

Attitudes toward male friendship in early New England were shaped in large part by the Puritan attempt to reform traditional patterns of sociability and manners, as well as by New Englanders' extraordinary reliance on family labor. Although taverns were available for men when they were traveling, Puritan leaders in New England frowned on tavern socializing. They limited the issuance of tavern licenses during the seventeenth century, thus restricting gathering places for conviviality among men.[7] Puritan leaders also eliminated the traditional feast days, such as Martinmas and May Day, which had provided occasions for sociability in English culture.[8]

Of course, sociability remained an important feature of preindustrial society, and adult men had plenty of opportunities to visit and socialize with each other. They could (and did) visit neighbors and relatives at home in the evenings and share a pipe and a mug of beer or cider. They could drink to one another's health, to patch up disagreements and remind one another of their commitment to good fellowship. For Puritan men as much as for other early Anglo-Americans, the capacity for friendly relationships was an important virtue. Plymouth governor William Bradford eulogized the minister William Brewster, for example, as a man "of a very cheerful spirit, very sociable and pleasant." The Puritan poet Anne Bradstreet described her father, Thomas Dudley, as "a prizer of good company."[9]

But while Puritans enjoyed a sociable glass of beer with their neighbors, they were committed to reforming traditional forms of sociable expression, including the rowdy and gregarious jollity in which men indulged at the tavern.[10] "Table talk . . . must be such as may edifie," warned the English Puritan writer William Perkins. Wit or "urbanitie . . . whereby men in seemly manner use pleasantness in talk for recreation, or for such delight as is joyned in profit to themselves and others" was permissible in conversation, but ridiculing their fellows or jesting at their expense was not.[11] Cotton Mather urged men in their speech to be honest, solid, useful, and never wrathful.[12] As it was important for men to display their commitment to well-ordered conversation, Puritan male diarists in New England were often self-conscious about how they spoke and presented themselves in social situations. Edmund Quincy, for example, resolved in the late 1660s or 1670s to be more careful "all the day long" of his discourse, to avoid using "foolish, jesting or taunting reproachful speeches," and to "abhor all liars tales & other stories, wanton songs [and] ballads." The rationale for purging these staples of traditional oral culture from speech was that social interaction itself was intended to serve God's purpose. In the future, Quincy resolved to himself, he would "[L]et all [his] speeches be serious, holy, inoffensive & edifying, weigh before hand what honor [his] discourse will bring to God, and what good to [his] friend."[13]

Social interactions were also supposed to be sincere and open, manifesting a conscience given up to the will of God; flattery, even to build goodwill, was deceitful. In other words, Puritans were supposed to come straight out and let their friends know what their shortcomings were. Minister William Brewster, for example, was eulogized as "inoffensive and innocent in his life and conversation, which gained him the love of those without as well as those within; yet he would tell them plainly of their faults and evils." Anne Bradstreet's father was "in manners pleasant and severe; the good him loved, the bad did fear."[14] Although they expected members of the redeemed community to feel sympathy toward one another, that sympathy required good Puritans to guard each other's souls, even at the risk of stepping on toes.[15]

Of course the social interactions of Anglo-American men in early New England were not all sober and austere. The diary of the Braintree blacksmith John Marshall provides evidence of conversations between men that were rich with stories and gossip. In a column on one side of the page, he recorded the occurrences that grounded his daily existence: work, weather, and Lord's day services. In a column on the other was his record of remarkable providences and notable events. Some of these events had potential religious significance, but they also included the scandals and stories that enlivened his life and stimulated his imagination. In February 1697, an earthquake caused "great terror" and a lively "discourse." There also was news of a French and Indian attack on some fishing boats, in which one man had been killed and six taken prisoner. In April Marshall reported in great detail the then-famous story of Hannah Dustin's escape from and murder of her Indian captors. There was gossip about suicides, drownings, accidental shootings; remarkable recoveries and mysterious deaths; and, in September, record of a surprise attack in which Indians killed or captured twenty inhabitants of Lancaster. "Our English fought manfully and killed divers of the Indians and finally drove them of[f] the island," Marshall wrote. The news must have come from Marshall's neighbors, as he had not been there, and no newspapers were being printed in New England at this time. No doubt they reassured one another, across a fence or over a mug of cider, that they would have fought manfully too.[16] Men's parables, advice, pointed reproofs, and expressions of love and approval continually defined, through discourse, the male community's expectations of other men. At the same time, their shared gossip and conversation allowed men to quiet their own anxieties about the precariousness of their lives and about their ability to perform their own responsibilities as men.

The social interactions of adult male neighbors and kin played an important role both in setting limits on the exercise of patriarchal power and in stabilizing patriarchal authority. This role was, essentially, to ensure that they all performed their duties as household heads. Male neighbors and kin could intervene in the interactions of a father and his son or a master and his apprentice, to ensure that (within a framework of appropriate filial deference and gratitude) the needs of the youth were being met.[17] Similarly, they could insist that a young man assume legal and financial responsibility for a child he had fathered, or that a married man limit his mistreatment of his wife.[18] Neighbors and kin who intruded into other families' interactions reminded men of their shortcomings and also demonstrated for the benefit of all who might be watching that men in general were reasonable, calm, and benevolent.

The conservative role of men's lateral relationships in helping to ensure that household heads fulfilled their family responsibilities was at least partly a traditional one. Traditionally, the concept of friendship was blurred with patronage and suretyship. The most common use of the term *friends* in the papers of seventeenth- and early eighteenth-century Anglo-American New England men referred to relatives or perhaps trading partners who might sponsor or assist a family if the father became unavailable. Sometimes "friends" were financial backers or the executors of wills. Boston merchant Peter Oliver appointed two men as overseers in case of his death, to supervise his wife's administration of his estate, calling them "my loving Choice Friends" and leaving them each ten pounds for their trouble.[19]

Usually, in fact, friends were relatives. When schoolmaster Joseph Green, writing to his brother who was at sea, referred to his brother's "friends" who "long to see you well come home," he meant himself, his other brothers, and his mother.[20] Plymouth town clerk and justice of the peace Josiah Cotton painstakingly copied down all of his family's correspondence for posterity as a way of paying "my dues to my Friends"; the friends he meant to describe were in fact the brothers and paternal uncles about whom he was writing.[21] When John May, a twenty-four-year-old settler in Woodstock, Connecticut, took three extended visits home to Roxbury, Massachusetts, during his first year in Connecticut in 1711, he recorded doing work for his father and going to see "friends." December's diary entries revealed that these friends were in fact relatives of the woman he was about to marry.[22]

Only one use for the word *friend* in seventeenth-century New England was specific to the Puritans. Christian friendship was supposed to exist between all persons who had shared the experience of conversion.[23] Christian friends were expected to admonish and remind one another of the word of God, and in this sense they too helped stabilize social relations. But the idea of Christian friendship also supplied a model for emotional bonding and intimate relationships between men: the love of Jonathan and David.[24] Occasionally this model could inspire a deeply emotional and affectionate relationship between two men, as it did in the case of John Winthrop, soon to become the governor of Massachusetts, and his fellow communicant Sir William Springe in the seventeenth century. Shortly before leaving England in 1630, Winthrop wrote Springe a letter in which he expressed feelings of love so exalted as to now seem quite extraordinary in a letter from one adult man to another: "I loved you truely before I could think that you took any notice of me: but now I embrace you and rest in your love: and delight to solace my first thoughts in these sweet affections of so deare a friend . . . I must needs tell you, my soule is knitt to you, as the soule of Jonathan to David: were I now with you, I should bedewe that sweet bosome with the tears of affection: O what a pinche will it be to me, to parte with such a friende!"[25]

Emotional expressions of love such as this between two men would have raised no eyebrows among seventeenth-century Anglo-Americans. Expressions of Christian love between converted, adult men were the very antithesis of the fallen passions—indeed were manifestations of the highest feelings a human being was capable of—because they were an extension of man's for God. It is an interesting letter from a modern perspective, since its writer appears entirely unconscious of the possibility that it expressed hidden homosexual implications, even though it expresses intense passion. Affective intimacy between adult men could be taken for granted in this society in a way that it no longer can.[26]

Youth and the Ambiguity of Friendship

While early New Englanders saw adult male fellowship as a social good, they frowned on another sort of male friendship. Close relationships between boys were suspect—not because they threw a boy's heterosexuality into question, but because they could threaten his relationship with his father or patron and disrupt his progress toward achieving an adult identity. New England boys from the age of ten or eleven were mostly socialized *not* in age-graded cohorts, as they are in modern, industrial-era schools, but in the familial settings of farms and shops, where fathers and masters could supervise their activities for most of the day. This was more than a pragmatic arrangement for organizing work; it also reflected the conviction that relationships with older men were more beneficial to a boy's social and moral development than relationships with peers.

Puritan and evangelical literature in the seventeenth and early eighteenth centuries continually urged youths and young men to prefer the companionship of their elders to the corrupting influences of their peers, an admonition that reflected the suspicion that youths were not yet capable of making rational, moral decisions. Minister Ebenezer Pemberton, in a sermon given in 1705 at the request of the merchant Andrew Belcher for the benefit of his son, twenty-one-year-old Jonathan, warned his listeners, "Youth is giddy and unthinking; they want the Wisdom and Experience of Age; their Spirits are all flame, their blood [is] hot and runs Races, . . . they will be endangered by everything they meet with." Later, he urged the young Belcher to "[f]requent not needlessly evil company, which carry a deadly infection with them."[27] Many fathers conveyed similar advice to their sons. Cotton Mather directed to his son Samuel, on the boy's departure for Harvard College in 1719, to "shun the company of all profane and vicious persons, as you would the pestilence. As much as you can, enjoy the company of such as may be your superiours."[28]

To some extent young men must have heeded their fathers, for it is rare to find mention of important peer relationships during youth in the surviving memoirs of adult Anglo-American men in New England before the eighteenth century. In the records we have, writers tended to place the greatest emotional and narrative significance on their relationships with fathers or other older men who sponsored them either materially or spiritually. For example, the letters that late seventeenth- and early eighteenth-century adult men in New England usually chose to copy and retain in their own personal records indicate that, to them, the ties most worth preserving were those of family, rather than ties of worldly or religious affinity outside the family. For some men, such as the ambitious town clerk Josiah Cotton, the ideological significance of family could be deeply practical, for Cotton knew he would be able to leave his children only small inheritances and hoped he could call on the "Friendship and natural Affection" of his more successful brother and other prominent relatives to provide them with patronage and opportunities for advancement.[29] Others, such as Joseph Green (whose only surviving parent was the widow of a Cambridge tailor), imbued family ties with religious and emotional significance, hoping that they would endure into the next world, knowing that his humble family connections offered little material benefit.[30]

Men who left spiritual autobiographies, too, tended to focus on their relationships with older males as the key relationships of their lives, generally crediting either fathers or pastors in bringing them to Christ.[31] These autobiographies typically fail to mention nonfamilial peer relationships before adulthood, or they treat them as a source of corruption, a trial that had to be overcome in order to succeed in a spiritual journey. Roger Clap remembered a turning point in his spiritual life when, as a child in England, some youths tempted him to play on the Sabbath but he turned them down.[32] In Michael Wigglesworth's autobiographical description of his years in college, peers appear only as competitors.[33] Another autobiographer recalled that "after [he] began to go to school and frequent the company of such as were as careless as [him]self of any things that considered their everlasting good [he] began to disrelish" the spiritual resolve instilled in him by his parents.[34] Secular autobiographies or memoirs followed a similar pattern. John Barnard remembered his schoolmates only for having gotten him in trouble with the schoolmaster.[35] Josiah Cotton's extensive memoirs contain virtually no information about childhood or even college friendships.[36]

To some extent, the absence of references to friends in seventeenth-century men's personal writings may reflect the limited opportunities most Anglo-American boys had for forming such relationships. Social life then was not age-stratified, as it is in an age of modern schooling. In towns and on ships at sea, youths had opportunities for socializing, but in the rural areas where most colonists lived, boys spent most of their time under the close supervision of older men in mixed-age households. Boys' closest age-mates in the large, interconnected families typical in early New England were most likely to be the brothers or cousins with whom they worked and lived. Boys had opportunities to form non-familial friendships while they were in school, but the duration of formal schooling was usually short, and even there, peer solidarity was discouraged. While boys and young men could engage in recreational activities like hunting and fishing or participate in militia training, these activities were sporadic rather than sustained.

Perhaps, too, boys and young men in this society had less need for close friends in the modern sense. When boys grew up knowing they would live their entire lives on land that bounded on that of their brothers and cousins, friendship would have melded with family in a way that made the two categories barely distinguishable. In England during the same period, in contrast, youths typically left home at around fourteen to go into service. Living in new places with relatively less supervision, they apparently had more frequent opportunities to form friendships and greater need for companionship.[37] For most New England farm boys, this need was less pressing.

At the same time, men's failure to mention peer relationships in memoirs does not necessarily mean they did not exist. Historians do have evidence of youthful peer group associations that belies the image created by parental advice and suggests why adult males might have wanted to forget or deny their youthful peer relationships. Even in godly New England, it seems that young men were more likely than their elders to indulge in the rowdy activities associated with traditional popular culture, at least until they married and settled down.[38] Ministers often complained about particular festive occasions, especially militia training days, that gave young men a chance to congregate in taverns and get drunk.[39] And in the evenings, after work was finished and parents or masters were in bed, youths seem often to have escaped from their houses to go "night walking," a shadowy and oft-condemned practice that seems to have involved mostly groups of boys and young unmarried men. Though evidence of such behavior can rarely be found in memoirs, court records reveal such youths harassing local householders, stealing fruit, throwing rocks at windows, knocking down fences.[40] We also find evidence in the diaries of men like Cotton Mather, who complained of the "knotts of riotous Young Men" who congregate "under my Window in the Middle of the Night, and sing profane and filthy Songs."[41] The youths' rowdy behavior seems often to have been specifically designed to ridicule adult authority, not through direct confrontation but through minor rule breaking and silly, though sometimes offensive, jokes and insults. In 1678, for example, youths Gershom Hawkes, Stephen Belding, and William Armes broke into the shop of William King, a tailor in Hatfield, Massachusetts. They then went down to the cellar of the shop, stayed there to play cards until very late, and defecated on the beam of King's loom before making their escape.[42]

Sometimes young men in company with friends also tried to flirt with or harass young women, an adventure that was likely to involve not only the thrill of interacting with the girl but also the excitement of avoiding being caught by her father. In Redding (now Reading), Massachusetts, in 1680, for example, householder John Brown described an evening encounter with two local youths who had awakened Brown's family late at night by throwing some stolen pears into his daughter's window. When Brown came to the window to confront them, the youths pretended to be drunken travelers who had mistaken the house for a tavern, "demanded Entertainment for them and their horses, and asked if [Brown] had a ever a Pretty Girle" within. They made noise like they were trying to break down the door. Brown recognized their voices and induced them to leave by threatening to expose them to their families.[43]

This kind of carousing by groups of young rural men (and occasionally women) had been at least partially tolerated in traditional England.[44] But Puritan New Englanders saw it as evidence that youths had a corrupting effect on each other, and specifically sought to limit and discourage just this sort of behavior.[45] Puritan reformers abolished traditional feast days, and also eradicated the revels, sporting events, and competitions that Elizabethan Englishmen had held on such holidays, in which young men were often the main participants.[46] Their conscious intent was to eliminate opportunities for youths to lead each other astray, and instead to maximize their contact with older males who could teach them to master their passions.

Perhaps, then, it was the Puritans' equation of manliness and responsibility that explains why the writers of memoirs so rarely mentioned friendships. Boys' rowdy behavior was not so much a proof of manliness as of frivolity. It was a sign that they were not yet men. When adult men wrote memoirs without recalling their adolescent friendships, or presented those friendships as obstacles to their later spiritual development, they may have been conveniently forgetting a phase of carousing in their youth. Manhood in this culture was achieved gradually, through identification with a father or master. In narratives of that achievement, relationships that were seen as delaying a boy's maturation may have been embarrassments rather than cherished memories.

The spiritual memoir of John Brock suggests that, in his mind at least, a deep divide separated a man who had experienced conversion, an important indicator of maturity and thus manhood, from the silly and immature boys who played tricks on adults. Brock became a college student at Harvard in the 1640s, at the unusually advanced age of twenty-three, after he had already become a covenanted member of his local church.[47] Brock's most important relationships immediately before and during college were with older adults, including his father and his pastor, his tutor at Harvard, and other adult male members of his church in Cambridge.[48] His younger classmates, in contrast, spent their time with each other. He described them as "taken with the world," "deceitful" (this after an incident involving adolescent pranks), and enamored of "vain" dinner conversation.[49] He described their relationships as "carnal friendship." However, as the younger cohort of students approached graduation, they began to have religious concerns and to be interested in following Brock's own more sober example. He considered their new interest in him to be a sign of "spiritual friendship."

So perhaps in truth young men did form friendships at a stage in life when they were not ready for the responsibilities of adulthood, and used those relationships to carve out a little freedom from the pressures of adult supervision. Yet they regarded those relationships not as a normal part of gaining their independence from parents, as we do, but as disrupting the process of becoming an adult. Even in the autobiography of Benjamin Franklin, often read as an antipatriarchal text, only one early peer relationship plays a role, and it is an ambiguous one at best. In recounting the story of his early life for his son's benefit in 1771, Franklin tells the story of only one intimate boyhood friend, John Collins, with whom he liked to debate and who helped him to run away from Boston at age seventeen in 1723. Because of Franklin's initial success in Philadelphia, Collins decided to join him there. But by this time Collins "had acquir'd a Habit of Sotting with Brandy." In the telling, his friendship with Collins now nearly became Franklin's ruin, as the other boy borrowed and spent his money and threatened to besmirch by association Franklin's rising reputation.[50] With his usual resourcefulness, Franklin found a sponsor willing to send Collins off to Barbados as a private tutor, where he could have a chance to redeem himself in a more regulated family setting without wrecking Franklin's own prospects.

Collins's role in Franklin's life story illustrates, as it was meant to, the potential for peer relationships to disrupt the vertical male relationships on which social stability and success depended. In Boston, Collins had provided critical support for Franklin, who wanted to break away from his master, to whom he was still technically bound by law if not moral obligation. But later, in Philadelphia, Collins threatened to subvert the patronage relationships on which Franklin's success now depended, and he had to be dispatched to the West Indies. His function in the story is as a symbol of youthful folly repudiated.

Many New Englanders remained suspicious of young men's friendships well into the eighteenth century, though the idea of friendship did gain a new legitimacy in the years before the American Revolution, especially among young urban men. This suspicion of young men's peer relationships was consistent with prevalent concepts of manliness. New Englanders, like other early modern Englishmen, associated youth with the passions; youths were an inevitable but dangerous and destabilizing part of the body politic. Young men were a danger, both to themselves and others, because they were ruled by their appetites, their hot blood.

This notion is the rough equivalent of our twenty-first-century idea that teenagers are controlled by their hormones. But rather than seeing these natural drives as a source of energy to be channeled in positive directions, early New Englanders saw them as dangerous to the young men themselves. Youths would become stable, responsible adults capable of controlling their passions only if they learned to identify with their fathers and other older adult males, and not with one another. This idea had a direct analogue in attitudes toward young men's sexuality.

Sexuality

The personality embodied in New England Puritans' ideal of manhood was an ascetic one. It was rational, godly, and resolute. The ideal man ruled his dependents with a firm but gentle hand, and he was mature, if not middle-aged. He might take pride in his physical strength and health, but he was not a sensual man. In fact, he would probably have criticized indulgence in sensual pleasures like fine clothes as effeminate, along with such other indulgences as libertinism, gambling, and courting women.

The question of Puritan sexuality has been hotly debated. Parameters of the debate are fairly clear: on the one hand, Puritans condemned giving in to the lusts of the body (outside of marriage) with a zeal unmatched by other seventeenth-century writers. On the other hand, Puritans rejected celibacy and idealized sexual love within the context of marriage, as well as the affectionate companionship that wives and husbands could provide to one another.[51] At issue has been the extent of sexual repression in Puritan New England.

Until recently, this debate has been informed by a sort of essentialism about sexuality—an assumption that sexual desires and their expression are natural and instinctive, and that societies encourage either their repression or their liberation. More recent contributions to the debate, under the influence of trends in cultural studies, are wary of this assumption, and some indeed point out ways in which sexual desires and orientations are themselves culturally constructed. The fact is that seventeenth-century New Englanders made assumptions about male sexuality that are virtually foreign to us. Indeed, they would likely have considered their ideal ascetic man to be the very model of male sexual potency, especially if he had five or six sons and some daughters as visible tokens of his virility. The sexuality of a young man prior to marriage, on the other hand, was much more problematic; it was a sign of effeminacy rather than manhood.

Early New Englanders' cultural ideal of manliness required boys to master the effeminacy of childhood and become rational, productive, and self-controlled. Their progression to manhood via a relationship with the father or another adult male helped give boys a sense of security while weaning them from the dependence and emotionality thought to characterize childhood. But becoming manly required boys not only to overcome childish feelings of dependence and narcissism but also to suppress an earlier identification with women, as well as their desire for female tenderness and affection.

Defining manhood in this way implied, in turn, a set of attitudes about adult male heterosexual desire. All adult men in early New England society had to achieve a heterosexual identity in order to live fulfilling and socially integrated lives, for the Puritans emphatically rejected celibacy. Only men who married and became the sexual partners of women would be recognized as having full manhood status. But at the same time, the feelings of longing that a man might experience toward a woman in the course of establishing that sexual relationship were viewed as potentially dangerous to his achieving a stable adult male identity. And those feelings were viewed as particularly dangerous to youths.

For this reason, early New Englanders fashioned a variety of social mechanisms to deal with the dangers to youths of sexual passion. In addition to a draconian set of laws intended to deter any deviant or extramarital sexual behavior, early New Englanders structured their social relationships so as to insulate young men and women from sexual experience. So long as they were dependent, young people were controlled by the family, which was supposed to prevent them from engaging in sexual relations. Even when they were placed out to live apart from their own families, boys and girls were subject to surrogate parental supervision, which guarded against youthful indiscretion.[52] Indenture agreements often contained provisions expressly prohibiting apprentices or servants from committing fornication or contracting marriage, as well as from playing cards, gaming, frequenting taverns, or keeping bad company.[53]

Supervision by older males, of course, did not entirely insulate boys from the effects of falling in love, which could be traumatic. For example, in the summer of 1676 Timothy Dwight, a young apprentice to Joseph Hull, fell into a "Swoun" and "kicked and sprawled, knocking his hands and feet upon the floor like a distracted man." After a day of worried questioning and expostulating with the young man, the family discovered that "his trouble arose from a maid whom he passionately loved."[54] Although Timothy was temporarily allowed to go to her, to cure his ravings, he was also counseled that this kind of passion was inappropriate because he had made it a "stalking horse" to his love for God.

Though the practice of placing out teenagers was meant to protect them from their passions, ironically it may sometimes have encouraged adolescent crushes. As servants in the houses of others, and living away from the comfort of their own families, youths might have sought companionship. Living in close contact with other adolescents of both sexes, either other servants or the children of the household, opportunities were presented. Romantic crushes must have developed easily in these settings. In 1709 John Leverett, president of Harvard, wrote to Timothy Woodbridge in Connecticut about his reasons for sending home Woodbridge's daughter Mary, a servant in the Leverett household. As Leverett explains, his stepson Thomas Berry, "a boy of not 15 years of age, and but a sophomore, has been smitten with her, by which he has been taken off from his studies . . . and reduced to a very inconvenient state; Distance and absence may cure a passion that may be greatly detrimental to my wife's only son and which can never be anything serviceable to your daughter."[55] Part of the role of a father and master in a household full of young people was to protect them from their own passions, changing living arrangements to separate teenagers from objects of temptation, and solemnly admonishing them not to forget that their first obligation was to God.

Early Anglo-American New Englanders' suspicion toward adolescent infatuations was buttressed by the common early modern belief that sex was particularly dangerous to boys and young men. Popular wisdom in England, and to some extent medical theory, suggested that sexual intercourse was actually physically dangerous to the health and reproductive capacities of young males before they reached maturity, in their mid-twenties (the customary age of marriage for men). Before the seventeenth century, parental and community pressure worked to control young men's sexual behavior. But as England's economy developed opportunities for labor outside the family in the seventeenth and eighteenth centuries and parental supervision became less effective—or less possible—a market developed for advice books to guide young men's behavior, including their sexual behavior. Writers consistently offered the same advice: "[I]f a man . . . especially in his youth gives way to frequent coition, it will cross his present health, debilitate his generative faculties, and entirely subvert his constitution by drying up the moisture of the body and damping that genial warmth so necessary to the human procreation," warned one widely read guide to sex published in multiple editions throughout the eighteenth century.[56] Similarly, a 1735 sexual advice tract warned young men that if they wanted to be able to father children once they married, they should "shun the soft Embrace Emasculant, till twice ten years and more Have steel'd thy Nerves."[57]

The concern of advice writers, and presumably parents, was not simply to control young men's sexual behavior so that young women would not get pregnant. At issue as well was how society understood and dealt with a particular transition in the lives of young men. In early modern English culture, the separation of boys from the realm of women was symbolically affirmed through their gradual integration into a male world of work and sociability. The Puritans were explicit about the need for young men to relinquish the emotionality and dependence that went along with childhood. But this relinquishment was not easy, and one potential pitfall along the way was romantic or sexual involvement.

Some psychoanalysts suggest that the issues of differentiation and merger that are so central to boys' development in childhood rise to the surface again when young men begin to have sexual relationships with women.[58] Reexperiencing a close emotional bond with a woman may provoke or renew ambivalence about separation and growing up. The cases of Timothy Dwight and Thomas Berry illustrate the dangers of romantic experience. The youths became so overwhelmed by their crushes that they were unable to function in their ordinary social roles. From the point of view of their parents and masters, such feelings were dangerous because they could lead to a destructive self-preoccupation or narcissism. The Puritans expressed their distaste for such behavior by insisting that decisions to marry must be made rationally and deliberately, and with parental supervision just to be sure.

One of the steps boys had to take to move out of the ambiguous identity of youth and become men was to prove to their parents—and also to themselves—that they were ready to act like men. Because they saw moral behavior as depending on the ability to bring the will under the control of reason rather than the passions, young Puritan men sought to prove their manhood by achieving mastery over their bodies and their fantasies. It seems apparent from surviving diaries that their struggles to gain control over sexual urges were not uncommon in the transition from teenage self-indulgence to adult manhood. Some of the spiritual diaries of men in their early twenties, for example, include frequently repeated resolutions to avoid an unspecified secret sin, presumably masturbation.[59]

Puritan men probably held themselves to a much higher standard of rational self-control than ordinary Englishmen aspired to. Part of what was innovative about Puritans' social practices was their attempt to in-

duce people to internalize moral restraint, rather than simply relying on
community pressure to shame those who violated customary norms. We
tend to look at this concern with sexual control as repressive, an attitude
born of our late nineteenth- and twentieth-century understanding of
masculine sexual urges and aggression as "natural" and instinctive, and
therefore at some level positive or desirable.[60] But what self-mastery implied was also the sublimation of desire and its redirection into productive work. For many seventeenth-century New England youths, sexual
self-mastery must have seemed less like repression than a test of their
own manhood. It signified that they were ready to leave behind the
world of longing and dependence on women and earn their place in a
world of masterful, self-controlled adult men.

This sense that self-mastery was a test of manhood is apparent in the
diary of Michael Wigglesworth, a young tutor at Harvard College in the
1650s. Wigglesworth was plagued by involuntary seminal emissions for
about four years, beginning at age twenty-two in 1652. He suggested
that the key to manly mastery was the same in love as it was in war. The
will must master the body's impulses, whether the desire was for sexual
release or to run away from a battle. But regardless of his exercise of will
while awake, Wigglesworth's body continued to master him when he
slept.[61]

One of the interesting things about Michael Wigglesworth's sexual
fantasies is that they involved his (male) students. Confessing in his diary to feelings of "fond affection to my pupils while in their presence"
provoked paroxysms of self-abasement and guilt. However, Wigglesworth felt guilty about his desires *not* because they were homosexual in
nature but because they showed his lack of rational control over his appetites. It was as unmanly to lust after women as to be a sodomite; indeed "in this culture sexuality itself whatever its object makes a man
effeminate."[62]

Wigglesworth's fear that his involuntary seminal emissions revealed
an unmanly lack of control over his body was paralleled by a belief that
the emissions were draining his body of vitality and weakening him
physically. He worried that his seminal emissions were the product of a
venereal disease contracted as a result of some unspecified "sin of my
youth," possibly masturbation or even some early illicit sexual encounter.[63] His fears are a good indication that ideas about the debilitating effects of early sexual release for males were part of seventeenth-century

popular culture, for he was so panicked about further "provocation unto the ejection of seed" that he was afraid even to read a medical book, for fear that it might inspire more dreams.[64]

The idea that sexual desire was unmanly was not unique to Anglo-American New England but was, on some level, widely accepted throughout early modern English culture. Throughout this period the opprobrious term *effeminate* referred not to a man with homosexual feelings but to one with "a strong heterosexual passion."[65] A man who succumbed to sensuality was thought to be "enslaved" to his passions, whereas to be manly meant to exercise rational control over the appetites.[66] Sexual love was potentially disruptive; it could make a man ignore his better judgment in order to please a woman. Excessive sexual love was seen as dangerous to reason, as well as to the firmness of the will. A long tradition held that a man in love lost his manly courage, and hence his ability to perform where it really counted, in the all-male world of battle. The belief that a courting man lost his manly courage goes back to the sixteenth century; as Romeo says to Juliet, after he has failed to fight with Tybalt,

> Thy beauty has made me effeminate
> And in my temper soft'ned valour's steel.[67]

By relinquishing his reason and giving in to his passions, a man in some important sense became unable to do what he needed to do to face life and succeed in it.

Courtship

Once a young man had achieved self-mastery (and, perhaps more important, proved to his parents that he had done so) he could begin to think about courtship and marriage. He was supposed to enter into marriage in a rational, deliberate way, choosing or acquiescing to a partner who would help to enhance both his own and his family's material and spiritual interests.[68] Love was not a prerequisite to marriage in seventeenth-century New England but was supposed to grow out of it.[69] Courtship was ideally initiated by the parents when *they* felt their children were sufficiently mature to handle married life. Marriages were in theory and practice economic and religious partnerships created to promote the financial and spiritual interests of the partners' families, but sexual love was usually also a factor. In fact most matches were created through some combination of financial negotiations by parents or other relatives and mutual attraction between a young man and a young woman.[70] But it seems that being swept away by romantic feeling could be a sign that a man was not yet mature enough to marry. For example, when Jonathan Hopkinson fell in love with and courted Hannah Palmer in 1675, becoming secretly engaged to her, his mother refused to consent to the match, saying they "were childish: & our beginnings was contrary to the way God's people went in."[71]

While a man was courting a woman, he was never seen as really manly. In late seventeenth- and early eighteenth-century Anglo-American New England, the image of a man courting a woman was always vaguely undignified, especially if he was in love with her. For example, in 1701 when Solomon Stoddard criticized men who wore wigs (a long-standing target for Puritans), he invoked the image of a courting man. Wigs were "*Light,* and *Effeminat,*" Stoddard argued, and subverted the "Masculine Gravity" and "Solemnity of Spirit" that manly men should properly display. Men who worried about their hair, and other emblems of courtly fashion, Stoddard went on to suggest, looked "as if they were more dispos'd *to court a Maid;* than to bear upon their Hearts the weighty Concernments of God's Kingdom."[72]

It was not only Puritans who treated courting men as objects of ridicule. The early modern usage of several words in the English language suggests how silly and undignified courtship made a man. The terms *spark, beau,* and *gallant* were all used to describe a man courting a woman, or a ladies' man. A spark was also a fop who "affects smartness or display in dress and manners." A beau was "a man who gives particular, or excessive, attention to dress, mien, and social etiquette; an exquisite, a fop, a dandy." Similarly, a gallant wore fine clothes, displayed courteous manners, and paid court to ladies.[73] Courtship evidently made men frivolous and effeminate.

What was unmanly about courtship? One famous courtship, conducted by a man in middle age and therefore at the height of his manly dignity, may provide some clues. Samuel Sewall, the merchant who was so proud at his first son's birth in 1677 and who struggled through his second son's adolescence in the 1690s, by 1720 had outlived two wives and achieved great professional success as a judge and an advisor to the governor of Massachusetts. Now, at the top of his career, he wished to marry the attractive and rich widow Katherine Winthrop. Recording the progress of his suit in his diary, Sewall revealed a wide crack in his usually dignified, august self-assurance. When he visited Madame Winthrop he was acutely aware of how he was being received, of her mood, and of how she reacted to everything he said to her. Encouraged when she received him with wine and marmalade one night, he was rebuffed by her "dark and lowering" expression the next.[74] Courtship had made Sewall vulnerable to the whims of a woman. Because he was courting a widow, who was able to make her own decisions about her future and her property, his fate depended directly on her will and preferences, not a situation to which he was accustomed. Young men who courted young women were spared Sewall's indignities to some extent, since at least part of the negotiation of a first marriage was conducted by parents over issues involving property settlements, and so young men did not need to feel personally responsible when a suit failed. But Sewall was directly subjected to Katherine Winthrop's scrutiny, and when she found him wanting, he smarted. Worst of all, even though their negotiation over Sewall's marriage proposal took place in private, both Sewall's and Winthrop's friends and family members were fully aware of their courtship. When she ultimately rejected him, the knowledge that the suit had failed was a matter of public interest for some time.[75]

Though Sewall did not come right out and say what it was about this courtship that made him feel vulnerable, the concerns he expressed about it had to do with his being forced to conform to the desires of a woman. Sewall himself claimed that his suit for Madame Winthrop failed because she demanded that he keep a coach and start to wear a periwig, expenses that he complained would have cost him 100 pounds a year and landed him in debtors' prison. Wearing a periwig would not really have cost him much, but his anxiety about it seems to reflect a deeper (and still pervasive) fear that women would unman their male admirers if they could. This fear was not unique to the Puritans. During the Restoration era in Europe it was common to poke fun at men who fell in love with women, suggesting that it made them into fops who cared only for their clothes and their appearance and lost the ability to do manly things like go to war.[76] Sewall's comment about the coach reflected another commonly expressed concern about love, that it could be costly and pose a threat to men's economic autonomy and competence. His concern may have been an emotional one as much as a financial one, though, building on the common stereotype of women as materialistic consumers whose desires to keep up with fashion would force their husbands into bankruptcy. One evening during his courtship of Katharine Winthrop, Sewall heard the governor observe that "in England the Ladies minded little more than that they might have Money, and Coaches to ride in." Sewall sardonically agreed that the same was true in New England.[77]

If the trials of courtship were difficult for a man as mature and experienced as Sewall, what might they do to a young and inexperienced man? Placing negotiations over courtship in the hands of older men provided a social mechanism for protecting young men from their desires, in addition to protecting family assets. The contrast between young men as pathetic, even comical neophytes and their strong, masterful fathers was portrayed quite explicitly in a story that appeared in a Boston newspaper in 1735 about a "young Gentleman of Durham, Connecticut" who had courted a young lady "with his solemn Protestations of Love, and ask'd for an approving Smile" for about two years. The woman, the paper went on to relate, had continually rebuffed his attempts: "[T]his at last so discouraged the fond Courtier that he gave over the pursuit; but being restless, he applys to his Father for relief . . . and he, being willing to help his Son in this difficult Case, immediately mounts his Horse and away, to the Parents of the young Woman; and discoursing half an Hour with them, they agree and strike up a Match." According to the story, the father, whose mastery (and money) had enabled him to do in half an hour what his son could not do in two years, rode home to give his son the good news. But a final twist in the tale drove home a moral about the danger of love matches, especially to the young. The son's happiness at his impending match was so powerful that it made him delirious, and having "los[t] the government of his Passions, in super-extatick Joy" he expired in the arms of his beloved.[78]

Some parental anxieties about early sexual experience were no doubt focused on its psychological effects. But there was also an economic dimension to their concerns, because sex could produce a pregnancy, and that would mean new financial burdens for men. To discourage extramarital sex, Puritan-controlled town governments before 1680 whipped both men and women who were proved to have engaged in fornication, a sanction that undoubtedly contributed to the low rate of premarital intercourse and premarital conception.[79] In addition, communities usually forced unwed fathers to pay maintenance for their illegitimate children. Moreover, older men could put substantial pressure on young men to force them to marry. Samuel Sewall, in the midst of trying to settle his son Sam into an appropriate calling in 1696, heard rumors that his ward, Sam Haugh, had impregnated a girl. Sewall gave him a talking to: "[I] told him if she were with child by him, it concerned him seriously to consider what were best to be done; and that a Father was obliged to look after Mother and child." The source of this duty was not so much his obligation to the mother as to the child: "Christ would one day call him to an account and demand of him what was become of the child: and if [he] married not the woman, he would always keep at a distance from those whose temporal and spiritual good he was bound to promote to the uttermost of his power."[80]

Fathers of pregnant, unmarried daughters often insisted on a marriage, and sometimes so did fathers of the young men involved, as for example when servant Martha Beale was seduced or raped by John Row, the son of her master. John's father, Elias Row, insisted that John would have to marry her and made an agreement to that effect with Martha Beale's father, at least if she should become pregnant. It is significant that the agreement was conditioned on the Beales' promise not to "noise the fackt aforesaid abroad," which suggests that giving a man a reputation for sexual misbehavior could seriously damage his credit within the town.[81]

The idea of a shotgun wedding appalls modern Americans, because we have come to think of marriage as promoting romantic bliss, denying its economic dimensions. Early New Englanders were far more frank about the economic purposes of marriage, and this was reflected in their ideas about manhood. Nearly all New Englanders assumed that a man was not really a man unless he could support a household of dependents. It seems to have been a widely shared assumption in New England culture that manly potency was linked to a man's ability to provide for a wife and children, an assumption reflected even in the vocabulary of courtship. Men who promised women that they would marry them if they became pregnant were implicitly asserting that they were old enough and economically competent enough to maintain a household. The twenty-year-old suitor of a young woman named Sarah Crouch, for example, told her he was as good as his rival, because "he could maintain her as well" as the other man.[82] Massachusetts law itself associated male potency with the ability to provide for a child, providing that a parish would be responsible for the care of a child begotten out of wedlock if "the reputed father is run away or impotent."[83]

It should be emphasized again that New Englanders' stress on rational self-control and the more general English treatment of economic competence as a prerequisite to male sexual maturity were not viewed as repressing manliness but as constitutive of it. Manliness, which implied not only moral qualities but also physical strength and sexual potency, required that a man be able to provide for and maintain control over his dependents. This kind of competence was not achieved until that stage in a man's twenties or even thirties when his father passed control of his property over to his son. In judging a young man's readiness for this transition, a Puritan father probably placed greater emphasis on rational self-mastery than other contemporary fathers, who may have focused slightly more on qualities like physical strength and the ability to manage a farm or a shop. But the concept of masculine gender was basically the same in either case. Mere maleness, a function of a man's "heat" from youth onward, was not enough to make a boy into a sexually mature man. Manliness was not a result of his nature but of his transcendence of youth.

Male Sexuality and the Balanced Body

While early New Englanders were anxious about the emasculating effects of sexuality and romantic love on young, unmarried men, their understanding of the sexuality of mature, married men was quite different. This contrast was particularly evident in medical ideas about the male body, as poor Michael Wigglesworth finally discovered. Early in 1655, when Wigglesworth was considering a marriage being negotiated on his behalf by his family, his worries about his body reached a new height. Fearful that his involuntary ejaculations had weakened him already, he worked himself into a feverish anxiety before finally consulting a doctor. Was it better for him to marry, to use "physick," or to remain single, he wanted to know. A Doctor Alcock offered calming and reassuring news. Wigglesworth's condition was the perfectly normal: "naturalis impulsus seu instinctus irresistibilis." In other words, his emissions were caused by the physical impulses produced by male sexual desire. The best possible cure, Dr. Alcock told him, was marriage, which would give him the regular sexual release that his body required. Indeed, the doctor had seen it work with another patient. Sex with his wife had not weakened that patient further but cured him, the proof of which was that this man "did very well after, and hath divers children living at this day."[84]

Medical theories about male sexuality were explained to lay Englishmen during the seventeenth and eighteenth centuries in a variety of books on sex and reproduction.[85] The theories proposed were loosely based on Galenist conceptions of the male body, which suggested that physical health depended on a body's ability to keep each of its humors in balance with the others.[86] A man's sexual potency depended on his ability to control or moderate his passion, and manliness was associated with maturity. Although male youths did not become truly sexually potent until about age twenty-five, these books suggested, men's potency continued to grow until it finally reached its peak in middle age.[87] At the same time, the sex book writers asserted that mature male bodies (as well as female ones) needed regular sexual release, and that a man's ability to perform sexually with his wife was a vital sign of manliness.

This popularized description of the human body explained several related aspects of gender and sexuality. First, it described maleness in terms of its superiority to (rather than its complementarity with or difference from) femaleness.[88] What kept the body running, its motive force, was the innate heat of the blood, which was fueled by the consumption of food and generated by the operations of the heart. Men's blood was hotter than women's, and it was this simple fact that determined gender. Second, it portrayed the body as an economic system in which the ideal state was a harmonious balance. What kept the body healthy was its ability to maintain an equilibrium among the four bodily humors—blood, phlegm, black bile, and yellow bile. Sex, for a man, could either promote or disrupt this balance.

Masculine potency was produced by the urges of the blood and the body's tendency to restore itself to balance. In the hot male body, some of the blood was transformed through the operations of that heat into "seed." Healthy male sexual impulses were seen to be inspired by "ticklings of the seed," that is, the need to release excess humors produced by the normal operations of the blood. The cooler female body, in contrast, was unable to change its blood into seed, leaving an excess supply of blood to be emitted every month during menstruation. Thus a man's acts of sexual intercourse, as one writer put it, were "proofs of his

heat and strength," because it was his hot blood that enabled him to
have seed in the first place.[89]

At the same time, virility required not just heat but moderation, because the body's humors had to be kept in balance. The virile man was a
rational, moderate man, not one ruled by his passions. In fact, moderation was the key to all physical health; as one text stated, "[I]t is food
moderately taken that is well-digested that creates good Blood, and good
Blood makes good Spirits, and enables a Man with vigour and activity to
perform the dictates of Nature." Moderate consumption would yield viable seed, which could then be planted in a fertile female body, always
ready to receive it, to produce the next generation's crop. Moderation
also led to happiness. The blood's heat enabled it to produce spirits that
determined a person's temperament. Moderate heat produced happiness, excessive heat generated anger, coldness created hatred.[90]

One of the things that strikes the modern reader of seventeenth- and
early eighteenth-century discussions of male sexuality is how they are
linked with the concept of economic competency. The Galenist model of
a body that had to be kept in balance had its analogue in the idea that excessive consumption and spending threatened the stability (as well as
the health) of a household economy, and in the commonsense notion
that the economic health of a household (or a nation) depended on its
ability to balance spending and debt with production and income—an
idea that underlay the earliest purely economic theorizing in the seventeenth century.[91] A man's potency depended on his rationality, frugality,
and ability to control his spending. Every popular treatise on the subject
reiterated the same set of concerns: men should avoid all excess, "for it
will allay the briskness of the Spirits, and render 'em dull and languid."
A man should "be careful that he does not spend his Stock too lavishly"
if he wanted to spend it well.[92] These manly qualities enabled him to
maintain a household without going into debt. Excessive longing for
sexual and sensual pleasure was viewed as a snare that could deplete a
man's physical strength, just as his desire for material pleasures could
tempt him into excessive spending and deplete his economic independence.

The perception of such feelings as effeminate parallels the twin notions that it was women's desire for sexual gratification that threatened
male health, and women's longing for material pleasures that was the
greatest threat to a household economy. Although moderate sex (the

kind a man would have with his willing but properly virtuous wife) was healthy, lust inspired merely by the desire to please a woman could make a man emit too much and destroy his health. The popular advice writer Nicholas Venette devoted many pages to the supposedly deleterious effects of "excessive venery" on a man's body. "The frequent caresses of women exhaust our strength and forces entirely; whereas moderately used, they preserve our health, and render our body more free and active than before."[93] Women were seen as having an unlimited desire for sexual intercourse. Their minds were less capable of rational perception, or distinction between right and wrong, and therefore were more easily influenced than men's by their own inner passions, as well as by outside influences.[94] Women were more lustful than men because their cooler, wetter bodies (unlike the hot, dry bodies of men) could not convert their humors into energy and activity as effectively as men's. They needed regular sex to dissipate their pent-up desire.[95] A popular stereotype portrayed women as harlots who could provoke men to sexual excess, disrupt the masculine economy, and lead to male ruin. The 1698 edition of *Aristotle's Masterpiece,* for example, warned of "harlots" who were "like a Horse Leach, ever craving, and never satisfied."[96] Women were not only sexually insatiable but also greedy and materialistic, and they would lead men away from the straight and narrow path to worldly competence "into places of danger, till they have caus'd them to ship-wrack their Fortunes, and then leave them to struggle with those storms of Adversity that they have rais'd."[97]

The model of manly selfhood that Galenic theory constructed was outwardly simple. Mature, moderate, and self-controlled men were manly, strong, and sexually potent men. Young, passionate men were effeminate, weak, and impotent. Manliness thus seemed to be a simple matter of self-control. But even within the terms of medical theory, women were always a destabilizing factor. Women could feminize even manly men.

Popular medical ideas about male sexuality in early modern Europe, then, paralleled the Puritan ideology of manhood. There was a clear bifurcation between youths, for whom sex was dangerous, and men, for whom it was healthy. This distinction would have been explained both in physical terms, by the idea that young men's bodies were unstable until they were fully developed, and in psychological ones, by the notion that youths were still ruled by their passions, while in older men rationality prevailed. What concerns underlay the ideas that youthful desire was so dangerous, and that sex for older males within the context of marriage was a source of health? Perhaps this construct allowed fathers to deny what would seem to be the obvious physical superiority of the younger men, and helped to justify their attempts to control their children.[98] Yet an underlying concern seems also to have been the pervasive anxiety about the effects of desire and fantasy on young men's ability to become capable, functioning adults. Like the suspicion of romantic love, fear of adolescent male sexuality reflected a general cultural suspicion of the emotions and of the influence of women—the same suspicion that underlay the cultural pressure to wean boys from dependence on their mothers.

Unlike in modern Western societies, then, neither peer relationships nor falling in love assumed a central place in young Anglo-American men's coming of age experiences in early New England. Both were viewed as a product of the passions, and as corrupting. A youth earned his manhood not by winning recognition from his peers, male or female, but by gradually earning the respect of his father. Only by learning self-mastery, rationality, and control over the passions—by mastering the desire and dependence associated with women—would he gain the mental, moral, and physical qualities necessary for him to assume adult male responsibilities.

3

Youth and the Challenge
of the Eighteenth Century

Although most Anglo-American fathers in New England had been able to provide livelihoods and competencies for their sons in the seventeenth century, demographic developments in the eighteenth century made this increasingly difficult. The practice of partible inheritance itself threatened to undermine the New England family system, for it was clear that lands would soon be subdivided to such an extent that the parcels would no longer be viable as family farms. Although a few generations of farmers in the seventeenth century had been able to head off the crisis by making use of previously undivided town land, by the eighteenth century property owners in most of the long-settled towns had run out of land to give to their children.[1] As their ability to provide for their sons by dividing up their land declined, fathers faced a new question: would they be able to continue to live up to the expectations set by the earliest generation of New Englanders? Fathers in different parts of New England faced this question at different times over the course of the century, depending on their economic resources and the stage of development of their local community, so it cannot be said that there was a single decisive moment of crisis throughout New England. But as the eighteenth century wore on, increasing numbers of fathers had to find new ways to live up to their moral obligation to settle their sons, and young men had to face the uncertainty of not knowing whether the new strategies were going to work.

The strategies varied. In some cases, sons spent more time working away from home and took more responsibility for their own daily lives and futures, which lessened their fathers' ability to make decisions for them. Other sons lived at home, continued to work for their fathers, and tried to earn extra money through seasonal employment, with the expectation of eventually saving enough money from a combination of wages and parental contributions to be able to purchase their own land. Some, if their families could afford it, received their portion in the form of an apprenticeship or an education that would prepare them to enter a trade or profession. Other strategies probably involved fathers as much as ever. Some fathers went into debt to purchase new land to give to their sons, generating income to repay their loans by increasing their holdings of livestock and then selling the livestock for cash to planters in the West Indies who imported their food from North America. And some fathers moved their entire families out onto the new land, for the sake of keeping everyone together.[2]

In the past, historians have often suggested that the most important result of these changes was to lessen fathers' control over their sons and to make sons more autonomous. Certainly the exaggerated interdependence typical of father-son relationships in seventeenth-century New England was eased in the eighteenth. The implications of this shift can, however, be overstated. There is little or no evidence to suggest that most eighteenth-century sons were eager to kick over the traces and leave their fathers behind. Rural New Englanders continued to think of the ideal man as a mature, responsible father and an independent property owner, despite demographic conditions that made those ideals harder to live up to. The core childhood experience on which these ideals depended, namely the gradual establishment of father-son bonds as a prelude to adulthood, continued to be at the center of male socialization.

Indeed, many eighteenth-century adult men continued to identify with their fathers or older male mentors, and they went to seemingly extraordinary lengths to avoid criticizing even the harshest and least helpful of fathers. Like seventeenth-century men, men who grew up in the mid-eighteenth century and related their coming-of-age stories in autobiographies or memoirs imagined themselves as having become men through the assistance of a good father or master, and not by overthrowing the father's authority. The memoir of Jonathan Burnham, born the fourth child of an Ipswich, Massachusetts, farmer in 1738 and apprenticed at age fifteen to a blacksmith, described his former master as "a good old man that built his house upon a rock and brought his family up in the nurture and admonition of the Lord." At nineteen, Jonathan left to enlist in the army, a common strategy for young men during the colonies' various wars with France, since they could use the bounty paid for their enlistment as a down payment on land. After his discharge Jonathan returned to work for his master, then served another two years in the army, then went back to Ipswich again. This time his master said to him, "Jonathan we read that a faithful servant shall be a dutifull son at length." Although the master had no farm to offer, he "gave me his eldest daughter to wife, who was a beauty and loved me as her eyes." In 1763 Jonathan and his wife moved to New Hampshire "on a place I bought where we lived and did prosper, for a most forty years."[3] Although it is clear that Burnham earned most of the capital for his eventual success on his own, his master retained a prominent role in Burnham's coming-of-age narrative as a kind of benevolent provider or fairy godfather.

John Cleaveland, the fourth son of a relatively prosperous Connecticut farmer, went to great lengths in his autobiography to reconcile his belief in the good father with the reality that his father had sometimes put his own interests ahead of those of his sons. John had wanted to go to school, but his father decided against it, a decision that John excused by saying that his parents' poverty had forced them to rely on their children's labor. John's father did not discover his son's calling for the ministry until the boy suffered an incapacitating injury while doing heavy labor at age seventeen. By then the father was more financially secure and was looking about for ways to settle his younger sons, so John was quickly prepared for college and sent off to Yale. He contained his ambivalence toward his father by highlighting his father's eventual recognition of his talents, and the two men remained close friends during John's adult years.[4]

Occasionally, despite his best efforts, the writer of a memoir was simply unable to construct a good father or father figure. Ashley Bowen was such a writer. The son of a Marblehead almanac maker, Bowen led a peripatetic early life; following the death of his mother not long after his eleventh birthday, Bowen's father more or less abandoned the family so that he could negotiate a new marriage with "a fine rich widow." To avoid the expense of supporting his son, the father bound Bowen out for seven years to a sea captain, a monstrous sadist who beat the boy unmercifully for entertainment. In his memoir of the experience, Ashley

Bowen recounted instance after instance of his own loyalty and attempts to please his master, for which he was rewarded with beatings and hostility. Finally he ran away, citing as grounds the fact that the master had abandoned his own wife and thus proven himself a bad man, not entitled to the world's respect.[5] Neither Bowen's father nor his master fit the cultural ideal. Even so, Bowen's memoir shows an adult man still going to extraordinary lengths to define himself in terms of a relationship with an older man.

Historians' emphasis on the authoritarian, repressive side of the father-son relationship in this society has produced a particular narrative of early New England history. According to this story, the decline of eighteenth-century fathers' ability to provide for their sons led to a diminution in patriarchal authority, which enabled sons to rebel against their fathers and emerge, after the American Revolution, as autonomous individuals. In the context of this narrative, our image of men as autonomous individuals appears to be a natural and inevitable fact: so long as the artificial constraint of patriarchal power is absent, don't men naturally wish to become autonomous? But in fact, there was nothing natural or inevitable in the eighteenth century about the cultural icon of the autonomous male individual. Sons' psychic reaction to their fathers' declining ability to provide for them was much more complex.

Despite their declining economic power, fathers remained emotionally central to their sons' lives, and sons continued to see the older men in their lives as strong male figures with whom they could identify. This tendency to imagine fathers as the centerpiece of a stable and prosperous society profoundly influenced the cultural imagination of New England society through the eighteenth century.

Of course, to argue that fathers and father-substitutes remained central to the emotional lives of New England men in the eighteenth century is *not* to argue that the relationships that defined manhood remained static. Young people who grew up facing increasing uncertainty about their future, knowing that they would bear at least part of the responsibility for earning their portion, were in certain ways more receptive to cultural innovation than earlier generations. Although the evidence of change in the lives of eighteenth-century youths is difficult to read, by piecing together strong evidence about the lives of urban and college-bound youths with sketchier evidence about rural young people, it is possible to discern some general shifts over the course of the century in the patterns of young men's lives. Chief among these changes was the growing importance of peer relationships and love in the coming-of-age experience of young men between the ages of fourteen and twenty-five. And as these relationships became more important, friendship and romantic love began to be reevaluated in a morally positive light, to a certain extent helping to ease cultural anxieties about the moral and psychological vulnerability of youth.

The New Sociability of the Eighteenth Century

One new influence in the lives of youths by the end of the seventeenth century was the growing visibility of the English gentry, especially in and around the port cities of New England. Although New England had been relatively cut off from the rest of the empire during the 1640s and 1650s because of political turmoil in England, metropolitan interest in the colonies revived following the Restoration in 1660. New England was gradually integrated into a trans-Atlantic commercial economy that also involved trade with the islands of the Caribbean, the Canaries, Newfoundland, and elsewhere. As a trading economy grew, a new class of merchants began moving into New England, settling in ports like Boston, Salem, and Newport. These new men tended to be, if not English by birth, at least more culturally identified with the English upper middle class and the English court than with colonial Puritans and middling farmers, and their cultural differences were often a source of shock and dismay for many local folks.[6]

A few New England men experienced the clash between the two cultures quite directly when they traveled and visited the English court. One such man was a highly educated twenty-seven-year-old New England Puritan named Jeremiah Dummer, who went to London in 1708 to serve as an agent for the colony of Massachusetts and kept a diary of his experiences. As a colonial lobbyist, he was expected to pay his respects at court, which since the Restoration of Charles II in 1660 had become the social center for London's fashionable lords and ladies. The contrast between the austere Boston of his childhood and court society at St. James's tested him. On his first day there, he wrote in his diary: "This day . . . I was entertained with the sight of all the great female beauties of the Court which pleased me to that degree I thot I could have gazed on them forever." His next reaction was to try to get control over his feelings: "But now . . . this seems a great fault and weakness in my mind. And my reason tells me I should be chiefly enamoured with virtue. I consider beauty is extremely Superficial, but Skin deep; if you take the finest woman in the world and strip off the epidermis, you'll see that the horror of her aspect will fright away the beholders, faster, than her charms attracted them before."[7] At first, Jeremiah coped with his feelings like a good seventeenth-century Puritan man was supposed to. He tried to use his reason to distance himself from his sexual feelings toward these beautiful women by imagining them as monsters.

Although most New Englanders did not have the direct experience with upper-class English social life that Jeremiah Dummer did, the growing importance and visibility of the English merchant elite in New England's cities forced many colonists to confront a new set of material and cultural influences, including gender ideals and styles of self-presentation that directly challenged older Puritan ideas. The merchants were part of a growing English upper middle class that, as England's commercial economy expanded during the Restoration and the eighteenth century, gained access to an increasing amount of wealth and used it to cultivate a personal style modeled after the style of the aristocracy. Women's dress became increasingly ornate and provocative, while men prided themselves in their sophistication, elegance, and good taste. Men also measured their manhood, in part, by their success in charming or seducing women. Unlike the Puritans, with their ethos of moderation and self-control, their sober dress, and their earnest commitment to marital fidelity, the English upper and upper middle classes inhabited a culture of display and open flirtation.

The influence of these new men and their cosmopolitan culture was most pervasive in New England's uppermost social groups. Jeremiah Dummer, whose own background and wealth allowed him to imagine himself as part of this upper middle class, abandoned the Puritan values of his boyhood, stayed in London to further his ambitions for advancement, and assumed a courtly style of masculine behavior. He had a high-profile affair, never married, and, according to a contemporary observer, eventually "grew a Libertine and kept a Seraglio of Misses round him to whom he was lavish of his favours."[8] Other men—those who hoped for success as merchants or urban professionals in New England—adapted to the expectation that men would wear wigs and English fashions (even if, like Samuel Sewall, they did so reluctantly). This process of assimilation, coupled with the familial encouragement of intermarriage between some of the oldest, wealthiest Puritan families and the new merchants, helped to create a distinct new urban upper class in New England.

Members of this urban elite possessed what were, for the Puritans, new and distinctive attitudes toward sociability. Rather than experiencing sociability within the community as an extension of the church congregation, with its commitment to moral reform, they imagined sociability as purely pleasurable—an opportunity to share interests and tastes with like-minded people. Instead of worrying about the corrupting effects of friendship, they celebrated it as a helpful adjunct to commercial relationships. Merchants and their associates created new, all-male spaces in which men could enjoy their friendships while conducting business: coffeehouses and gentlemen's clubs, for example.[9] Success as a merchant in the early modern Atlantic world required social connections, the more extensive the better. While the wealthiest men had family ties with English investors, giving them both financial backing and enduring investment relationships, other ambitious men tried to expand their access to credit and capital by broadening their social connections.[10] Coffeehouses and exclusive clubs allowed men to expand and deepen ties with fellow merchants and other colleagues, whom they praised in an increasingly explicit celebration of the ideal of friendship and amity among men. Clubs like the Society of Freemasons, whose first New England chapter was founded in Boston in 1733 by a group of wealthy merchants and gentlemen, claimed to be based on a mutual commitment to the ideals of friendship and sympathy.[11] By the 1730s, the obituaries of gentlemen had routinely come to describe the deceased as "a kind and obliging Friend" or as "warm and sincere in his Friendships."[12] Ships were commonly named *Friendship* or *Amity*.[13] Poems on the subject of friendship were common.[14] *Friendship* was the buzzword of the eighteenth century.

Within this newly gregarious urban milieu, middling young men began to carve out new patterns of sociability of their own, forming clubs and groups with other youths, not for the purpose of sharing ribald amusement but for mutual self-improvement. College students, for example, began to form groups to debate religious and philosophical issues. Both Edmund Quincy and Ebenezer Parkman were members of a North End religious society that met on Sabbath evenings, and also of the Wednesday Night Club, which met at Harvard during the 1720s.

Members of this group, about half of whom became ministers within a few years, presented essays or speeches and engaged in "Disputations and Observations thereupon." Members were required to behave consistent with "Morality, . . . a Religious or Civil Life" and could be fined or removed from membership for their failure to live up to the group's standards.[15] Their pragmatic commitment to improving one another's debating skills while at the same time keeping each other on the straight and narrow was not unlike the rationale behind the Friday evening Junto that Benjamin Franklin formed in 1727 after moving from Boston to Philadelphia—a group of aspiring young clerks and artisans who hoped to acquire both the social polish and the reputation for moral probity that would enable them to succeed as tradesmen.[16]

Even further along the cultural spectrum from gentlemen's clubs were the young men's groups formed specifically to provide members with spiritual sustenance and mutual moral oversight. The church in New England had a long tradition of allowing or encouraging lay meetings among the converted.[17] Toward the end of the seventeenth century and at the beginning of the eighteenth, New England ministers began to encourage the creation of meetings specifically for young men, to promote piety among the members. These societies appear to have been more common at first among middling, urban men, where the need was greater, than among rural populations. John Barnard joined such a group in Boston after he graduated from college in 1700.[18] Ebenezer Parkman likewise entered a "Friday Evening Association of Batchelors" in Boston's North End in 1722, a society that had been in existence since 1677. Some of these groups welcomed ministerial input and supervision or were initiated by ministers, but others were entirely independent of a formal church.[19] Several religious societies were also established at Harvard College during this period.[20]

One of the major stated purposes of these groups was a commitment to Christian friendship, or mutual spiritual "watching." The North End group, for example, came together "to avoid those temptations & abandon those courses that by Sad Experience we find our Youth to be exposed or inclined to." The members agreed that boys or men who repeatedly failed to attend meetings or "live[d] scandalously & prove[d] a discredit to the Meeting or a dishonour to Religion" would be barred from the group in the future.[21] A late manifestation of the Puritan movement for the reformation of manners, these young men's groups were organized around a concept of mutual spiritual solicitousness that required them to be brutally honest about one another's moral failings. Their philosophy of friendship was stated by Ebenezer Parkman in the aphorism, "A friend like a Glass will discover to you your own infirmities."[22] But though these groups grew out of Puritan and other reformed Protestant traditions of moral reform, they were something new. In no sense was their discipline imposed by fathers or legal authorities; these were voluntary associations in which young men themselves assumed the responsibility of disciplining one another.

Young, middling urban men no doubt pursued different aims in joining religious and self-improvement societies than merchants did in going to the coffeehouse. One major benefit of membership in a young men's society was reassurance at a critical life stage during which boys were still uncertain whether they could successfully make the transition from dependence to their adult social role. Such societies emerged at a time when more and more young men were feeling unqualified for full communion in the churches of their parents.[23] Although occupational data on these men's groups is limited, a study of a Charlestown Christian young men's society has shown that most of its members came from families in the middling ranks of artisans and tradesmen, neither the richest nor the poorest families in town. Most were themselves apprentices.[24] We can surmise, then, that these youths' success as adults would depend less than it traditionally had for rural young men on their loyalty to their fathers and more on their ability to find and please customers in a commercializing economy. The responsibility of mutual governance and simply the security of being part of a group may have given these young men confidence that they could indeed assume adult responsibilities.

Perhaps the most significant cultural effect of these young men's groups was to give a new legitimacy to the idea of friendship between young men, since the reason for their association with each other was not to rebel against patriarchal authority but to take mutual responsibility for each other's moral welfare. In contrast with the subversive, "corrupting" influence of boys who got together to harass adults and flout authority, the young men in these associations explicitly presented themselves as promoting virtue and morally upstanding behavior. This rationale for friendship, too, seems to have helped raise the value that young men placed on their friendships. It is around this period that we

begin to see collections of letters attesting to lifelong friendships between men who had formed bonds in their youth, like the letters that
Ebenezer Parkman and Edmund Quincy continued to exchange
throughout their lives. These letters possess a formal, classical feeling,
perhaps because the writers were so self-conscious about the moral rationale for their pursuit of friendship, even when they were discussing
such intimate subjects as courtship and masturbation.[25] But even if these
young men seem to us moralistic and stiff, we should nevertheless recognize that their behavior challenged the expectations of a patriarchal
culture. In assuming responsibility for overseeing each other's behavior,
they were making the claim that youths possessed moral capacities that
had not previously been recognized.

In addition to the genteel celebration of friendly conversation and the
Protestant notion that friends could offer one another mutual moral
support and oversight, a new, almost euphoric optimism about friendship, sociability, and human interaction came to pervade urban culture
in New England during the eighteenth century. This optimism about
friendship was buttressed by developments in moral theory associated
with the Scottish Enlightenment, sometimes referred to as sentimentalism. These moral philosophers expressed a new, optimistic idealism
about commercial society, which they thought would produce personal
relationships based on mutual sympathy.[26] Sympathy, or disinterested
friendship, would provide a new basis for social stability and cohesion,
which would in turn create a more benevolent, moral world. This optimism was a marked turn away from seventeenth-century anxiety about
the corrupting potential of the passions.

Some evidence suggests that sociability came to play a greater role,
too, among the farming families who made up the majority of New England's population. Encounters between men in taverns became a more
ubiquitous feature of rural and small-town life as the number of taverns
rose quite dramatically during the eighteenth century.[27] And in particular it was their teenage sons and daughters who seem to have found
the new "polite" style of self-presentation intriguing. Puritan ministers
noted young women's wish to emulate the new fashions, and inveighed
generally against the younger generation's desire for "Courtly Pomp and
Delicacy."[28] Signs that patterns of sociability among rural young people
were changing include descriptions of young people's parties, or "frol-
ics."[29] While it might be overstating the case to claim that young people

were developing a newly distinctive youth culture, the evidence does suggest that young people were spending time with one another and developing important relationships, independent of adult supervision.

Manhood and Courtship in the Eighteenth Century

The new merchant elites in New England towns and cities had their own styles of courtship and self-presentation. Rather than demanding that men and women remain modest and rational in one another's company, they welcomed flirtatious heterosexual encounters at new kinds of social events like dinner parties, salons, and balls.[30] Genteel women were increasingly valued not for their modesty and industry, as in Puritan culture, but for their beauty and vivacity. Men were admired not for their rationality and responsibility but for their wit and discernment.[31] The facility to observe and comment on female beauty became a point of distinction that marked a man as truly refined, and men vied at balls and other events to be thought the most refined connoisseur of the charms of the women present.[32] (Gentlemen also believed themselves entitled to comment on the attributes of any woman they saw on the street, and ordinary women like shopkeepers' wives and daughters seem to have been particular targets for harassment.)[33]

But like the Puritans, these men remained deeply suspicious of romantic love. Because they so obviously participated in world commerce, these merchants have often been taken as the heralds of a more modern culture and have been seen to have introduced more modern ideas about family relations. But insofar as modernity includes an acceptance of romantic love as the basis for marriage, this assumption cannot be sustained. The English merchants who resettled in the colonies at the end of the seventeenth century aspired to live and behave like aristocrats and gentlemen, and this meant, in part, displaying a marked distaste for too much emotional closeness. Their genteel ethos called for detachment and moderation in social interactions, and they disdained displays of enthusiasm, passion, and intensity as rude and unrefined. The writers of eighteenth-century books and essays on manners addressed to would-be gentlemen advised young men to avoid love's snares by associating with many women and refusing to fix their fancy on any one of them, and they commonly took a cynical view of what a man had to do to win a woman. If he commented on her physical beauty and called himself her "devoted Slave," it was said, he could not fail. Writers were self-consciously ironic; one author suggested, for instance, that letter writers mix their protestations and vows of love with "Three Thousand Lies, Fifty Pounds weight of Deceit, an equal Quantity of Nonsense, and treble the whole of Flattery."[34] Although not all gentlemen adopted it, the pose of the libertine, who earned his manhood by seducing women without marrying them, was very much a part of genteel culture. For New England's merchant gentlemen at the end of the seventeenth century and the beginning of the eighteenth, it was still unmanly to fall in love.

For men lower down on the social scale, either rural or urban, evidence of ideas about love, courtship, and seduction is hard to find, but evidence about certain aspects of their sexual behavior is readily available. We know that over the course of the eighteenth century in New England's population as a whole, there was a pronounced increase in the number of young women who went to the altar already pregnant, a clear indication of an increase in the incidence of premarital sexual intercourse. The rate of premarital pregnancy began to increase in most New England communities after 1680, reaching such high levels after 1750 that it has been estimated that as many as one-third of all brides were already pregnant when they married.[35] Also, the rate at which young men denied their moral responsibility for pregnancies and contested bastardy claims by young women rose after about 1690. Criminal sanctions against men for fornication gradually diminished, presumably as a more diverse population was unwilling to impose shaming punishments on sons for their failure to live up to stringent reformed Protestant standards of self-control.[36] Some historians have taken this evidence as proof that the ideal of the libertine was replacing older ideals of manly responsibility among New England's youth, and some young men probably did win prestige among their peers by appearing to toy with women. However, young men's attempts to play the rake were usually checked by mechanisms of social control that required them to play the man and marry their lovers. Evidence of the rising rate of premarital pregnancy must be read in connection with the comparatively low rate of births outside of wedlock.[37] These statistics suggest that although Puritan strictures against premarital sex were losing force, the traditional expectation in English yeoman society that men would marry their lovers and support their children remained relatively unchallenged.[38]

At least two mechanisms developed before 1750 to ensure that men would marry the women they were courting and would thus live up to their parents' idea that a man was measured by his ability to support his children. Communities were apparently still willing to coerce men who fathered children out of wedlock into marrying the mother of their children. Although surviving court records do not show precisely what legal mechanisms were used after 1730 to induce men to marry, it is likely that they were most often initiated through quasi-civil petitions for child support brought before justices of the peace.[39] In Massachusetts and Connecticut, systems had apparently evolved by about 1740 for the imposition of maintenance orders either after or in lieu of bastardy actions brought in lower-level criminal courts.[40] The monetary sanction for bastardy was the cost of child support for the first four to five years, usually assessed at two and a half shillings weekly for a total of twenty-five to thirty-two pounds. In Massachusetts, for example, the mother would go before a justice of the peace and swear out a complaint against the alleged father. On the basis of that complaint, along with the testimony of her midwife, she would be awarded an order for child support.[41] Evidently, however, a man could avoid either trial or enforcement of the judgment if he married the woman, in which case the support order would not appear in the record books. In a 1738 case, for example, Gill Belcher agreed to marry his pregnant lover, Mary Finney, and was married by the justice of the peace on the spot.[42] (This case appeared in the records only because Belcher alleged that he had been too drunk during the proceeding to know what he was doing and immediately appealed to the Governor and Council of Massachusetts for an annulment.)

The other option for a man was a private settlement. If settlement negotiations were begun early enough, a man could offer a settlement in exchange for a promise to keep the affair secret.[43] Such cases illustrate, at the very least, that a man's reputation for "manliness" among his parents and relatives in early eighteenth-century New England continued to depend on his not being identified as sexually promiscuous or irresponsible. The behavior of Ebenezer Thompson in 1726, after getting his girlfriend Lydia Wyman pregnant, illustrates how important it was to him to at least maintain the illusion that he was a responsible, mature man. His greatest concern was to avoid publicity. Going to the Wyman family house in Woburn, he pleaded with Lydia to publicly deny that the child was his, for "he had denied it so much to his friends that I can't not leave you now & would pray that you would not expose me." Evidently he believed his reputation with his relatives rested on their belief that he was chaste and capable of exercising sexual self-control before a marriage that they would sanction.[44] But before Lydia would let him go, he had to answer to *her* claims on him as the price for her silence. "You know you have had to do with me time after time," she said, reminding him that as part of their sexual relationship he had implicitly assumed a responsibility to support any child he might father. Ebenezer's response to her is most telling: "[I]f she would go away," he said, "he would come and see her and give her something and I will be manly to you."[45] He would prove his manliness to her, however halfheartedly, by quietly providing for her and the child.[46] (There is no record of how much he promised to pay, though Lydia's brother suggested forty pounds, significantly more than the cost of a child support order). The existence of such cases suggests that the personal costs of fathering children out of wedlock remained high for men rooted in small New England communities, even if the communities were no longer willing to insist that young men abstain from sex before marriage.[47]

Scholars have long suggested that in the mainland Anglo-American colonies, as well as elsewhere in the English-speaking world, control over marriage transactions moved away from parents and into the hands of sons and daughters during the eighteenth century.[48] Young men, rather than their parents, became responsible for initiating courtship, and young women gained the power to consent or to refuse. No longer were their own negotiations subsidiary to parents' financial negotiations over a young couple's future. But although it is clear that young couples in the eighteenth century gained much more control over their sexual lives, parents retained some power to oversee their decisions. Legal mechanisms to force men to marry their lovers worked because parents continued to supervise and be involved with their daughters' courtships.

Understanding courtship procedures in rural areas of New England helps us to see how parental oversight worked. When a young man decided to proceed beyond mere flirtation, he was expected to ask the woman's family if he might call on her. There followed a number of visits to the house, where most sustained courtship activities were likely to take place. A courtship by a young Cape Cod ship's captain named Benjamin Bangs, for example, was probably fairly typical. When his ship was wrecked in December 1747, Bangs was taken in by the family of Mr.

David Rawson in Braintree, where he met Rawson's daughter. After staying for a few days to see about the ship, Bangs went home, but he returned for visits to Miss Rawson half a dozen times over the next few months. During those visits, having come a considerable distance, he stayed through the night at the invitation of the family.[49] It is likely that during those overnight visits, Bangs and Rawson's unnamed daughter slept in the same room or even in the same bed, getting to know each other during the late hours and talking about a possible future together. By the 1730s, many New England parents had apparently decided that they would allow their children to engage during courtship in an old-fashioned Welsh custom called bundling, sleeping together in the same bed while fully clothed.[50] Critics of bundling charged that it created too great a temptation for ordinary mortals, and they were probably at least partly right.

Some families in mid-eighteenth-century New England apparently took a casual attitude toward the formal rituals of courtship and simply assumed that if a couple slept together at night, they must be planning to get married.[51] This was the assumption, for example, in the family of Huldah Reed, a young Woburn woman living with relatives in 1749. The father of the family testified that "while she lived with us Samuel Kendal came to see her sundred times, as I thought Courted her, and they seemed very fond of each other, and would go together alone into her bed Chamber when he came, & would be together alone as long as they pleased." One night in particular, "he and she were alone together the biggest part of the night, for after we were in Bed, I heard them talking &c Several times in sd night, in the room where we left them when we went to bed."[52] Despite the appearance of laxity, these visits were supervised, for if parents did not know what went on in beds at night, at least they knew *which* young man was courting their daughter, and if a pregnancy resulted, they would know whom to hold responsible.[53]

Despite the persistence of legal mechanisms to reinforce the traditional linkage of manly sexuality with economic competence and support for dependents, more and more men were resistant to being forced to marry, even at the risk of becoming known as rakes or libertines. Men became more willing to contest bastardy claims after about 1690.[54] Some men also, evidently, became more forthright about denying their moral responsibility for their lovers' pregnancies. By the middle of the eighteenth century it was becoming slightly more common for men to refuse settlements until they had been dragged into court, suggesting that they cared less about the publicity those suits would bring. In 1750, for example, Samuel Stone declined to marry Huldah Reed and entered into settlement negotiations with her only after being brought to court, on the urging of the judge.[55] Similarly, Ephraim Keith, Jr., a recent Harvard graduate reading law in Taunton in 1763, was presented with a warrant on the complaint of a local family that he had gotten their daughter pregnant. With the help of a lawyer, Ephraim got his father to settle the matter out of court with the woman's family rather than enter "Some disadvantageous Accommodation of the Matter," presumably a marriage.[56] Afterward, Keith described his behavior as "the [mere] Pecadillo of begetting my own Likeness" and expressed his "Resentment on the Account of the disingenuous Conduct of my inhumane Persecutors."[57] (However, he still had to apologize to his father.)[58]

What would eventually undermine New England's system of parental oversight of courtship was not so much male irresponsibility as an emerging set of ideas about the nature of courtship and marriage. Beginning around the 1740s, New Englanders became engaged in a lively debate about the relative merits of romantic and marital love.[59] Certain writers in newspapers and journals began to describe marriage as "the most perfect State of Friendship" and to take the position that "no Man can be a fine Gentleman . . . that makes a bad Husband."[60] Advice books, such as the widely read *Oeconomy of Human Life,* began for the first time to take the position that love was not to be feared when it was directed toward a modest and virtuous woman. Indeed, love was a refining passion: "Shut not thy bosom to the tenderness of *Love:* the purity of its flame shall enoble thine heart, and soften it to receive the fairest impressions."[61]

Part of what made possible this reassessment of romantic love in the eighteenth century was a reevaluation of the role of the emotions in moral life. In a transatlantic cultural shift associated with the emergence of sensibility and sentimental moral theory, educated and middle-class people in eighteenth-century Britain and Anglo-America were developing new attitudes toward the feelings.[62] Puritans in the seventeenth century had followed the prevailing theory of psychology, which conceived of the mind's faculties as hierarchically ordered, with reason superior to the passions. The conversion experience essentially tamed the will, making possible its voluntary submission to reason. However, the new Scottish school of moral philosophy suggested that the psychological

impetus for virtuous behavior came not from reason but from innate social affections, or feelings. Around the same time, evangelical Protestant
theology began to suggest that the conversion experience operated directly on the emotions, sanctifying and purifying them. Rather than reason, then, it was the emotions or affections that became directly responsible for virtue.[63]

This new attitude toward the feelings in moral theory led logically to a
reassessment of various aspects of personal life. If the feelings were not a
disruptive, morally dangerous force that needed to be controlled by the
rational faculties, then young people did not need to be protected from
them by their fathers. Moreover, young men did not have to learn to
master their passions in order to become functioning adults. Instead,
they had to learn to cultivate and experience the finer feelings or affections that were responsible for true virtue. Also by this logic, women,
who had always been thought more emotional than men, would no
longer be an obstacle to male virtue but could potentially help men to
develop their affections and mature into moral, socially useful human
beings. Like friendship, heterosexual love could become a medium
through which young people could influence one another to become
moral adults and good citizens.

This new attitude toward the emotions in moral theory was accompa-
nied by a new set of attitudes in popular culture toward romantic love.
While the traditional hostility toward love and women was still expressed by a few skeptics who saw love as emasculating, it became increasingly common for men in the mideighteenth century to celebrate
love as a manly passion. Samuel Quincy, a Boston area lawyer, wrote to
Robert Treat Paine in 1755, waxing enthusiastic about the "invigorating
& Soul-inspiring Passion LOVE! which while it evidences a manly gen-
erous Spirit, at the same time convinces us that you are sensibly touch'd
with all the endearing Delicacies of Female-Tenderness."[64] Nathan Fiske
copied similar sentiments into his commonplace book in the mid-1750s:
"A Tenderness for the fair Sex is the noblest Present we have received
from Heaven. 'Tis a delicacy in sentiments that distinguishes us from the
rest of Animals, and the finest inventions are owing to a strong desire to
please."[65] It even became possible to say that a man who avoided courting women was unmanly, because he was not brave enough to risk rejection. John Adams, for example, in his diary ridiculed Parson Wibirds because "he ha[d] not Resolution enough to court a Woman."[66]

As the experience of falling in love became an expected precursor to marriage, the experience of wooing and winning a woman emerged as a much more central rite of passage to manhood, relatively speaking, than it had been in the past. We know this, at least in part, because of the centrality of the experience in men's own writings. In young men's commonplace books, for example, courtship and the vulnerability that it inspired suddenly became a common theme in the middle of the eighteenth century. It has been observed that entries about women and sex in the commonplace books of two eighteenth-century southern men, William Byrd and Thomas Jefferson, clustered around certain particularly traumatic events involving powerful women. The same is true of the commonplace books of a number of middle-class New England men in the mid-eighteenth century, who wrote many pages of poetry and letters on love, courtship, and the pain of rejection while they were in their early twenties, the age of courtship.[67]

Anthropologists have observed that most premodern societies require boys to submit to trials or rituals through which they must pass to become real men.[68] Early New England youths, too, underwent trials before they could become men. Seventeenth-century Puritan boys proved their manhood by enduring tests of their loyalty and devotion to older men. In the eighteenth century, New England youths had also to prove their manhood by showing that they were able to court and win a woman. And although courtship may not have been as arduous a rite of passage as some societies impose on young men, it certainly had its risks.

By convention, it was the man who began a courtship and the woman who decided whether or not it would continue. A courting man, therefore, was in perilous territory. One danger, of course, was making the wrong choice, especially when a young man did not have a father nearby to advise him. But once he had decided, an equally serious risk was that he might be rejected.[69] Advice books acknowledged both problems, but especially the potential humiliation that a man could face if the woman refused him.[70] To guard against that, a man must not reveal his feelings too quickly, warned one popular handbook:

> [I]f you give [your passion] too large a scope, instead of being master of it, it will be the master of you; and you will, thenceforward, lay your weakness so open . . . that the pleasure of tyrannizing will be irresistible . . . [never] mention love, till you are in a manner certain, she is

half ripe to make it the first petition in her prayers; and, even then, let it be so mixed with raillery that in case you have deceived yourself in your conclusions, you may, without a blush, laugh off your own disappointment and her triumph together.[71]

Worst of all, a man should never let it be publicly known that his courtship of a woman had failed. When John Adams was visiting Hannah Quincy in the late 1750s, his father warned him that neighbors and relations were all talking about his presumed courtship of her, and Adams worried about the consequences: "[T]he Story has spread so wide now, that, if I don't marry her, she will be said to have Jockied me, or I to have Jockied her, and he says the Girl shall not suffer. A story shall be spread, that she repelled me."[72]

If men did allow their feelings to get out of hand, the pain of rejection could indeed be acute. When Adams was in fact rejected by Hannah Quincy, he was obsessed by thinking about her. Referring to Quincy as "Orlinda" (for it was common among educated Anglo-American writers to refer to individuals they were courting by classical pseudonyms), Adams wrote to his friend Richard Cranch, "If I look upon a Law Book and labor to exert all my Attention, my Eyes 'tis true are on the Book but Imagination is at a Tea Table with Orlinda, seeing that Face, those Eyes, that Shape . . . I shall soon I fear go mad for I have had no Idea but that of Orlinda, that Billet and Disappointment in my head since you saw me."[73]

Aspiring lawyer Robert Treat Paine wrote two letters to Ellen Hobart while attempting to regain his self-esteem after she had refused his request to begin a courtship in 1763. It was a point of honor, he said, that "calls upon me to free myself from the Suspicion of trifling levity on the one side, & Servile Captivity on the other." Presumably, neither would be considered manly. Moreover, it was important to him to demonstrate to her that he could master his feelings after being rejected. He did not want her to think he "had Conceived some resentment of yr. treatment or . . . that my Mind was too weak to bear a disappointment—either of which imputations would in a greater or less degree be ill founded."[74]

As courtship became more central in men's coming-of-age experiences, the individuals who mediated those experiences were changing. No longer did fathers serve as the sole gatekeepers to men's entry into full manhood status; fathers shared that responsibility with the women whom men were courting. Because of this new role, women were able to assert their own views about manliness, and to make them matter. Women's increasing part in defining the terms of male self-presentation in courtship was reflected in New England's print media. For example, *American Magazine* published a parable about courtship in 1744, featuring a libertine who asked a lady if he could court her. The lady responded with a letter advising her suitor to reform his character.[75] An essay submitted to the *New Hampshire Gazette* in 1761, titled "The Choice of a Husband," explained what the writer wanted in a husband: he should be young (twenty-five), rich, and unencumbered by debts; "good natured and friendly, sincere and well-bred." He should not be a coxcomb or a braggart, should be a patriot ready to fight for Britain, and should possess a benevolent and sympathetic heart.[76] Women commonly told their suitors how to behave. Several of the women courted by Robert Paine, for example, told him he was a libertine and that they did not like it. The unidentified "Lavinia," who Paine courted unsuccessfully in 1757, gave him advice about the kind of woman he should marry, and in 1763, Ellen Hobart accused him of "unmanly Toyings," to which he responded with a letter assuring her of his respect for women.[77]

While older stereotypes had suggested that women would turn men who fell in love with them into coxcombs and fops, these new descriptions of courtship suggested that women would use their influence to reform men's characters and make them more manly.[78] Whether ideals of manhood changed as a result of women's influence is not entirely clear. Women may have helped to popularize the eighteenth-century ideal of the "man of feeling" by insisting that men exhibit greater emotional sensitivity toward them during courtship.[79] Others simply expected men to live up to an older ideal that required men to be sincere friends and responsible husbands.

Although they now asserted their desire for respect and increased emotional intimacy before marriage, most rural women probably did not expect men to be dramatically different from the men they had known all their lives, including their own fathers. The message conveyed by Mary Dodge, a gracious and evidently lovely Massachusetts woman who was simultaneously courted by two men in the early 1740s, was that her chosen man should be mature, responsible, and devout. Her favored suitor was John Cleaveland, who by then was an evangelical minister at Chebacco, in Essex County, Massachusetts. Cleaveland self-consciously repudiated the genteel style that many young men of his era were trying to copy. He wrote to Mary, saying, "I am not acquainted [with] the World's Mode of Courting and Therefore shall not practise according to the Same, but honestly Speak the meaning of my Heart, as a Widower of 60 years age would do."[80] Mary had meanwhile received a passionate love letter from her cousin Ezekiel Dodge, a young student at Harvard, to whom she indicated in no uncertain terms her preference for evangelical over genteel manliness. "I am not transportingly pleased with Aetna's flaming strains," she wrote back to Ezekiel. "[I]t is that Gentle Flow that makes glad the City of God; and God has (I trust) inclined me to make choice of one that has been favoured with a Drink from the same." Dodge's letter (apparently a frantic declaration that threatened suicide if his love went unrequited) was "very unbecoming one that sustains the characters of a *Rational Gentleman, A Scholar, A Christian or a Believer* in Christ, and a *Candidate* for the *Gospel ministry*." Had he "wholly subjected his Judgment and Reason to the Government and Direction of fluctuating Passion?" she wondered. Was his threat of suicide "the Language of Solid Judgment and Reason? or only of Raging Passion?" Mary Dodge suggested to Ezekiel that she considered this kind of unrestrained passion unmanly.

> [M]y kind Advice to you is that if you design ever to joyn in Wedlock with any person and duly regard the solemn ordinance according to divine appointment, that you Let Judgment and Reason have their proper place, that you do not quit your Lawful Studies in the Search of Trust to follow *ignus fatuus* and idle fancies . . . then you'll be in the way to serve God in your Day and Generation in the Relation of a Gospel-minister *(which is a great Relation)* of a Christian and of a head of a Family as the Lord should prepare the way for you.[81]

A few weeks later, Mary Dodge wrote to Cleaveland to let him know that he was her choice, indicating the manly qualities she admired in him:

> Dear Sir
>   It is with the greatest Pleasure that I improve this opportunity of Expressing my unfained Desire, that you may Be A Workman [for Christ] . . . that you be strong in the Grace That is in Christ Jesus, That so you may Endure Hardness as a good Soulder of Jesus Christ, and I Rejoyce much that the Lord is making use of you To build up his Kingdom in other Places as well as in your one.[82]

The mature, level-headed John was, in her eyes, the more manly of the two.

It is fairly clear that Mary Dodge and her chosen suitor, John Cleaveland, assumed most of the responsibility for their own marriage negotiations. One consequence of this shift in the control over marriage choice from parents to children was certainly to give young men and women more autonomy. But it also produced an important change in the social mechanisms for reforming manners in eighteenth-century New England. Though Mary Dodge and John Cleaveland were still part of an evangelical Protestant culture, John was induced to conform to that culture's moral expectations not only by his fear of and identification with his father, but by his desire for Mary, his lover. Women, through courtship, would become increasingly responsible for the inculcation of manners and morals in men.

It is worth noting that this romantic system of courtship, with its increasing emotional perils for men, also gave friendship between young men its greatest importance. As young men increasingly faced not only the risks associated with occupational choices but also the risks of courtship, friends became an ever more important source of solace and support. Sometimes friends shared their fears of rejection.[83] Sometimes they wrote to console each other, or to ask for consolation. Male friends also facilitated each other's sexual adventures. Once, for example, Robert Treat Paine wrote a pair of love letters for a friend, possibly as part of an intended seduction.[84] Although the men who wrote letters documenting such connections were all members of the elite, depositions in fornication or bastardy proceedings occasionally reveal that less educated young men in small towns and villages, too, gave each other alibis, moral support, and valuable alliances while negotiating the seas of courtship.[85]

The new ideas about friendship that had been developing since the beginning of the eighteenth century helped to make popular a sentimental ideal of friendship among young New England men.[86] Examples scattered through surviving papers confirm that conventional expectations of friendship between middle-class young men after about 1740 envisioned sentimental relationships as a socially acceptable possibility. The papers of Yale classmates Noah Welles and William Livingston beginning in the 1740s, Harvard classmates Jeremy Belknap and John Chipman in the late 1750s, and Princeton classmates Joseph Brigham and

Ephraim Wheelock in the 1780s all provide examples of apparently intense, emotionally expressive male friendships.[87] Two other such friends were Harvard classmates Robert Treat Paine, the only son of a Harvard-educated minister turned merchant, and Ezekiel Dodge, the only son of a middling trader from Abington, Massachusetts, and the unsuccessful suitor of his cousin, Mary Dodge of Ipswich. In 1747 Ezekiel was twenty-four years old, older than any of his classmates and, unlike them, old enough to have become involved in a serious courtship. In January or early February, he had sent his passionate proposal of marriage to Mary Dodge, and in mid-February he had received her stinging letter of rejection.

It was apparently in the months following this rejection, when he was feeling particularly vulnerable, that Ezekiel Dodge developed an intimate friendship with Robert Treat Paine, who provided him with plenty of emotional solace. In fact, Ezekiel's love for his friend may have become something of a substitute for his thwarted feelings for Mary. While they were both still in Cambridge in May 1747, before the beginning of summer vacation, Dodge wrote a letter to Paine that can be described only as a passionate declaration of his friendship for the younger boy. The letter was also a defense of the value of friendship. "Friendship is that dilectable bond by which friends are united, than which nothing Can be more pleassnt," wrote Dodge, referring to the biblical friendship of David and Jonathan and continuing optimistically, "[T]hanks be to my jenial Stars that it was my happy lot to Contract Such an acquaintance with you that the Silver Cord of friendship hath rap'd [wrapped] our Souls in Such a glorious Concord."[88] What Dodge was getting at was no mere metaphor but a deeply emotional, tangible experience of love for his friend. He went on to describe his feelings for Paine as "anxious Love and ardent affection," and professed himself unable to find words to describe them: "When I think of representing my anxious Love & my ardent affection to you alas! my fainting muse folds up her wings unable to Sustain the task—wt. words Shall I Speak or what numbers Shall I Chuse to paint my arddent passion & my warm desires. Suffer me to break of with venting a few pasnate desires & weaping forth Sum broken accents—may heaven ever protect you whose prosperity is my hapyness & whose misfortune is my misery."[89]

While the tone of these letters between friends is surprisingly emotional, young men also styled their friendships as a kind of mutual moral surveillance, not unlike that of Edmund Quincy and Ebenezer Parkman a generation earlier. The friendships of Paine, Dodge, and the three or four other youths in their circle appear to have coincided with a period of spiritual searching for all of them, and all of the friends except Paine began careers in the ministry shortly after graduating from college. Paine himself was admitted to the covenant in Boston's Old South Church in April 1749, at the unusually young age of eighteen.

No longer did Christian virtue require young men to be guarded with their feelings. The flowery language and emphasis on emotional expression in sympathetic male friendship creates for us a certain amount of ambiguity in the meaning of young men's love for one another.[90] These boys described the feelings of friendship as delectable, captivating, as filling their hearts with flame.[91] Their actual level of intimacy is hard to know. Certainly it was common for college students to share beds, just as men shared beds when traveling. Israel Cheever addressed Robert Paine, his former college roommate, as his "Dear Chum, with whom I have lain warm so many Nights," but a humorous comparison between "bosom friends in the Night" and bed bugs dissipated any sexual implications.[92] Ezekiel Dodge was the least restrained of any of the writers, and it may be that some mutual uneasiness with his level of emotional involvement led him in subsequent letters to reiterate that his love for Paine was Christian love, and that his affection for other members of their college literary club was "hearty."[93] Perhaps the references to "ardent affection" and "passionate desires" had to be stabilized with a dose of masculine bluster lest they get out of hand.

Or perhaps the meaning of sentimental friendship was stabilized by the fact that it usually occurred at a particular stage in young men's lives, a stage connected with issues of emerging sexuality and vulnerability toward women. Many more examples of such friendships among middle-class Anglo-American men are to be found in the early nineteenth century, usually between young men who had not yet begun courting women. Perhaps sentimental friendship was a kind of practice run, offering youths the opportunity to express feelings in a new language and to try out intense attachments to others outside their families before they became involved with women.[94]

As in earlier times, youth in the eighteenth century was seen as a transitional stage of life in which young men readied themselves to enter permanent relationships with women and occupy the roles their fathers had occupied before them. Unlike the past, though, eighteenth-century youths were supposed to negotiate this stage not by learning to master their passions but by taking risks, falling in love, and assuming a new share of the responsibility for their own behavior. The emotions associated with youth were no longer so frightening, and could even at times inspire true benevolence.

The long-term significance of these changes in the meaning of love and friendship would be immense. Over time, increasing expectations for emotional satisfaction in courtship would change cultural definitions of marriage and transform the experiences of women and men. But these changes were still decades away. In the short term, changes in courtship affected the experiences of youth and bachelorhood but did not change the central definition of manhood. In the eyes of the majority of adults, bachelors were never really men. Only when men married and left the liminal community of bachelors did they become real men. Just like their Puritan ancestors, eighteenth-century New Englanders defined as men only those who had achieved a competence, married, and become fathers.

4

Manhood and Marriage

In April 1686, Cotton Mather was twenty-three years old, unmarried, and the pastor of Boston's North Church. Despite his youth, he was becoming accepted into the ministerial community, whose members invited him to participate in a prayer group, or conventicle, which consisted of themselves and their wives and met at their various houses. Obviously pleased, Mather wrote: "tho' I were a young Man, yett Owner of neither Wife nor House, nevertheless they did mee the Honour to *meet* and *fast* at my Study, on 21 d. 2 m. when I preached to them, on Gen. 32.26."[1] Because he was (evidently) an exception to a general rule, Mather's private little boast reveals an important dividing line in the community of males in early New England. On one side were the men whose youth or condition of servitude placed them in a dependent relationship with others. On the other side were the householders whose ownership of "Wife [and] House" gave them full membership in the male world.

Once a man achieved a competence—that is, obtained the property or income necessary to support a household—and married, he had in theory achieved full manhood status. Ordinary Anglo-Americans in early New England measured manhood by a man's ability to produce and provide for a wife and children. Defining manhood in terms of a man's economic productivity was a corollary of the early modern assumption that marriage was an economic endeavor. Much as had been true for yeomen in early modern England, the nuclear family in New England was the basic unit of production and consumption. It existed to help men and women support their economic needs and procreate.[2]

98

The most pious Puritans, however, required more, suggesting that marriage should serve a spiritual goal and that love should be part of an ideal marriage. These ideas were all involved in their effort to reform society by strengthening family relationships. At the same time, most early New Englanders did not believe that marriage existed primarily to affirm a couple's romantic commitment or to maximize their spiritual happiness. And even given the growing expectation of romance in courtship in the 1740s, a romantic concept of marriage would not be widely accepted until after the American Revolution.

Husbands as Providers

Becoming a husband was an economic act as much as a personal and social one. Assuming the availability of assistance from his family (which middling young men before about 1740 tended to be able to count on), an industrious man would generally be able by his midtwenties to acquire enough property or income-generating work to marry, and a successful marriage would help him to prosper. Once a man had secured a competence, marriage became a helpful—indeed necessary—means of preserving and augmenting that living.[3]

Men usually began planning to marry and begin a sexual relationship with a wife at around the time they became independent property owners. In fact, the acts of marrying and building a house were often symbolically linked; in medieval usage, the term *husband* connoted ownership of a house.[4] John May, a twenty-four-year-old man who left his home in Roxbury, Massachusetts, to start a farm among kinfolk in Woodstock, Connecticut, in 1711, spent most of his first year there clearing land, planting, and building a house. At the end of November, as soon as the house was finished, May went back home to Roxbury to get married, and he brought his wife home to Woodstock at the end of December.[5] James Freeman, a Barnstable, Massachusetts, man who also left home at the age of twenty-four, sought his fortune as a schoolmaster and trader in Halifax, Nova Scotia; he too began talking seriously about marriage while he was building a house.[6]

Before the 1740s, Anglo-American New England men approached marriage with great economic realism, usually undisguised by romantic metaphor. For example, John May's diary for 1711, which was used almost entirely to record the economic transactions of shared work that structured his life, reflects a clearheaded sense of the continuum between productive and personal life. A sampling of his diary entries for the week of December 11 follows:

> Decemr 11 was Roxbur lecture
> Decemr 12 i cut wood for John Ruggles
> Decemr 14 Isaac Child holpt me cut wood for John Ruggles which made it 3 days
> December 16 was the Sabbath
> Decemr 18 A Great Day's Work.[7]

December 18 was May's wedding day. After a year of industrious labor directed toward making this step possible, he apparently sensed no irony in describing his marriage in terms of productive endeavor.

Even in the mid-eighteenth century, when men and women had increasing expectations for emotional expression in courtship, men could still speak about becoming husbands with the same pragmatic realism with which they kept accounts of transactions with neighbors. Almost any man's strategy for becoming an economically independent householder explicitly included finding a partner able to provide the female labor needed for successful housekeeping. As James Freeman wrote to his cousin back in Boston in 1751, "[consider] the great want I am in of a Wife or a Mestress (either might do) and you will be tempted not to wonder when the news comes of my being a Husband." With chagrin he wrote, "I . . . Scaulded my Legg in a very pittifull manner indeed with the water in the Teakittle" and suggested that he was spending altogether too much time managing household affairs.[8] Having a woman to take care of the cooking, the garden, and other household labor enabled a man to devote his time to men's work.

In an important sense, marriage also served to make a man a full participant in the transactions of trade and sociability that defined the world of adult householders, because it made him more economically stable and productive. By acquiring a "Wife [and] House" he became a more efficient producer, a more reliable neighbor, a more creditworthy trading partner. He also gained authority over dependents and no longer had to submit to the authority of his own father or master.

But a man's new status as an autonomous householder did not mean freedom from responsibilities, and a married man's fulfillment of his moral obligations would be measured by a community of like-minded adult males. A husband had the legal and moral duty to provide his wife with food, clothing, shelter, and firewood, and to assume responsibility for her debts.[9] According to Benjamin Wadsworth, a husband was supposed to "indeavour that his Wife may have Food and Raiment suitable for her. He should contrive prudently, and work diligently, that his Family, and his Wife particularly, may be well provided for."[10]

According to the Puritans, a husband also had a moral duty to love his wife, a requirement that was as strong in the seventeenth century as it was later on. For example, Samuel Man, first minister of the Congregational Church of Wrentham, Massachusetts, advised that "the husband should love, provide for, and be tender-hearted to the wife."[11] By the mid-eighteenth century the duty to love one's wife included higher expectations of emotional expressiveness, and love was being talked about not only as a duty but also as a source of happiness.[12] The good husband had such qualities as an even temper, agreeability, and constancy.[13] He confided in his wife and was supposed, in turn, to be her dearest friend.

But from the point of view of ordinary New Englanders throughout the colonial period, the most basic element of a man's duty to his wife remained economic support. To act like a man in the context of marriage meant to support a wife and children.[14] John Winthrop stated one of his society's most fundamental assumptions about manhood while on board the ship *Arabella* in 1630: "A man must lay upp for posterity, and he is worse than an Infidell that provideth not for his owne."[15] Almanac writers in the eighteenth century were less morally zealous but just as pointed when they satirized, in humorous verses such as the following, the husband who spent all his money and neglected his family:

> He that for Drink neglects his Trade
> And spends each Night in taverns till 'tis late
> And rises when the Sun is four hours high,
> And ne'er regards his starving Family,
> God in his mercy may do much to save him
> But woe to his poor Wife, whose Lot it is to have him.[16]

Neighbors, families, and towns could put considerable pressure on husbands to fulfill their obligations to cohabit with and provide for their wives. In 1705, when George Lason petitioned the governor and council of Massachusetts to be allowed to live separately from his wife, a mob threatened "to pull down Lason's house" and set it on fire.[17] After

Ebenezer Medberry of Rehobeth drove his wife out of his home in 1764, the community became actively involved in trying to convince Ebenezer to take her back in. In this case, Ebenezer's failure to house and support his wife was particularly egregious, since the house from which he had ejected her had been her property, acquired through inheritance from a previous husband. As neighbor Silvanus Martin told Ebenezer, "[I]f I was in his place since the woman was endowed by the income of the estate of her deceased husband & now destitute, If I was he it should never be said, if I could not live with a woman, that I robbed her of her dowry. I should resign a sufficient support & not abridge her of her clothes or let her go begging."[18] Although Ebenezer refused to be reconciled to his wife again as a husband, since he felt no affection for her, he ultimately promised "he would provide for her & she might live in a room of the house."[19]

Neighbors also expected a man who fathered children out of wedlock to support those children. Before a man could abandon a pregnant lover or a woman who had borne his children, he had to answer to his neighbors—or move to a community where no one knew him. In the 1750s William Haskell, for example, had an affair with Tabitha Lufkin, a Gloucester fisherman's wife, while her husband, Stephen Lufkin, was at sea. Haskell told a companion, Thomas Jacques, that he was thinking of leaving his own wife and children to take Tabitha to Rhode Island. "I asked him whether he intended ever to return if he had gone away," said Jacques. "Not till the fall," replied William. "It is time for me to look out," William continued, for Tabitha was pregnant, and "I Suppose I Know who must father it." His plan for "fathering" the child was to provide Tabitha with a house in Rhode Island, to go on a sea voyage until after the child had been born, and then to come back home and "settle with his creditors and make sale of what he had and leave the effects in somebodies hands for his wife and children" before rejoining Tabitha. How willing he would have been to continue to provide for two wives was never tested, since he and Tabitha never did run away together. Still, he continued to declare his commitment to Tabitha in financial terms; after she was arrested for adultery on the complaint of her husband, Haskell declared dramatically "that he would stand by this said Tabitha as Long as he had any Estate Left him."[20]

Certainly there were good economic reasons for neighbors to pressure husbands to support their wives and children. Members of New England communities assumed a legal obligation to provide support for the destitute, and if a husband did not fulfill his obligation to support his family, the responsibility would fall to other household heads. But the fact that money was at stake should not mislead us into thinking that early New Englanders had purely instrumental motives for holding men responsible for their dependents, for ideas about manhood were as intricately woven into the web of their culture as in any other society. Middling English people like them measured manliness in terms of productivity and responsibility for dependents, behavioral and moral traits that were assumed to accompany property ownership and householder status. Peasants may have measured it in terms of rough strength or courage, the gentry in terms of their ability to command deference from their social inferiors. But middling New Englanders measured manhood in terms of a man's ability to provide for his wife and children.[21]

To some extent, seventeenth- and early eighteenth-century Anglo-American New Englanders assimilated Puritan moral ideas about marriage into their concept of marriage as an economic endeavor. The Puritans' idea of marriage superimposed a spiritual partnership on the economic one, so that husbands and wives became spiritual helpmeets as well as partners in the production of children and economic necessities. But husbands saw no incongruity between the economic and the spiritual goals of marriage. Michael Wigglesworth, courting a widow in 1690 after the death of his second wife, assured the widow that "[t]he spiritual as well as outward good of myself and family, together with the good of yourself & children, [are] my Ends inducing me hereunto."[22] As a newlywed in the early 1700s, Josiah Cotton penned a set of "rules for marriage," resolving that he and his wife would devote their family to serving God. But what he most remembered about his first year of marriage in his retrospective memoir was the fact that "we spent . . . not much short of 100 L in housekeeping, which somewhat exceeded our income."[23] The bottom-line measure of the success of his marriage was financial.

Divorce was difficult to obtain anywhere in colonial America, and informal separation was probably the only recourse for many unhappy couples.[24] Still, the Puritan legal systems of Connecticut, Massachusetts, Rhode Island, and New Hampshire permitted divorces on a broader basis than the courts in England or most other Anglo-American colonies. Coming as they did from middling and lower-gentry families, the Puritan founders of these colonies were more committed to the notion of marriage as a voluntary contract, and less concerned than the upper-gentry leaders of other colonies about the possibility that divorce could disrupt clear lines of succession to property. Partly for this reason, the Puritans allowed marriages to be dissolved as a result of an egregious breach of their terms by either party.[25] And though divorce was not common by modern standards, in New England it was accessible to people across the economic spectrum, unlike in England, where it could be obtained only through a costly legislative process in Parliament. Thus divorce records provide evidence of popular expectations of husbands among a broad segment of New England's population.[26]

Such records tend to confirm that the most central obligation of husbands, even as late as the 1770s, was to provide economic support for their dependents. Before 1770, the most common single grievance among women seeking to terminate their marriage was desertion and nonsupport by their husbands, although this grievance was often coupled with other allegations, such as adultery or cruelty.[27] Men were more likely than women to leave a marriage, since they more often had the mobility and the economic resources to set up lives (and sometimes bigamous marriages) elsewhere. Still, the sheer volume of petitions based on desertion and nonsupport suggests that families and neighbors were far more likely to offer their support for divorce petitions brought by wives whose husbands were not supporting them than by wives whose husbands were abusive or unfaithful.[28] At its most basic level, marriage was an economic venture, not an emotional one.

In skirmishes between family members and neighbors struggling to interpret and deal with a troubled marriage, husbands were often evaluated for their adequacy as providers. Catherine Cobb, it seems, frequently criticized her husband, Elijah, a storekeeper in Taunton, Massachusetts, for failing to provision the table. Joseph Cobb, a relative of Elijah's, had stayed with the family for several days in about 1763, and he recalled that "every Day when I Came home to Dinner I heard Cathrine . . . Complain[ing] (as she sat Seesawing in her Chair) of her husbands Not Providing Necessaries of Life." Joseph's deposition goes on to reconstruct the following dialogue between Elijah and Catherine:

> *Catherine:* I have No Bread; No Meat; No Rum nor No Sugar No Molases; No flax Nor Wool, Nor Nobody to help me.
> *Elijah:* Caty why Do you talk So you well know that we have all these things in the Store to Sell & you may use Any of these things as you Please.

Although he denied failing to fulfill it, Elijah nevertheless acknowledged that he had a duty to provide "victuals" for the table. Neighbors and family members assessed the Cobbs' marriage using the same fundamentally economic criteria. "Cobb [Elijah Cobb] kept a good house while I lived there," testified John Cooper, who had lived in the house as a boarder. Catherine's mother agreed, at least according to one witness, "for, said the Madam, Caty Wrongs Her Husband; . . . he Provides well for her."[29]

Discussions of an unsuccessful marriage, whether among neighbors or between witnesses before a judge, very often focused on whether both parties had made the expected economic contribution to the marriage, whether that was an issue in the case or not. When Russell Knight of Lancaster, Massachusetts, sought a divorce from his wife, Mary, on the grounds of her adultery, neighbor Hannah Meriam testified that he provided for his family "as fare as his Circumstances would admitt," but that Mary "did not take a prudent Care of the store her husband laid in."[30]

Stephen Lufkin, the Gloucester fisherman, sought a divorce from his wife, Tabitha, in 1760 on the grounds that, in addition to committing adultery while he was away on fishing trips, she had "unnecessarily run him into debt & wasted his substance."[31] Tabitha countered by submitting her own petition for divorce, cataloguing how he had failed *her* in his husbandly duties, mostly by failing to provide for her wants or to pay for her purchases. "If I could not eat such as he did I might go without, let me have what stomack I would, good or bad"; he "denyed to pay for a braid of sider which I bought in his absence, which I had nothing to drink but water for seven or eight months." She said he had even found fault with her "for buying cloath for a coat for him," telling her to "be gone out of the doors and not to come in again" and "I was forced to humble myself on my knees to him before he would be reconciled with me." And now, Tabitha added, he "has stript me so bare that I have neither money nor clothes for my Comfort. My father went to him to borrow an apron and a coat and he would not let him have them nor nothing else."[32]

A man's work in "providing" encompassed more than simply the physical labor he performed in growing crops, fishing, or earning an income for his family. Statements in the Cobb, Knight, and Lufkin cases reveal an important assumption about the difference between male and female economic contributions to marriage. The husbands in each of these families acknowledged their duty to "provide for" or "provision" their wives and families. To "provide" or "provision" implied, in the seventeenth century, not only productivity but also foresight, preparation, and planning. The husband's role in providing, then, was associated with rational planning and suggested that what he produced had long-term value and permanence.

Mistresses Knight and Lufkin were criticized for failing to take "prudent care" and for "wasting" what their husbands provided, or running them into debt. Good wives, in this construction, were cast as conservators of the husband's goods and property, rather than as producers. Bad wives, conversely, were excessive spenders who depleted the family's supplies because they could not control their appetites.

What was the origin of this fear that women would deplete men's property? It is a convention in the historiography of the family to distinguish the economically productive role of women in the preindustrial family from their role as consumers and emotional nurturers in the modern, consumer-oriented family.[33] But it seems that early modern families made their own distinction between men's and women's work: the work done by men was considered productive, while the work done by women was performed for the purpose of conserving what men had produced. Good wives conserved men's wealth, while bad wives spent or wasted it.

The stereotype of the greedy and lustful wife is an old one. Concerns about waste and spending dating from the medieval period reflected a traditional assumption that the objective of household production was to guard against want and hardship, rather than to create wealth or material comfort.[34] Moreover, fears about women's propensity for excess may have been a residue of Reformation-era suspicions of women's passions. A symbolic system in which women represented the dangers of excess or self-indulgence reinforced the notion that a reasonable, mature male was needed to protect the family from debt and ruin. Might such symbolism also have reflected an inchoate fear that men could lose control, slide back into a puerile dependence on women? The image of the wasteful wife could serve as a hortatory reminder to men of the dangers of giving in to women's demands.

Meanwhile, the depiction of men as producers and providers, especially of commodities like rum and sugar, seems to have been a new one. Older uses of the term *husband* dating from the fifteenth century suggest that husbands had once had the primary duty of conserving family resources. A husband was not only a man joined to a woman in marriage but also "the manager of a household or establishment . . . a steward," and "a saving, frugal, or provident man; an economist."[35] The seventeenth- and eighteenth-century notion of men as producers and women as conservators (or spenders) was more suitable to an economy in which surplus production and capital accumulation were becoming possible and property was no longer conceived merely in terms of conserving scarce resources.

Concerns about greedy, wasteful women continued to be voiced in the mid-eighteenth century, perhaps because they were interwoven with anxieties about women's rising consumer expectations. In the 1750s and 1760s, when the Cobbs, the Greens, the Knights, and the Lufkins were battling over the fate of their marriages, New England's inhabitants were beginning to participate in a growing consumer economy. From 1750 to 1773, the American market for imported consumer goods rose by 120 percent.[36] Various types of manufactured goods, including the rum, sugar, and molasses mentioned by Katherine Cobb and the cloth for Stephen Lufkin's coat, became available for purchase from suppliers outside of local exchange networks. Anglo-Americans' rising participation in this consumer economy acquired political implications as the meaning of consumption became an issue leading up to the American Revolution.[37] One dimension of this issue, apparently, was men's resentment of women's changing consumer behavior, for stereotypes of spendthrift women or women obsessed by fashion were a common image in Anglo-American print literature in the mideighteenth century.[38]

These portrayals of "bad" wives did not go uncontested by Anglo-American women in early New England, for women's labor and informal trading often contributed considerably to family wealth, especially in the generally expanding economy of eighteenth-century New England.[39] Tabitha Lufkin, for example, offered a spirited defense of her own economic contribution to her marriage: "My husband says that I wasted his goods Judge you Gentlemen whether I have or not We came together with little or nothing and now we have some hundreds a pounds of household stuff some hundreds of pounds at Interest and my husband has Been in no way to git it only By fishing without it Be this Last voyage he has more then all his Brothers can show put them all together and If I had wasted it how could he have it now."[40] However, the stereotype obscured a wife's productive contributions to a marriage while also placing the burden of providing for a family on the shoulders of her husband.

Men who accused their wives of adultery not infrequently framed their complaints in terms of conservation and waste, suggesting how closely linked in their minds were their identities as husbands and as independent property owners. When Benjamin Green petitioned for divorce from Jemimah Chadwick, he laid out what had been his hopes for the marriage, saying he had "flattered himself from his own Industry and her Prudence and good behaviour" that they would enjoy "great felicity in that state." His job had been to produce a sustenance for the household, hers to manage prudently what he provided. When Jemimah disappointed his expectations by being unfaithful, he conflated her physical and emotional betrayal with her uncontrolled desires. "[B]y her levity & secret Extravagance all his Substance has been spent and your Pet'r runned considerably in Debt," he complained. The adulterous wife was a danger to her husband's emotional well-being and his economic well-being, suggesting that his sense of his manhood was inseparable from his sense of economic competence. Jemimah had also borne a child that she admitted was not his.[41] It is unclear whether his primary grievance was her excessive spending or the fact that her spending was going to support another man's child. In Benjamin's mind, the categories were confused; she was supposed to prudently manage his property in goods as well as his property in her chastity, but instead she had squandered both.[42]

Husbands as Procreators

The popular view of husbands as providers was interwoven with popular as well as medical, legal, and moral ideas about men's sexuality within marriage. Manliness for most early New Englanders was less a function of possessing a male body per se than of occupying the social role of independent household head and father. In a dependent male, the body was a source of dangerous passions, dangerous to the self as well as to society. Youths could be overcome by their passions and desires, and they needed wiser, more rational men to guide them away from their own weakness. Once a man had achieved a competence and married, however, he had in theory attained full manhood status. No longer required to demonstrate his deference to an older male, his new social status gave him authority and political capacity. It also changed the meaning of his sexuality.

Advice books' counsel to married men on matters of sex was rooted in the same suspicion of excessive desire and consumption as the sexual advice offered to bachelors. Sexual intercourse should be moderate; men were cautioned not to waste their precious seed. "Husband your Vigour well; if ought or Health, Or Offspring numerous, beautiful, and strong, Or Pleasure weigh."[43] The "Bridegroom should remember that 'tis a Market that lasts all the Year, and be careful that he does not spend his Stock too lavishly." At the same time, now that a man was married, the converse must also be kept in mind: copulation should not take place too seldom, "for both these are alike hurtful."[44] Within marriage, sexual intercourse was to be moderate and regular, for "love that is prudently managed, causes health, inspires courage, and renders us agreeable."[45]

After marriage, it seems, the male body became less a danger and more a source of potency and pride. Although the economic model of the body was the same in discussions of both marital and premarital male sexuality, mature, married men faced less danger of running out of "vital fluid." In fact, early modern advice writers perceived a relationship between age and virility that was the inverse of ours. Even though it was conceded that boys as young as sixteen and seventeen had sufficient vital strength to beget children, advice writers warned that to do so could endanger their future potency. Instead of believing men to reach their sexual peak in their late teens, it was thought that men's ability to beget children "constantly increases till 45, 55, 65, and then begins to flag, the Seed by Degrees becoming unfruitful; the natural Spirits being extinguished, and the Heat dried up." The moral: "Age in Men hinders not Procreation, unless they be exhausted in their Youth, and their Yard shrivell'd up."[46] It must have been as evident to eighteenth-century men as it is to us that nineteen- and twenty-year-old youths had certain sexual capacities superior to those of their forty-five- and fifty-year-old fathers. Nevertheless, a broad cultural association between manliness and economic competence, as well as a lack of differentiation between sexual potency and fertility, seems to have made plausible the view that the sexual potency of mature, married men exceeded that of dependent males.

Advice about marital sexuality in seventeenth- and eighteenth-century New England came not only from medical sources but also from Puritan moral reformers and even guides to manners. Although the Puritans (like most contemporaries) viewed romantic love before marriage as spiritually dangerous, they viewed love within marriage as a spiritual good and a source of earthly happiness. Unlike earlier Christian moralists who idealized celibacy and condemned even married sex as carnal, the Puritans accepted and celebrated sexuality within the context of a Christian marriage.[47] Pious Puritan husbands often idealized the love that they felt for their wives and the harmony, both spiritual and physical, they experienced within marriage. For example, John Saffin, a seventeenth-century Puritan emigrant from England, had a happy twenty-year relationship with his wife, Martha, whom he called "My Dove" and "The dear companion and joy of my life" in elegies written after her death.[48]

The manly vigor of a married householder was measured less by his ability to maintain self-control and more by his capacity to father children and support them. According to one advice writer, a man proved his manhood in many ways, from acting courageously to demonstrating his reasoning capacity, but it was "particularly in generation, where he communicates himself, and . . . gives proofs of his heat and strength."[49] A man who produced a large brood of such "proofs" was considered manly indeed. Although the obituary writers of New England's urban papers usually celebrated the manly courage, reason, and virtue only of elite men, posterity would remember even an ordinary tradesman like Peter Flowers of New London because of his extraordinary procreative capacities. As a newspaper noted of the seventy-five-year-old journeyman butcher in 1761, "By three wives he had born and baptized, thirty eight children; twenty by his first, six by his second, and twelve by his third, who survives him."[50]

Distinct beliefs about premarital as opposed to marital male sexuality made good functional sense in a society like New England's, which placed such emphasis on a man's ability to become economically independent in adulthood.[51] So long as a young man was still dependent on parental support, procreation was a threat to his future autonomy, a drain on his ability to save. Moreover, premarital sex with a woman not approved by the family could also threaten his ability to enlist parental support in the acquisition of property. But once a man had married and attained the independence of a propertied householder, fathering children would have become an asset to his autonomy. Economic production in seventeenth- and eighteenth-century New England depended to an unusual degree on family labor. Because farmers on such marginally productive land could not afford to import servants, they relied on their maturing sons to provide the heavy labor on their farms.[52] Although children were still an economic liability during their early years, after they reached the age of fourteen or fifteen, when most fathers were entering their forties, children could contribute significantly to family prosperity. Sons allowed a father to increase the area he was able to cultivate, and thus increase his wealth.

So can we assume that once a man married and began a regular sexual relationship with his wife, his manhood was finally secure? Not necessarily. In addition to the possibility that he might fail adequately to provide economic support for his wife and children, various other dangers might still threaten manhood. One danger was excessive love or sexual feeling for his wife. Puritan moralists warned that marital love must not become too passionate, lest it overshadow a person's love for God and disorder his or her mental balance.[53] They warned that carnal love should be kept in bounds by a rational soul. Similarly, seventeenth- and eighteenth-century medical writers warned against the dangers of excessive passion within marriage and counseled moderation—for health reasons. John Saffin metaphorically conflated physical and spiritual aspects of love when he copied in his commonplace book a passage contrasting marital love with that "disordered Love meerly carnall which is as Different from Amity as the burning sick heat of a feaver is from the Naturally kindly heat of a Healthfull Body."[54] Medical advice writers suggested too that reason should limit the excesses of the body. Both types of writers, then, continued to warn about the need for moderation.[55] Even in adulthood, a man's longing for a woman had to be kept within bounds.

During the eighteenth century, virtuous love began to be described in somewhat different terms. Love became delicate and prudent, producing harmony and pleasure. What had changed was that virtuous love could now be felt during courtship as well as marriage; in fact, it was the emotion that courting couples looked for to indicate that a marriage would be happy.[56] This shift should perhaps not be seen as a break from the Puritan celebration of marriage but rather as an extension of it, for the spiritual love of two truly sympathetic partners was if anything an even higher good than the rational love of husband and wife.

Lust, on the other hand, was still considered excessive and debauched both the soul and the body. Advice writers still issued dire warnings about the consequences of sexual excess by married men.[57] Advice writers coupled their warnings about wasting seed with cautions that men should not try to perform superhuman feats with women in order to prove their virility. Nicholas Venette, for example, suggested that readers "ought to look upon as fabulous" the story that Hercules impregnated fifty virgins in the space of twelve hours. Not only was this kind of performance unlikely, it was also bad for a man's health. Herculean sexual performance would "weaken and enervate" men; "their seed becomes barren, and their privy parts refuse to obey them."[58] These books offered men a rationale to assuage their fears, if they had any, that their wives expected them to be like Hercules.

An important element of a man's role as a husband was his capacity for sexual performance, and here, too, his manhood could be threatened. Husbands had a legal duty to cohabit with and engage in "conjugal fellowship" with their wives.[59] And Anglo-American women were not reticent to assert their right to have sexual intercourse with their husbands. Mary Knight, for example, complained to her neighbors in the 1760s that her husband, Russell, would not sleep with her. Russell acknowledged that he had sexual duties within the marriage but presented them as contingent on Mary's performance of her wifely obligations. According to a witness in their subsequent divorce litigation, Russell told Mary "that if She would only behave in any Shape as a Wife ought to he would not be wanting for any thing he could do for her by Night or by Day to what belonged to the Part of a Husband & more especially that Part which was so natural to all Mankin[d]." It was Mary's fault that he would not sleep with her, said Russell: "[I]f she would only leave off her bad carriage & be kind & courteous & be prudent of what he had brought to the house & would behave like other women he could overlook & forgive all & would lodge with her."[60]

Women also sought judicial help in getting out of marriage with an impotent husband. An impotent man could not impregnate his wife, defeating the very purpose of the marriage, and male sexual impotence was at least in theory grounds for the legal termination of marriage at the instigation of the wife.[61] Moreover, as one advice writer warned, any man who was "debilitated" in the sense that his "Yard be so feeble that it will not strait of Erection . . . ought not to marry, or if he does, he must be contented if he finds his Wife looking for that Satisfaction which he is incapable of giving."[62]

When Elizabeth Bredeen petitioned the Massachusetts governor and council in 1744 to have her marriage to Joseph Bredeen annulled, she argued that he was "naturally and incurably so defective in his body, that he is utterly incapable of procreation." Furthermore, she told the council, her husband's sexual deficiencies had put her "in a very infirm low state of health actually brought upon her as she is advised by the peculiar circumstances of the said Joseph's body."[63] His incapacity meant not only that he could not reproduce but also that he could not give Elizabeth the regular sexual release on which her health supposedly depended.[64] Her complaint to the court in effect asserted that she had a right to sexual satisfaction, at least insofar as it was linked to procreative activity within marriage.[65]

Witnesses in the divorce case brought by Judith Walker against her husband, Simeon, in 1773 on the grounds of his alleged impotence further reveal the popular belief that a man's competence as a husband was intimately connected to his ability to satisfy his wife. Two men testified that Simeon's private parts were of exceptionally small size, and that "it is commonly reputed in the Neighbourhood that the sd Simeon is not qualified to be a Husband."[66] In fact, Simeon's genitals were a neighborhood joke.[67] But Judith Walker had been happy enough with her husband in the past. Once a neighbor named Tom Temple had asserted "that her Husband was not a man," to which Judith had responded that "her Husband was as much a man as poor Tom Temple, she believed," and she went on to say that "she didn't know but he was as much as any man, and was as much of a man as she desired."[68] But after several years of a childless marriage, a miscarriage, and a period of living apart, Judith Walker changed her story and sought a divorce. For his part, Simeon Walker vehemently denied that he lacked manly endowments, even inviting the judges to ascertain "his sufficiency for a Husb[and]" through a physical examination if they wished.[69]

It seems, then, that eighteenth-century Anglo-American New Englanders expected the ideal husband to be physically potent and virile, capable of meeting his wife's sexual needs and of impregnating her. The problem was that the only real judge of a man's performance was his wife. Like Judith Walker, a woman might say at one moment that her husband was a competent husband, and then change her mind the next and say that he was not. Fortunately for men, another aspect of the early modern European understanding of sexuality offered a source of proof of a husband's virility that obviated his need for his wife's approval. Seventeenth- and eighteenth-century Englishmen did not clearly distinguish sexual performance and fulfillment from fertility. Most doctors of the period, as well as advice writers, thought a woman incapable of conception unless she had experienced orgasm.[70] Thus, a woman who became pregnant provided visible evidence of her husband's sexual competence.

If a man who fathered a dozen children demonstrated his virility to the world, the reverse was also true. Barrenness was a major concern of advice book writers, and the audience they addressed was not limited to female readers. A woman could fail to conceive because of a "want of Love in the Persons copulating" or a lack of ardour or intensity in the man. Various dietary supplements were suggested to increase male vigor, including the testicles of roosters and various other animals; the meat or eggs of partridges, quails, and pheasants (because all these birds had the virtue of "being extremely addicted to Venery"); boiled turnips and parsnips; and a variety of herbs and spices.[71] Advice books reassured men that barrenness was usually the fault of the woman, but who could be sure? A Restoration-era English tract suggested that a wife who did not become pregnant might begin to call her husband "a Fumbler, a dry-boots, . . . a goodman Do-little" or "a John Cannot."[72] And there is at least some anecdotal evidence that barrenness could be a major source of unhappiness for Anglo-American husbands, as for their wives. A New Haven husband and his wife had a childless marriage of many years' duration. He had, neighbors thought, a "somewhat violent" temper and "a natural Moroseness of Disposition," but ordinarily kept himself "under a tolerable restraint." In 1759, however, he beat his wife to death and hanged himself, no longer able to contain his rage and disappointment at having failed to become a father.[73]

Husbands as Masters

Only when a man finally obtained the property that could give him economic independence, usually with the help of his father, was he really recognized as a man. Finally he could build a house, marry, and assume his place as a full member of the community of householders. Marriage even changed the meaning of his sexuality, making it a source not of danger but of potency and pride. Yet manhood status in early New England was never completely secure. Men had to continue to prove their manhood by providing for wives and fathering children. And most of all, men had to maintain control over their households. As a husband, a man had the right to command his wife's obedience, and she in turn labored under legal disabilities that might well discourage her from challenging his authority.[74] It has long been recognized that the Puritan reforms that encouraged men to be responsible husbands and fathers also strengthened men's authority as household heads. And this was the contradiction at the core of the Puritan attempt to reform traditional social life by strengthening the patriarchal family.

The powers and the obligations of husbands were understood in terms of an analogue, on the level of everyday experience, to seventeenth- and early eighteenth-century theories of political economy. Like its classical counterpart, early modern political economy assumed that the people of a nation needed a ruler to guide and order their economic behavior so that their own greed and self-interest would not lead them to chaotic and self-destructive action. Economic activity would produce a benefit to the public only to the extent that it was conducted within this hierarchical political and moral framework.[75] By analogy, women's sensuality and less-developed rational capacity made them likely to succumb to lust and temptation, endangering the economic health of their families with their extravagance and waste. Husbands, with their supposedly greater capacity for reason and self-control, were needed to manage and rule over the productive behavior of households so that they would not fall over the precipice of indebtedness into bankruptcy and starvation.[76] It was men's rationality that qualified them for the role of foresighted provider—and authorized husbands to guide and govern their wives.

What, if any, were the limits of husbands' authority over wives in the eyes of their contemporaries? Adult men seem to have struggled with competing commitments in assessing this question. Puritan communities differed from other early modern English communities not so much in their beliefs about male authority as in their insistence that husbands try to live up to the ideal of rationality in their dealings with their wives. Just as communities pressured fathers to live up to the ideal of fatherhood, neighbors could remind husbands of their duty to demonstrate self-control with their wives, and they could invoke the government's coercive power to insist on it. For example, when in March of 1705 Experience Chamberlin showed her neighbor some bruises she had received in a beating by her husband, the neighbor immediately lodged a complaint against Jacob Chamberlain for abusing his wife, and on the following day tithingmen Jacob Bacon and William Ward were at his house to ask questions. Experience told them her husband had "beat her with his fist upon her head so that he stounded her" and "beat her with a stick." Jacob Chamberlain was bound over to the July Court of General Sessions to answer a charge of abusive carriage.[77]

Puritan New Englanders disliked violent husbands. When they described a bad husband, they often coupled accusations of violence with those of unwillingness to provide for dependents. Benjamin Wadsworth, in the midst of an encomium to the good husband, broke off: "O man, it may be thou art idle, lazy, dost take no care to provide Necessaries for thy Wife and Family, but instead of this, dost take to Tipling, Gaming, Ill Company, dost tarry out very late and unseasonably, and then comest home drunk, vomiting, or raging like a furious beast; if tis so, thou art exceeding vile and wicked."[78] Similarly, a 1684 petition by Mary Litchfield to allow her daughter, Mary Streight, to be divorced, asserted that Mary's husband, Henry,

> instead of provideing for her tooke from her, her wearing apparrell, And left her almost naked more like an Indian than A Christian swearing most Abominably, threatening to split her open, calling my Daughter Mary Dam'd whore, Commanding her to give him his hatt, and several Times beating and abusing her, since which time he hath never come nigh my Daughter nor provided for her, neither for meate, Drink Cloathing nor Lodging, neither had my Daughter any way to subsist but what she earned for a considerable time by hard working.[79]

The specter of the heathen savage reminded the court of the dangers of an improperly governed family. The civility and social order that the Puritans so hoped to create in New England were deeply threatened in the absence of a responsible male household head who could provide the necessities of life for his dependents and give them proper moral guidance.[80]

Yet despite the reality of sometimes bestial husbands, the question of whether a man was entitled to govern his dependents if he could not govern himself was a question early New Englanders went to some lengths to avoid having to answer. Despite persistent evidence that not all men were rational and that no man was always in control of his passions, neighbors clung to the idea that men were more rational than women under ordinary circumstances. In part, they were bound to a conceptual framework within which men's violence was perceived as disciplinary, excessive cruelty by husbands was seen as a temporary lapse, and women's assertiveness was construed as emasculating. A man was never really able to master his household unless his wife cooperated. Perhaps the male community's unwillingness to truly condemn violent men grew out of an uncomfortable awareness of the limits of men's authority, and of their dependence on women.

The assumption that adult men's use of force was generally disciplinary made it difficult to sustain a characterization of male domestic violence as irrational or motivated by passion. Husbands accused of excessive violence simply asserted that they were providing rational and righteous discipline for their sinful or unruly wives. For example, Mary Homer told a neighbor on a Sabbath day in 1694 that "she dard not to come into the house for an hour & half the reason was because her husband stood with a cane in his hand to beat her & a hammer to throw at her." When the neighbor came to investigate, Michael cast himself as a husband calmly disciplining a disobedient wife, explaining that "if it pleased God to give him a little more strength he would cane her stoutly." Then, as if to emphasize the rational, deliberate nature of his action, "he sett a little while as if he considered of it & said again that he would cane her stoutly."[81] Once he had convinced the neighbor to leave him alone with Mary again, however, Michael showed less restraint, threatening, Mary reported, that he would "stab me and . . . break my limbs."[82]

Neighbors tended to become involved in domestic violence cases only in extreme circumstances, when it appeared that a wife was in danger of serious harm. Cases involving wife abuse that did appear in court tended to be those in which the husband's violence was extreme, probably because these were the cases in which neighbors could build a consensus that the man was acting out of passion rather than administering discipline. Neighbors of Dr. Henry Smith of Dorchester, Massachusetts, for example, testified in an assault prosecution in 1700 that Smith's wife and daughter had burst into their house one evening, followed by Smith himself. Smith, "seemingly in a passion," had commanded his wife to come home and accused her of having just then been in bed with another man (which both wife and daughter denied). Smith thereupon picked up a firebrand, pretending to use it to light his pipe, and jabbed his wife in the mouth with it, so that blood came out of her mouth and coals fell down the front of her dress. On other occassions, Smith had threatened to kill his children.[83]

Witnesses seem to have been horrified by the behavior of the men in these cases. Yet even in the face of persistent evidence of violence within a household, early New Englanders sent women back to live with abusive husbands once immediate danger was past, admonishing both parties to live together peaceably. Cases of wife abuse ordinarily did not result in divorce proceedings. The legal remedy available to a woman like Experience Chamberlin (or, more precisely, to the community) was to seek a peace bond against her husband, in effect subjecting him to a fine if she could prove he had mistreated her again before the next judicial term.[84] The practical remedy in most such cases was for neighbors to send the woman back home and to admonish the husband to behave in a manner more befitting a rational Christian husband. The intent of either remedy was not primarily to improve the situation of the woman but to place pressure on the man to govern his temper. Unable to imagine a world in which women and children lived without men to govern them, neighbors convinced themselves that obviously violent men were capable of self-control, and that families were better off with bad men than with no men at all.

In occasional troubled marriages the husband was rational more often than not, and it was the wife who was violent. Such marriages presented moral lessons about the proper order of things, providing useful illustrations of the contrast between manly self-control and reason and female irrationality. Stories about such marriages also functioned to portray men who put up with emotional women as paragons of self-mastery and virtue. A number of men in difficult marriages made a show, at least for their neighbors, of their forbearance and control in their dealings with irrational, even violent wives. Russell Knight, for example, who sued his wife, Mary, for divorce in 1766, was to all appearances a model husband for many years before that time, despite his trying wife. Jonathan Knight, a male relative of Knight's, testified that Mary had at times "threatened [his] Life & Swore by God [she] would have [his] hearts Blood." She also once "flung a Pine torch in his face & he carried the scar of it a good while." Despite these provocations, Jonathan said, Russell Knight always "behaved in my sight & hearing with the Greatest patience imaginable."[85] A witness supporting the divorce petition of Elijah Cobb quoted Cobb's wife, Katherine, as saying that "she Loved a Dogg beter than she Did him," to which Elijah was said to have responded, "I wonder you will say so for I Have a Good Respect for you."[86]

Other cases offered moral lessons about the extreme provocations that husbands must be prepared to deal with. For example, when Major James Richardson, a self-identified "gentleman" from Leominster, Massachusetts, sought a divorce from his wife, Hannah, in 1772, witnesses averred that he had been a model husband. Phinehas Butler testified that to his knowledge the major had never struck his wife "or ever so much as spoke in Anger," even though his wife had often threatened "to be the Death of him," chased him and other members of her family with a sharp knife, and threatened to burn down the house.[87] Nathan Rugg testified that during the ten months he lived with the family, the major "always behaved with extraordinary patience towards her[;] when she used to abuse him, whether she was drunk, or sober, she was almost always exceeding troublesome in the family and intollerably so to him raving at him," breaking chairs and trying to kill him and the children.[88] Jotham White said he had not "ever heard [the major] when his patience seem to be quite gone say anything worse then that he must and would board hir out if she did not behave better, this I have often wondered at his patience of which he has as much as any person I ever knew or he could not have behaved with So much moderation to her."[89] Such self-control reinforced the presumption that men were more rational than women.

The troubled marriages chronicled in divorce records of the period represent extremes of behavior and not the typical eighteenth-century Anglo-American New England marriage. But at the same time, they reveal a structure of belief about gender as well as the limits of the Puritan attempt to reform male behavior. When New Englanders imagined the good, stable society, they pictured rational, moral husbands at its core, ruling over, providing for, and planning for women and children, who lacked control over their appetites and passions. Men's authority, of course, was unstable insofar as everyone realized that men also had bodies, appetites, and passions over which they could lose control. But even when faced with real evidence that an adult man had succumbed to his passions, neighbors clung tenaciously to the belief that household heads were rational defenders of virtue, protecting the world against the forces of passion and misrule. A conception of manhood that divided the world into rational men and passionate women and boys often required the use of force to maintain discipline. But that use of force was the problem.

5

Manliness and the Use of Force

On the morning of August 29, 1679, Malden, Massachusetts, neighbors Thomas Shepard and Samuel Blanchard both got up early to work in their fields before the sun rose high and hot in the late summer sky. A rail in the fence dividing their property had mysteriously come down. Blanchard impulsively called out to ask whether Shepard had taken it out on purpose to allow his swine to feed on the ripe corn in Blanchard's field. Shepard took umbrage at this inquiry and more words were exchanged. Then Shepard, his honor impugned, crossed over into Blanchard's field and beat Blanchard's face bloody. Blanchard sought his revenge later by reporting Shepard's assault to local officials, averring the he "would leave the court to judge by [Shepard's] threatening words and sly and secret actions . . . what manner of man it was who smites his neighbors secretly."[1]

Our image of Anglo-Americans in early New England is not generally of men fighting over family honor. Puritans' insistence on the strict control of anger, particularly within the family, and the stability and homogeneity of early New England communities contributed to a low rate of reported crimes of violence.[2] We have seen that Puritan men were unusually concerned about family commitments and took seriously their role as the rational moral leader of their household. We might therefore expect to find that they created radically new definitions of manhood that did not depend on the defense of honor. But manhood status among Anglo-American men in early New England was tied not only to a set of moral qualities associated with fatherhood but also to property ownership, and when their claims to property were challenged, some men resorted to force to defend their manhood. In fact, some Anglo-American New England men apparently assumed, as other early modern Englishmen probably had, that as adult men and freeholders, they had the *right* to use force to defend their manly authority and their property if it was threatened.

Historically in Western culture, there have been deep links between the idea of manliness and the use of force. Medieval literature and language connected the notion of manhood with physical strength, power, and vitality. For example, the word *virtue* was originally closely related to the Latin *virtus,* meaning simultaneously manliness, physical strength, force, and energy. The word *courage* implied the possession of physical qualities such as lustiness, vigor, and vital force, and could also be used to describe anger, haughtiness or pride, boldness, or sexual vigor and inclination.[3]

These physical connotations of manliness and virtue were no longer explicit by the sixteenth century. Both the Renaissance and reformed Protestantism contributed to a progressive inculcation of norms of self-discipline and respect for the authority of law in English society, largely through their emphasis on the importance of household heads and fathers in maintaining control over their dependents.[4] These fathers and household heads were supposed to serve as models for the rest of society of self-control and respect for law. But because this system of social control depended first and foremost on the assumption that fathers and masters could use physical force to "correct" lawbreakers, manhood status continued to be associated in covert ways with the use of force. Patterns of behavior and belief revealed by prosecutions for minor assaults suggest that men believed themselves morally entitled (or at least honorbound) to use force against other adult males if their manhood—their status as a property owner—was somehow infringed or challenged.

Use of Force by Adult Men

Consider, for example, the dispute between Shepard and Blanchard. It was a dispute (as well as a set of disputants) with a long and apparently contradictory history. At first glance, Thomas Shepard's background seems to identify him with an older set of ideals for manly behavior emphasizing physical strength and courage. The son of an English emigrant who had settled in Malden in 1651, Thomas Shepard had a reputation as a man with a short fuse. In 1671, at age thirty-one, Shepard had been presented to the county court for assaulting Samuel Sprague and calling him a "base villain." In the context of this dispute, Shepard seems to exemplify an openly aggressive style of masculine behavior posed in stark relief against the rational, self-controlled ideal of Puritan manhood. Thomas Shepard had told Sprague, "[W]henever I see you my spirit rises & Wherever I meet with you I shall remember you." "What dost thou meane to play the fool," Sprague replied. "I am Resolved I will not strike." Sprague kept his resolve, even when Shepard taunted him with "reviling speeches."[5]

But the facts of Shepard's later dispute with Blanchard present a more complicated picture, suggesting the difficulty of drawing a bright line between traditional ideals of manly behavior and those of Protestant English settlers in early New England. Both Samuel Blanchard and Thomas Shepard were middling landowners, each holding more than one hundred acres in Malden, as well as additional acreage elsewhere, during their lifetime. Samuel Blanchard was a regular attender of meetings at Malden's First Church, though he was not admitted to communion until 1681. But so was Thomas Shepard; in fact, he had been formally admitted to communion in 1677. Nor were the Blanchards entirely peaceful folk. They, too, had a history of conflict over the boundaries to their land; the town of Malden had had to settle a dispute between the Blanchards and John Guppy, Shepard's predecessor on the adjoining lot, in 1665.

Despite the fact that their conduct violated their church's norms for moral behavior, the Shepard-Blanchard dispute was not easily resolved, and it continued for two more generations. After Samuel Blanchard moved away from the farm in 1680, Blanchard men from his brother George's branch of the family continued to share a boundary with Thomas Shepard, and the long-standing boundary dispute that went with it. Hard feelings between the two families were smoothed over for a time, after George Blanchard's son Joseph married Shepard's daughter Hannah in 1681. But nineteen years later, when the Blanchard family's presiding patriarch, George, died at age eighty-four in 1700, the dispute between the two families resurfaced.

After George's death, the Blanchard family land was divided up among his sons, and the Malden farm went to the two youngest sons, Joshua and Abraham. As the inheritors of the family's property, Joshua and

Abraham also inherited the family's title dispute with the Shepards. That same year, in 1700, Shepard swore out a warrant for the arrest of his thirty-five-year-old neighbor, Abraham Blanchard, who had come into his field, pointed a gun at him, and then run at him with a pitchfork "as if he would run the tines into his belly," and had also chased Shepard's dog with the pitchfork and shot at it.[6] Three years later Shepard and the Blanchards were in court again, this time because one of the Blanchard men had plowed up, fenced in, and started to grow crops on portions of the road between the two sets of farms.[7]

The Shepard-Blanchard feud, if we may call it that, continued to escalate. At the end of the summer of 1707, Shepard (now sixty-eight years old) dug or ordered his servants to dig a deep pit in the road used by the Blanchards, rendering it impassable. He later admitted he had done it to spite Joshua Blanchard, who drove his cattle along that way.[8] Joshua Blanchard was furious. One Sunday in October, Shepard arrived on horseback on his way to church, followed by his wife and eighteen-year-old granddaughter, just in time to see Blanchard closing a gate in order to block the path along which the Shepards customarily traveled. Shepard, irate at this insult, threw down the gate with his staff and began to ride his horse over it. At this, Blanchard struck Shepard's horse with a board, knocking Shepard off, and told Shepard that he "went to meeting to serve the Divel" and "if I had him alone I would give him his due."[9] Witnesses said they heard Blanchard call Shepard an "old Thiefe," "Thievish Rascall," and a "Jackanapes." Finally, after a litany of epithets, Blanchard cut to the core of his grievances and told the neighbors that Shepard "had Stolen the value of five pounds a year for Sundry years in Grass both from him sd. Blanchard and his father in his time."[10] At last, in April of 1708, both Joshua Blanchard and Thomas Shepard were prevailed on, probably by court-appointed arbitrators, to issue a joint statement of reconciliation and promise to live together in the future as "Good and Christian Neighbors," on pain of forfeiture of a peace bond.[11] Their dispute did not resurface in the courts.

Given the common modern assumption that violent behavior in a society is indicative of social discontent, the most interesting feature of the Shepard-Blanchard dispute is the fact that none of its participants was socially marginal. Both of the disputers were white adult male property owners, married, and the heads of households. A glance through any county court docket from seventeenth- or eighteenth-century New England would reveal that, except for the fact that theirs lasted so long, fights such as Blanchard's and Shepard's were fairly typical in early New England. Ordinary, middling men (and women) often engaged in a grandiose, narcissistic style of verbal combat when they disagreed with one another, a practice that resulted in frequent slander prosecutions.[12] In their exchanges of insults, men sometimes came to blows. And litigation growing out of these disputes was as likely to involve middling people as the poor.

To examine patterns in fights between males in early New England, I have analyzed various kinds of records generated in misdemeanor assault prosecutions for the county courts of Middlesex County, Massachusetts.[13] Because of its mostly rural population, the circumstances of Middlesex County assault cases probably were fairly representative of those found in New England generally, though the records of incidents occurring in its two important towns, Cambridge and Charlestown, do occasionally reveal certain distinctly urban manifestations of male violence, like sailors' brawls. Assault complaints filed in the years from 1680 to 1760, years for which data are most readily attainable, reveal that the most typical assault complaint featured a property owner who used force to defend against a challenge to his alleged property rights, sometimes assisted by his sons, servants, or wife.[14] The average participant in these cases was age thirty-five, married, and, as indicated, an owner of property—not, as would be typical in a modern industrial society, under thirty and marginally employed.[15]

Between 1680 and 1710, the years for which the most complete records are available, very full information on the causes of underlying disputes is available in thirty separate cases of male-on-male assaults.[16] Twenty-one of these cases involved fights between men acting in their private capacity (not related to law enforcement). Of the private disputes, the vast majority, approximately sixteen out of the twenty-one, involved disputes over land or personal property, mostly livestock. Besides the twenty-one private disputes, nine cases involved assaults by property owners on constables or other law enforcement officials who were trying to arrest them, serve process on them, or seize their property. Thus in sixteen out of thirty cases (53 percent), the underlying cause of violence between men was a mature man's attempt to claim or defend a claim to real or personal property, while in nine (30 percent) it was a mature man's attempt to resist the authority of a law enforcement official.

What can these cases tell us? Because the records provide no information about unreported assaults, they are a problematic source for measuring the rate or incidence of violent behavior. We cannot say that these events were the only fights between men in this thirty-year period. However, the circumstances of reported assaults probably can tell us which kinds of violent behavior people found socially threatening enough to justify bringing a legal action. Patterns in the underlying causes of assault prosecutions suggest that the men most likely to be prosecuted for assault were not the volatile, aggressive young men whom we would expect to find getting into fights but instead the adult male household heads on whom moral and religious authorities relied to maintain order over dependents. Presumably, young men's fights could be dealt with by families, while adult men's fights could not. Adult men were therefore more likely to be dealt with by the legal system.

The pattern of prosecutions thus appears to reveal a system of social control that relied mostly on private, paternal authority to maintain order. But in addition these cases may tell us something historically important about the unacknowledged limits of that system. The very notion of the godly father or householder as the bulwark of social order depended on the assumption that a man was entitled to use force to assert his authority over unruly dependents. By extension, he might sometimes have used force to subdue other disruptive people. In early modern societies, the state did not possess a monopoly on the lawful use of violence, and its private use was a permissible and even necessary mechanism for the maintenance of social order.[17] In New England, assumptions that male property owners were entitled to use force to defend their rights remained embedded in the English common law rules and practices that operated there until the nineteenth century. So adult manhood continued to be implicitly associated with the right to use force.

In addition to providing evidence about patterns of prosecution, the depositions and other witness statements generated by the Middlesex assault prosecutions show us what kinds of insults got men upset enough to fight. They also reveal the ways in which ordinary men and women assessed, justified, or condemned violent male behavior. The cases tend to support the conclusions that adult men's identities were deeply bound up with their property, and that adult men did believe they had the right to use violence under certain circumstances.

For example, reports on the assaults that grew out of private disputes often included an allegation that one man had crossed another's boundaries. Like the Shepard-Blanchard feud, a dispute between Thomas Richardson and Simon Crosby of Billerica in April 1689 follows the common pattern. Around the middle of April, Crosby was burning off a field to prepare it for cultivation, and he assigned his eldest son, nineteen-year-old Simon, to "service" the fire so that it did not burn out of control and cross onto the property of Crosby's neighbor, Thomas Richardson. "When I ran to the fence," the son reported later, "I found the fire had run throw." After watching until the fire burned itself out, Simon saw that it "did but little damage," so he returned to where his father was working at a neighboring sawmill. Shortly thereafter, Thomas Richardson showed up at the mill with several other men. "With both his fists bent [he] tould my father that if that he had him in place he knew where he would make him feele it and drawing near to my father he took hould of my father either by the shoulder or the collar and gave my father a shuff forward and . . . severall provoking speeches and then went away."[18]

Men invoked a variety of conventions to justify their use of force in disputes like this one. One important criteria was whether a man had been physically situated on his own property at the time of the fight. In the litigation of an assault claim by Amos Marrett against Edmund Goffe of Cambridge, for example, a major question was who had been on whose land. Marrett claimed that Goffe had first attacked him "under a pretence of my being upon his land." But Marrett had retreated onto his own land, he said, while Goffe, "being upon my own land and [within] my own fence . . . did again . . . assault me." For his part, attempting to make Marrett look like the aggressor, Goffe testified that he and Marrett had met in the public highway.[19] To attack another man on his own property was presumptively illegitimate. Joseph Spaulding, a Chelmsford farmer, testified that his fellow townsman Thomas Chamberlain had offered him "much abuse as he was at worke upon his owne ground by striking him with a raill."[20] Spaulding's emphasis suggests that being attacked on his own property was at the core of the "abuse."

If being on one's own land conferred a kind of immunity from legitimate attack, being physically situated within a house (either one's own or another man's) seems to have conferred an even higher level of protection. Frances Chope, for example, appears to have claimed a right to be left in peace, based on the fact that he was staying in the house of his father-in-law. Solomon Green and his wife had marched into the house to demand that Chope return some personal property. After engaging in some "high words," Green "challenged [Chope] out of doors." Chope understood this as a challenge to fight and refused to leave the house, "saying he knew not but [Green] might murder him."[21] His physical presence as an invited guest in his father-in-law's house was a factor in deciding whether Green's threat of force was unlawful.

Men also sought to characterize as moderate or reasonable the use of force to defend property, another factor in determining whether the action had been lawful, and thus manly. In retelling the story of a violent incident, men involved in these cases often tried to characterize their own actions as moderate and controlled and their opponents' as resulting from their surrender to their passions. For example, when John Eames saw a table he owned about to be carried away in a cart by John How and ordered his son and son-in-law to go and take the table out of the cart; afterward he asserted that he had done only what was reasonable and necessary to recover his property. In recounting the story of his dispute with John How over the table, he described How as making a "furious" attack on Eames's son. Eames, however, claimed to have repelled the attack with only "one small blow in the face," just enough force to rescue his son.[22] Of course, the real issue in this dispute was who owned the table, or at least which of the men had legitimate reason to believe he was the rightful owner. The characterization of one man's violence as moderate and the other's as furious was talismanlike; it suggested that the man who appeared to have greater mastery over his passions in fact had the clearer conscience, and thus the better right.

Another convention used to determine whether the use of force had been legitimate or illegal was its openness. For example, attackers who hid in the bushes or secretly damaged the property of their antagonists could be assumed to be acting improperly. When Samuel Blanchard charged his neighbor Thomas Shepard with being "sly and secretive," he was suggesting that his foe had violated the norm of manly openness in his actions.[23] Philip Goss of Lancaster forcibly reclaimed his hog from Nathaniel Hudson, who had found it eating his corn. Under some circumstances, recovering one's own property would have been excusable. But Hudson emphasized that Goss had rushed out of the bushes to attack him, by which he meant to suggest that Goss knew his behavior was illegal.[24] This criterion was almost certainly derived from the medieval legal and moral doctrine that a man who approached his foe openly showed he had a clear conscience, whereas a furtive or secretive approach evidenced immoral purposes.[25]

In a contest to present oneself as a rational man who had been unduly provoked, it was helpful to portray one's adversary as rebellious and disrespectful of authority. Men who had reputations for unruly, antiauthoritarian behavior were less likely to be convincing in their claims to be defenders of legitimate family and property interests. For example, Samuel Morrow of Redding had come to court in 1706 to seek redress for an assault by his brother Daniel and Daniel's wife, who had called him a dog and chased him and his cows out of a field with a stick. But Samuel was known as a man with a nasty temper and a penchant for questioning authority. Four acquaintances recalled seeing him bashing someone on the head with a club and saying "that if the governor had been there he would have served him the same."[26] As a man with seditious tendencies, it became impossible for him to claim to be rational, moderate, and righteous.

These statements suggest a belief that force used to defend propertied authority was righteous violence. It could be characterized as rational, moderate, and not really violent at all. There are striking parallels between the language men used to justify their behavior in fights and the language used to describe disciplinary force imposed by a master or a social superior upon a servant. Evidence of conventions about disciplinary force is difficult to find in the records of assault cases, since most uses of physical force against servants were deemed perfectly legitimate and left no trace in litigation records except where it was alleged that a servant had been treated with unusual brutality.[27]

However, retaliatory force used by a servant *was* perceived as illegal and occasionally resulted in an assault prosecution. A 1701 Boston incident, described in the records of a criminal assault prosecution there, suggests the extent to which "moderate" violence by social superiors toward servants and slaves was deemed socially acceptable. In October 1701, three men working as laborers at Castle Island witnessed an exchange between Captain Timothy Clarke, the overseer of the work project, and a free black laborer there named Adam. After receiving an order from Clarke, Adam "shewed himself very surly" and refused to obey. Clarke "with a small stick which he then held in his hand struck his [Adam's] tobacco pipe out of his mouth, gave him a shove with his hand and struck him a blow over the shoulder with his stick." The men's deposition gave no indication that they thought this behavior at all extraordinary or improper. Instead they emphasized the small size of the stick and the fact that Clarke had been provoked by Adam's "surly" behavior. In contrast, they saw Adam's reaction as excessive and violent. "[T]he said Negro in great fury and rage shoved the Captain again, wrested the stick out of his hand and broke it," and tried to hit Clarke over the head with his shovel. The white laborers rescued Clarke, and Adam was imprisoned for assault.[28]

Even when there was no particular legal reason to do so, men often tried to frame their threats or acts of violence as disciplinary acts. In so doing, they sought to cast themselves as patriarchal figures upholding the norms of righteous behavior rather than as provocative or contentious disrupters of peaceful social relations. For example, in a separate incident on the same day as Richardson's confrontation with Crosby, Crosby's seventeen- and fourteen-year-old sons, Thomas and Joseph, saw some of Richardson's hogs come into their family's field. When one of the boys went to chase the hogs off their land, Richardson himself appeared with a long goad, which he brandished at the boy, "and said he would drubb him before the week was out."[29] By threatening to "drubb" the boy, Richardson sought to construct his own use of force as a punitive or disciplinary act, presumably to punish the boys for letting the fire burn Richardson's land.

We recognize in these descriptions of violent incidents the ex post facto attempts of people involved in litigation to provide legal justification for their behavior. But for these men, such rationalizations were as much constructed by culture as they were imposed by law. Most of the men were household heads, fathers, and masters. They thought of manly men as the rational members of society, responsible for controlling the disorderly impulses of women, slaves, and young people, through force if necessary. They also thought of themselves as providers with an obligation to protect their dependents from the unruly or rapacious tendencies of outsiders. They did not like to think of themselves as disrupting social peace. Their theories about themselves as defenders of the law and chastisers of boys and servants might not always have given them a legal defense for an assault charge, but they offered a plausible basis for denying or justifying the aggression. The man who hit his opponent with "only a small blow," the captain who used only a small stick against the black laborer, the man who confronted his enemy in public—all manifested their virtuous self-control at the same time that they displayed their physical power and authority.

What else, if anything, lay beneath New England men's altercations over fences? The most likely source of social tension in the villages where they lived was the growing scarcity of land for fathers to distribute to their sons. For example, in 1679, when Thomas Shepard was the more active aggressor in his dispute with the Blanchard family, he was forty years old and had five sons to provide for. The prospect of being unable to purchase additional land for his sons (and thus of failing in his obligations as a household head and a father) would have been very real. Meanwhile his neighbor Samuel Blanchard had no sons at all. Later, when Blanchard's nephews Abraham and Joshua became the aggressors against Shepard, they had their own concerns about land. As the two youngest sons, they had received relatively small shares of the estate, although Joshua, at least, managed to prosper later in life. It may be that the festering resentments that burst out in these conflicts between farmers originated in the growing anxiety New England fathers felt about their inability to provide for their children.

Beyond psychological explanations, it may be that early American men believed they had a legal or quasi-legal right to use violence in defense of property rights under certain circumstances. Claims to property in early modern England were somewhat less absolute and more unstable than we assume them to be today, and even the common law assumed a certain level of publicly demonstrative private action by property owners as part of the process of claiming and maintaining rights to land. Title or legal rights to property could be acquired in a number of ways other than by grants to title by the sovereign, such as by adverse possession. According to *Blackstone,* an eighteenth-century treatise on the English common law, property rights could be gotten through the "mere naked possession" of property, which was perfectly good evidence of legal title "till some act be done by the rightful owner to divest this possession and assert his title." In fact, mere possession could eventually "ripen into a perfect and indefeasible title" if the rightful owner took no steps to assert his rights. In other words, in a dispute like the ongoing one between Shepard and the Blanchards, if Shepard had begun to use a field owned by one of the Blanchards and that Blanchard had not taken some act to oust him or at least publically object, after a generation or so Shepard and his family would have acquired a species of title to the land.[30]

Most attempts to claim rights to a neighbor's land were probably not meant to take property rights away from another person so much as they were based on a belief that such rights had already been granted. A legal category of rights known as prescriptive rights appears to have been at stake in many of the disputes found in the Middlesex County court records. Several kinds of interests in property, including rights of way, which allowed one property owner to pass over the land of another, and rights of common, which allowed one property owner to use another's land for a particular purpose (usually for grazing livestock), could be acquired through prescription, or long usage with the express or implied consent of the owner.[31] A property owner's failure to object to such a use of his land could be construed as evidence that he had consented to it. At the same time, proving that consent had been given could be difficult, especially when the original neighbors who had made a tacit agreement were dead. Owners who had been accustomed to using a path, fishing in a pond, or taking firewood from a woodlot could find themselves renegotiating their rights when a new owner came onto the scene.

Demonstrative and potentially violent behavior by property holders was encouraged not only by English common law doctrines about property but also by traditional mechanisms for proving the existence of prescriptive rights, mechanisms that would still have been part of English rural custom in the seventeenth century. Often, the public behavior of the parties, rather than some formal document or rule of decision, determined the existence of such rights, which were established less through formal sources of proof than through the memories of witnesses.[32] Loud, openly demonstrative assertions of rights functioned to establish the legal basis for assertions of property rights in disputes by making it clear to potential witnesses that a man had a long and well-founded expectation of enjoying those rights, or that his right or title was superior to that of an interloper, or that he had not consented to a particular use of his property.[33]

Displays of violence in these situations, then, rather than being illegal acts that had to be justified after the fact to avoid punishment, were in some sense public affirmations of a man's status as a property owner. They established and proved the existence of property rights, and were part of a quasi-legal tradition of violence built right into the English legal understanding of property and property transfers. This tradition appears to have encouraged various self-help tactics in defense of property rights. Sometimes such actions were collective, sometimes private. Some men appear to have invoked claims to higher law in defense of their property, when formal legal claims failed or were unavailable. For example, John Bigelow of Cambridge objected in 1680 when his neighbor Jacob Bullard removed a fence that Bigelow had believed marked the boundary between their property. Bullard argued that he had rights of common to use the pasture on what Bigelow had thought was his property, and therefore had a right to take down his fence if he chose to. Bigelow's response was a mixture of befuddlement and righteous indignation. He conceded that Bullard might be legally in the right, said a witness, who added that even if Bullard "knew so much law," Bigelow said he would "find a way to deale with him, and if he could not do it by law he shall do it some other way."[34] In 1702, Samuel Law of Concord was charged with (and convicted for) killing a horse that was damaging his field. Asked by witnesses "why he did not take the laws of [the horse's owners]," Law answered that his neighbors and fellow townsmen "had been such divels to him that he would not, but he had a law within himself and that he would make use of that."[35]

Stories like these provide evidence of the deep importance of property to men's sense of themselves as men.[36] But they also reveal an expectation that manhood had to be defended when challenged. Rather than a secure status arrived at in adulthood and conferring authority on its possessors, manhood in this culture remained elusive and problematic. The threats to property that provoked the fights surveyed here were mostly trivial, involving symbolic challenges rather than real economic injuries. But they were vigorously defended against, in terms that echoed the culture's discourse about manhood.

These cases also have implications for how we understand the political history of New England. A legal or quasi-legal tradition giving property-owning males the right to use force in defense of their property could potentially undermine the stability of political authority, even in law-abiding early New England. It was not uncommon for Middlesex County property owners to attack or chase away constables who came onto their property to collect rates or enforce court orders. Between 1680 and 1711, nine incidents of resisting arrest or legal process appeared in the Middlesex County courts—representing nearly a third of all litigated assaults. For example, in 1684 Concord constable John Wheeler attempted to enter the house of Robert Blood with a warrant issued by the town, assisted by several armed men whom he had deputized to help him. Blood, however, summoned his grown sons Robert and Josiah to back him up and suggested that the constable and his men were armed thugs without legal authority. Declaring to Wheeler, "[Y]ou art a rascal & a thiefe, you are come to rifle my closet and steal my goods as you did before," he demanded that the men "go off his ground and said you have nothing to do here."[37] Blood had ongoing trouble with the town of Concord; in 1685, when another constable attempted to arrest Blood for his refusal to pay his rates, father and sons, with the assistance of another man, threw the constable and his men off their property.[38] When constable Joseph Allen, Jr., of Watertown entered the house of Thomas Waite in 1707 and tried to attach some of the furniture inside, Waite issued a tirade, "uttering Many Terrible Promises & Threatening Speeches, Declaring Time after Time that if he did not get out of his House He would Knock Him Down."[39] Just as in cases of ordinary assault, the fact that a constable had physically entered a man's property, especially a house, seems to have inspired a fair number of men to resist arrest or the attachment of property.[40]

This tradition of quasi-legal uses of violence was at the center of rural violence in Anglo-American yeoman farming communities throughout the eighteenth century, and it continued for many years after the American Revolution. Especially in backcountry areas of North America with poorly developed legal institutions, groups of men collectively resorted to demonstrative and sometimes violent behavior to assert themselves when their property was threatened.[41] Some historians have taken the violence of northern land rioters as a manifestation of revolutionary resistance by the socially dispossessed against legally constituted authorities in New York, Vermont, and Maine.[42] But the fact that these rioters were property owners, as were the participants in various regulator movements throughout the colonies, suggests that they perceived themselves as defending rightful legal authority, not attacking it.

More significant, it may well be that men accepted demonstrative and often violent behavior as a legitimate tactic for defending their manhood and their property rights, especially when legal institutions and officials were perceived to be failing in their duty to protect them. These men's confidence that their actions were legal and just would have been based on a long tradition providing that, as propertied men, they were entitled to use violence to defend their rights and to discipline or chastise intruders who entered their lands and homes unlawfully. Such actions by the small farmers and craftsmen who made up most of the northeastern population during the Revolution, as well as the various agrarian conflicts that preceded and followed it, expressed both a traditional sense that independent property ownership conferred a kind of sovereignty on ordinary adult men, and the conviction that men must defend that sovereignty when challenged.

Use of Force by Youths

One of the most striking features of the assault cases that appear in the Middlesex County court records is that younger men were much less likely than men in their thirties to be prosecuted for their involvement in fights and assaults. Out of thirty cases in the sample between 1680 and 1710, only four involved men under age twenty-five who became involved in fights on their own. The remaining twenty-six involved fights between men in their thirties, forties, and beyond. Of course, young men, unmarried men, and marginal men like servants were all just as capable of physical force as mature, married heads of households. Nevertheless, young males appear in these records much less often than a modern reader would expect. It is improbable that youths in Middlesex County were so docile or obedient that they never fought with other youths. More likely their disturbances were dealt with by fathers or masters, and thus were kept within the family. Their absence from the court records suggests that the patriarchal system of social control was working.

At the same time, occasional records do provide evidence about the kinds of violent behavior in which young men typically engaged. Sometimes, instead of being dealt with in the county courts, young men in the fifteen to twenty-five age group were brought before a justice of the peace to be admonished or fined. Once in a while they appeared as codefendants in assault cases because they had helped their fathers during disputes, such as when nineteen-year-old Simon Crosby, Jr., was made a party in the Richardson-Crosby dispute.[43] On other occasions, depositions make clear, youths became involved in fights to demonstrate their loyalty to their fathers or masters, but were excused from prosecution on the assumption that they had been acting under their fathers' direction, like Eames's son in the dispute over the table.

When they became involved in fights on their own, young men exhibited patterns of behavior very different from those of older men. When young men in their teens and early twenties committed aggressive acts, they seem to have invariably been involved in such activity at night, when they were able to escape from adult supervision and associate with each other. And when they did become involved in fights, they had a much more difficult time presenting their behavior as legitimate or lawful, as there was a presumption that young men's violence was disruptive.

References in depositions and other sources to disruptive nighttime behavior suggest that most of it involved less serious offenses like smashing pumpkins or pelting houses with apples. When youths did commit more serious assaults, they could be prosecuted in the county court. Samuel Everton, age twenty-three, was convicted in 1696 of a breach of the peace for fighting with Jonathan Fosdick, age twenty-six, as well as "uncivill outrageous carriage at the house of Nathanl Adams at an unseasonable time in the evening."[44] William Shattuck, Jr., a young man in his early twenties, was presented in court twice: once in 1702 for seriously beating twenty-one-year-old Samuel Perry, and again in 1704 for "riotous carriage sometime about midnight" with two other youths.[45]

A 1681 incident involving Frances Wilson, a young, recently freed apprentice about twenty-two years old, provides revealing details about young men's late-night activities. The case also illustrates how difficult it was for males to claim the legitimate right to use violence when they were minors and not yet property owners. Wilson, according to his own testimony, "having occasion to go to Redding to look after a horse," decided to go visit some of the family members and neighbors of his former master, having "not seen them for more than a twelve month."[46] As it happened, this visit was also the occasion of several late-night sprees for Wilson and a couple of young acquaintances. Late on a Wednesday night, Wilson and one or two other young men, looking for some excitement, stole some pears from a widow's orchard and threw them at the house of Adam Colson. Although Colson was probably at home, the first person who went out to reprimand the boys was his black slave.[47] "What is the reason you steal Goody Daston's peares?" asked Colson's servant. At being chastised by a slave, Wilson became defensive and angry. "You Black Dog I will knock out your brains," he shouted back, and then he declared to his companions that "he would be the Death of that Black Dog if ever he could lay his hands on him."[48] Stones began to fly, and one of them hit Colson's servant in the stomach. Colson's wife, Mary, came out into the yard, where she joined in the fray, calling to Wilson that he was a "devilish damned drunken rogue."[49] Wilson's companions had by this time vanished, but the overwrought Wilson yelled back that if Colson's wife and his servant "would come over the Rails he would Dash [them] in pieces." Goody Colson threatened to beat Wilson's brains out and began to heave stones at him, whereupon he called her a witch.[50]

Records created during the ensuing legal battle over Frances Wilson's culpability for assault make it clear to us that both sides had acted violently. But what is interesting about the dispute are the various conventions and strategies used to establish whether that violence was legitimate (and hence manly) or illegitimate (and therefore rebellious). Both Colson's servant and his wife derived their authority to threaten and throw stones from Adam Colson's status as a property owner. They could claim, with some justification, to have been defending their family's property (and peace) from a late-night disturbance by unlawful intruders. Supporting their version of events, neighboring farmer John Brown testified that late at night on the previous Sabbath, Frances Wilson and another young man from Redding had awakened his family as well by throwing stolen pears through the window. They had lied about their identity and acted obstreperously.[51] Brown's story portrayed Wilson as an unruly boy out to challenge the authority of householders and disrupt community order.

Wilson's alternative version of what had happened illustrates how difficult it was for dependent members of society, not only unmarried and propertyless young men but also slaves and women, to assert moral authority through the use of force. In the heat of the fray, Wilson had sought to discredit his adversaries through insults, calling the slave a "Black Dog" and the woman a whore, a mother of bastards, and a witch. Appearing in court to defend himself on Adam Colson's complaint for assault, he "humbly craved" the chance to apologize for his behavior, but explained that all he had intended was to reprove Colson's wife and servant for using angry words. Rather than a boy being scolded by a householder's representative, Wilson claimed he had been a free white man acting to uphold the moral order against a challenge by a disrespectful black servant, and that he had lost control only when provoked (presumably as any reasonable man would be) by a scolding woman: "Whereupon his dame came out and fell a talking very hard and especially to me . . . Now I must confess, though I was called a divilish damnd drunken roague and divers other provoking words she spoke, I am sorry that I should not rather bear them patiently than to reply so angrily as I did, seeing it would have been more honorable to God and comfortable to myself."[52]

In support of this story, Wilson's former neighbors and mistress testified that when they had known him as an apprentice, "his behavior was modest civell & curteous to his neighbors who were his equals and respectfull to them that were his superiors, and not given to quarelling or contending with any."[53] Although Wilson was on shaky ground here, he did his best to portray himself as an ordinarily rational man who had simply been disciplining an unruly slave and a scolding woman. To buttress this self-construction, he called character witnesses who described Colson's slave as habitually violent and rebellious. Two men recalled incidents while they were on the night watch when Colson's Negro had refused to halt on command, "and gave us . . . bad language in bidding us for to kiss his ass and such ill language."[54] David Barheller testified that he had once seen Colson's Negro quarrel with Goodman Burnam's boy and threaten to cut off his ears.[55] Apparently Wilson hoped that he could clothe himself with responsibility and authority by contrast with a woman and a black male symbol of disorder. He was convicted despite his efforts.

Evidence of young men's behavior raises the possibility that among young men manhood meant something different, something divorced from the virtue associated with property holding and independence, something more like simple physical courage. It took nerve to ride up to a house in the middle of the night and shout insults at the owner, knowing full well that the man in the house probably had a gun. And an occasional case involving a fight between young men suggests that some youths made explicit associations between masculinity, courage, and physical strength, without attempting to connect them to the defense of property or order. William Shattuck, a youth in his early twenties, for example, provoked Samuel Parry, another youth, to fight with him by taunting him and calling him "a little sort of man."[56]

Still, the things young men did when they got together at night suggest that their actions, too, were shaped by the gender ideology of their patriarchal culture. Mature men's violence demonstrated their authority as men. Young men's violence challenged or made fun of that authority.

Raids on apple orchards, rocks or fruit pelted at windows and doors, smashed pumpkins, and disguised identities were not assertions of authority. They were jokes, tricks, acts of ridicule. They were a way for youths to thumb their noses and express their resentment toward householders and, in particular, toward the houses themselves, which symbolized older men's authority and manhood and were so important to adult men's identities. Such acts were a way to suggest that particular men were not as manly as they liked to think.[57] But they were also a way for young men and boys to vent their angry feelings toward symbolic targets, so that they could avoid actually having to confront their anger toward the fathers and masters who had so much power over them.

Codes that defined the legitimate uses of male violence for Middlesex County farmers were the codes of a yeoman society in which the only men who were socially recognized as real men were family heads and freehold property owners, and institutions of authority other than the family were weak. The ways in which male aggression was provoked, justified, and excused confirm once again that, in this culture, male identity was deeply tied to dominion over land and the acquisition of householder status. Many ordinary New Englanders apparently believed that independent male property owners and patriarchs could legitimately use violence to shore up their authority in a variety of circumstances. Dependent males (young men, servants, and slaves) however, could not. Independence was the crucial determinant, in men's minds, of their right to use force.

We can expect that ideas about manliness and appropriate uses of force were similarly constructed in other yeoman freehold areas of North America. In several other colonial Anglo-American subcultures, however, willingness to use force may have been as closely bound up with concepts of manliness without involving the defense of property. In the world of seamen and pirates, for example, fighting was habitual, and ideas about the loyalty that shipmates owed to one another, the importance of defending their collective honor, and other values may have contributed to a somewhat different set of ideas about the relationship between manliness and violence.[58] Members of the English aristocracy and gentry, too, possessed a highly elaborated code of violence—very different from that of New England yeomen—that found expression in the rituals and customs associated with dueling.[59]

When rural Massachusetts men encountered men from these other subcultures from time to time, most often in the colony's coastal towns and cities, they found them foreign and threatening, in part because their rituals were hard to comprehend but also in part because their rituals made a show of what New Englanders interpreted as passionate excess. Even the relatively sophisticated Boston Puritan merchant Samuel Sewall watched with horror as, with great pageantry, a duel between military men in Governor Andros's company was announced in Boston in 1687.[60] Over the succeeding ninety years, provincial New Englanders continued to come face to face with the occasional English gentleman with his sword at the hilt, ready to defend his honor. An encounter in Salem, in Essex County, in 1713 between a Lynn, Massachusetts, yeoman named Joseph Jacobs and one Charles Blessington, Esquire, illustrates the culture shock that such behavior could cause. Although the circumstances of their first meeting are not known, Jacobs evidently offended Blessington on the street, whereupon Blessington ran back to his lodging to get a sword and returned to where Jacobs stood. "God damme you you Rascal I will learn you more manners," he cried. "I won't be affronted by an rascal in your country!" Then he punched Jacobs on the breast and "flourished his sword over said Jacobs' head divers times," said the sheriff, "threatening of him like a mad distracted man."

In reading the local sheriff's eyewitness account of this event, one has the sense that the sheriff had to struggle to understand what was going on and how he was supposed to behave; in his retelling, events seem to be taking place in slow motion. "When I first saw . . . Blessington appear in the street with his sword in his hand and running toward said Jacobs in a rage I concluded that sd. Blessington—being a very passionate man—would have drawn his sword and have done some mischeife before I could have time to come to them to keep the peace." Finally, the sheriff ran up and announced to Blessington "that I came to keep the peace and that it was my office to keep the peace and I was then in the execution of my office and I will keep the peace." Blessington, apparently startled at this assertion of authority by a country farmer, called the sheriff "a changeling and a rascal" and told him "that it was a company of fools" that had put him into office.[61]

Anglo-American farmers in early eighteenth-century New England thought of themselves as moderate and rational men, quite unlike these passionate, violent gentlemen. And yet the farmers also had a concept of manly honor. A yeoman farmer's honor lay in his ability to pass on a competence to his sons, and in his sovereignty over his own domain. In some sense, a New England man defended his honor by asserting his right to defend his property, along with the authority and independence that went with it. And though they often condemned violence and anger, New Englanders also assumed that the use of violence or force was a prerogative of independent, adult manhood. And indeed it was. For so long as the family's effectiveness as an instrument of social control was thought to depend on the ability of fathers and masters to suppress disorderly behavior in women, children, and youths, manhood status would continue to give men the right to use some degree of force to uphold their authority. The ideal of rational manhood was in some ways a fiction, a denial that violence was a component of manhood, even though everyone knew it was.

Patterns of Violence from 1711 to 1762

After about 1710, patterns of violent behavior between males in Middlesex County, to the extent they can be discerned from surviving records, began to show signs of change. Between 1711 and 1762, in the forty-two individual assault prosecutions in which the underlying dispute is known, only thirteen (31 percent) involved disputes over land and livestock, and twelve (29 percent) involved cases of abuse of authority or resisting process.[62] Legal historians have often noted the rising incidence of civil litigation in New England during the eighteenth century, a development that indicates increasing public confidence in the ability of the courts—as opposed to churches or town meetings—to resolve disputes in the region's expanding economy.[63] Also, the rate of serious violent crime in Massachusetts generally fell during this period.[64] Perhaps the declining visibility of violence in defense of property in Middlesex County court records reflected a growing confidence that the legal system would protect men's property rights without resort to self-help.

Or perhaps the decline in violent conflicts over property was a sign of changing conceptions of property. During the eighteenth century, paternal strategies for settling sons shifted away from the seventeenth-century pattern of dividing existing lands among all the sons to instead providing cash gifts or new land obtained by purchase. Increasingly, land was also used to produce commodities to sell, to generate the cash needed to make these settlements. Land was itself becoming a commodity to be bought and sold, rather than serving as the main mechanism through which a man asserted his authority over his sons and fulfilled his moral obligations to them.

But the process of social change in eighteenth-century New England was not without its casualties. Assault prosecutions in Middlesex County reveal a rising incidence of fights or violent confrontations between men who identified themselves as gentlemen and men who identified themselves as laborers, suggesting that Middlesex County was becoming an increasingly stratified society.[65] They also show an apparent increase in the seriousness of violent acts committed by youths (though not necessarily a greater incidence of youthful disorder), suggesting that some young men may have felt a deepening resentment toward a patriarchal system in which they were less and less certain they would be able to participate. Taken together with the decline in the relative number of fights over property rights, these changes are consistent with a picture that has been drawn by historians, of eighteenth-century New England as a society in which the likelihood that young men would become yeomen landholders in adulthood was shrinking and social stratification was on the rise.

The most noticeable change in the circumstances accompanying violent male behavior after 1711 was the increasing number of disputes that took place in or around taverns. As Puritan control over the licensing of taverns diminished in the eighteenth century and the number of people living in settled, urban areas grew, the number of public houses in New England rose. In Middlesex County, the total number of taverns increased from 38 in 1701 to 119 in 1740 and 176 in 1760.[66] The increased presence of taverns brought some of the all-male sociability characteristic of English yeoman society back into New England. In taverns, men could affirm feelings of good fellowship and solidarity with other men to whom they were not bound by family ties, ritually affirming those feelings by drinking to one another's health. But taverns also loosened inhibitions and provided new venues in which men could engage in violence to challenge or defend each other's manhood, as vividly illustrated by an incident at a tavern near the mercantile town of Salem, in Essex County, in 1689.

On the evening in question, three young men, Ralph King, John Newell, and Thomas Witt, came into a tavern belonging to King's father, after traveling together for some time. While the three drank together, Newell and Witt (apparently continuing some earlier argument) made an insulting comment about King and his father. Angered, King reached across the table and struck at them. The father entered, commanded peace in his house, and brought them all a drink. Newell took the drink but theatrically refused to pledge good will to King because "he had a grudge against him." While King's father was in another room, Newell downed his drink, took King by the collar and hauled him into the tavern's entryway, where he and Witt put out the light and attacked the third youth, stamping on his face, neck, chest, and stomach. "Why did you not cry out for help?" asked a neighbor later, as King lay dying of his internal injuries. Replied the youth, "I thought they would laugh at me and call me a coward."[67]

Within the space created by taverns, norms governing the expression of aggression were not closely tied to the authority bestowed by property ownership. Aggressive posturing in tavern disputes tended to be more flamboyant than in late seventeenth-century disputes over property. Physically demonstrative insults were common and most often involved the face, the head, or clothing. A common technique of insult was to damage a man's clothing, particularly his hat. In a tavern in Groton in 1719, John Chamberlain, a laborer who was doing farm work for the tavern owner along with eight other men, became engaged in joking word-play with farmer Joseph Spaulding. The mood turned angry, and Chamberlain knocked Spaulding out with a punch. While Spaulding was unconscious, Chamberlain and his companions removed his hat, cut slits into it, and threw it in the fire, and they also cut slits in his coat. Before Spaulding came to, someone put a bridle over his head.[68] (The bridle was a traditional punishment in England, imposed on assertive women to remind them that, like horses, they must submit to their husbands and masters. Here, it seems to have been used to insult Spaulding's manhood.)

Another insulting gesture was for a man to spit on his hand and rub his wet fingers across the mouth of another, usually while repeating mocking or insulting words.[69] In 1755, John Hill of Billerica insulted Daniel Lock of Chelmsford by "filliping" him on the chin and spitting in his face.[70] To effectively insult a gentleman, one might damage or pull off his wig, put one's fingers in his eyes, or wring his nose.[71] In this theater of gesture and insult, the status claims being enacted by men's expressions of aggressive feelings were less tied to the authority bestowed by property ownership. They were instead bound up with the codes of dress and deportment that determined the identification of a new class of merchant gentlemen, and which were apparently affecting the self-awareness of men in other social groups as well.

Taverns brought men of different classes and backgrounds together and increased men's contact with a wider world. Although this experience may have had a leveling influence on New England society as a whole, interactions within taverns were as likely to create and reinforce a new consciousness of class distinctions as to smooth over status-related tensions.[72] But it may also be true that taverns created a space in which laboring men could assert that they were better than gentlemen on the grounds that they were more masculine.

A vivid example has been left to us in a case that started at a Woburn tavern in 1720. On a chill January night, one Timothy Richardson and a group of drinking companions burst into the tavern, where a local gentleman named Francis Leathe was sitting by the fire with three friends. Leathe and Richardson were evidently acquainted. Leathe rose from his chair with an exaggerated show of politeness and offered to let the newcomers sit down. Richardson and his companions ignored him, went to another corner of the room, and ordered drinks. After an interlude of drinking, Richardson sauntered over. "Do you want your ten shillings?" he asked. "I would be very glad," answered Leathe, "but I did not ask you for it now." Richardson persisted: "[Y]ou came for it the other day when I was not at Home. But if I had been at Home, I would a broke your Neck out of Doors."[73]

The ensuing dialogue was both highly ritualized and out of control. Richardson escalated his insults as Leathe tried to ignore him. "You little Dog," Richardson growled. "Leave off," replied Leathe, "I would not quarrel with you tonight." "You dare not," Richardson countered, "you darst as well die. I shall take you and stamp you into the ground and shitt upon you, and if I don't, I wish I may be burnt to Ashes in a minute." Leathe got up and called for the bill, and started to go into the other room. Richardson followed him out and "hunched" him in the side. "If it cost me Fifty Pounds," he called back to his friends, "I will be revenged on that little dog." As Leathe left the tavern, Richardson called out, "If I cannot whip every Leathe ever born I'll be damned." Finally, Leathe managed to mount his horse and start up the road for his house. A few minutes later, Richardson pursued him on a borrowed mount, and hit him across the back with a club.[74]

A decade earlier, this dispute might have been acted out in another setting. Leathe would perhaps have arrived at Richardson's farm, armed with a warrant allowing him to seize some personal property to satisfy a trivial debt and assisted by a couple other men. Richardson might have questioned the legality of the warrant and brought out his sons to chase them off his property. But when a dispute like this was instead acted out in the venue of a tavern, neither man's position was grounded in the authority of property ownership or law. Leathe did not have a warrant, and Richardson was not on his own land. The negotiation of moral legitimacy thus became more dependent on physical gesture, bearing, and language. Through such means, Leathe suggested to the assembled public that he was genteel and Richardson was common, while Richardson displayed his ostensible strength and courage in contrast to Leathe's timidity and weakness.

The other new pattern of male violence revealed by Middlesex County court records was the apparently increasing level of violence that involved disruptive behavior by youths. Evidence from court records cannot tell us whether the activities associated with night-walking were actually becoming more common, but it does suggest an increase in the level of violence associated with reported incidents. The youths who were prosecuted for nighttime misbehavior during the mideighteenth century went far beyond practical jokes; their actions terrorized the occupants of houses, sometimes for hours. In one incident, the teenagers and youths who attacked a house were alleged to have been "armed with clubs, swords, axes, forks and guns," and to have fired a gun at the house.[75] In another, three youths were presented for attacking the house of Joshua Parker while he was away, and threatening to break in and rape his wife, Parnel.[76] Two other descriptions of attacks on houses also alleged assaults or attempted assaults on the women inside, suggesting that young men's resentful actions against householders were becoming more sexually charged and explicit.[77] Such attacks were of course a way to insult a husband's manhood, since they suggested he could not protect his wife even in his own home.

Nevertheless, these changes in the patterns of male violence should not obscure certain basic continuities. Despite the weakening of paternal power, no new paradigm for thinking about manhood had emerged in New England by the 1760s. Householders in eighteenth-century Middlesex County, Massachusetts, as in the seventeenth century, imagined their manhood as bound up with their property and their houses.

They continued to defend their manhood by fighting with men who challenged their authority as householders, even if those men were constables. Boys continued to attack the houses of older men in order to ridicule or insult their claims to manly authority. In some sense, both groups confirmed through their behavior that men who had houses, property, and independence had a greater claim to manly authority than youths. Their acts suggest that the Puritans' framework for thinking about manhood still held its grip on the New England mind.

6

Manhood and Politics

Politics is ordinarily thought of as a realm separate from the private and personal realm of gender relations. But in seventeenth- and eighteenth-century New England, political rhetoric interpenetrated with the language of gender. In particular, perhaps because men were the main political actors, political writers and speakers sought to portray their leaders as manly, or to call into question the manhood of those they opposed. Indeed, the very ways in which political relations were conceptualized often built on assumptions about manhood and gender relations. It would be too simplistic to say that political disputes were *caused* by concerns about gender. Nonetheless, the gendered rhetoric of politics gives us a new perspective on the ways in which social change was related to political events in colonial New England.

Many scholars have suggested that the American Revolution involved a final repudiation of patriarchal assumptions about the family and politics in colonial America. They argue that the decline of patriarchal power within New England families helped to make possible, emotionally, the overthrow of a patriarchalist conception of government and the adoption of a republican, contractual political theory. One of the most powerful (and pervasive) images in American revolutionary rhetoric was the image of the brave, manly American resisting the authority of the tyrannical parent government of England. The force of this image, these scholars would suggest, drew from the transition from patriarchal family relations to a new, affectionate style of family life and an ideal of autonomous personality.

But a look at the gender symbolism in New Englanders' political rhetoric from 1676 to 1776 suggests a different conclusion. The patriarchal

146

or patrifocal ideal of manhood did not die out during the eighteenth century but instead displayed remarkable persistence. Even though the social conditions that had strengthened patriarchal power within families in the early colonial period had changed, giving young men and women the chance to face life's choices, challenges, and risks with more freedom than in the past, a conception of manhood centered around the achievement of propertied independence and the father-son bond remained at the center of cultural expression. It seems that the satisfactions of that bond were hard to abandon.

This final chapter will look at the ways in which images of manhood were deployed in political debates between 1676 and 1776 in order to better understand how New Englanders' ideas about manhood shaped political discussion. Three particular episodes in New England's political history will be explored. During the first two—the overthrow of New England's colonial governor Edmund Andros in 1689 and the currency debates of 1720 to 1745—events took place mostly in Massachusetts, the most prosperous and politically important of the New England colonies. In the third episode, during the 1760s and 1770s, first Massachusetts and then all of New England would become the crucible of the American Revolution.

Writers and participants in all of the debates drew on images of manhood in trying to persuade readers of their arguments and to make sense of political issues. Although these images could be used to support strikingly different arguments, the images themselves were the products of a patriarchal culture. Political writers in each of the three periods invoked the metaphor of the bad ruler as a tyrannical father. All argued that the fathers of families had the ultimate responsibility for protecting their sons' economic security. And all portrayed manly men as responsible fathers and independent household heads, as much at the end of the period as at the beginning. To understand this is to understand that the ideas that shaped the American Revolution in New England were as much a product of parenthood's cultural ascendance as of patriarchy's decline.

Rulers as Fathers

In the earliest years of New England's history, the ideal of patriarchal manhood helped to support a hierarchical and deferential political culture. The earliest governments in New England had been run by local

Puritan leaders, with minimal interference from the English Crown. Although the franchise in the colonies was relatively broad compared with England's (all adult male church members had the right to vote in town government and to vote for the town's representatives to the assembly), voters almost always deferred to the judgment of the Puritan magistrates, obediently returning the same men to office year after year.[1]

Once every year, seventeenth-century Massachusetts ministers explained their theory of government in election sermons given before an assembly of magistrates and freemen in Boston. They saw government not as we do, as an expression of the will or interests of voters, but as an agent of God responsible for enforcing divine will and ensuring compliance with the law. In their annual election sermons, the ministers often invoked the ideal of the good father to buttress the authority of the colony's Puritan magistrates: These men, they explained, were "nursing fathers, who are betrusted with the care of the child."[2] The analogy between fatherhood and government was not unique to the Puritans. It was common throughout the Anglo-American world in the sixteenth and seventeenth centuries; it had been an idea important to the growth of the monarchy, and in the 1640s the patriarchalist Sir Robert Filmer used the analogy to articulate a defense of absolute monarchy as a natural parallel to absolute paternal authority.[3] During the period when the Puritans held political power in Massachusetts, ministers there shared the view that a father's right to command his children could be used as proof of a monarch's right to rule his subjects.[4]

However, the Puritans' conception of government was never genuinely Filmerian, for neither Puritan rulers nor Puritan fathers had absolute authority. Rather, they held power in a form most closely resembling a trust from God. Much like Puritan fathers, Puritan rulers had a special responsibility to seek their subjects' spiritual welfare, which meant that they had to promote religious purity. The analogy between the special trust of rulers and that of fathers was often made explicit. In 1667, for example, Jonathan Mitchel had reminded the magistrates in Massachusetts that since God loved the people like a son, rulers must care for them on God's behalf like a father would care for a child, promoting their moral and spiritual good. Rulers were fathers writ large, not simply because of their authority but also because of their care for the people's spiritual well-being. Above all, rulers were "nursing fathers . . . to the church."[5] Upon them devolved the ultimate responsibility for promoting God's will and religious purity within New England's holy commonwealth.

By no means did the Puritans ever embrace the idea of a democratic society. They were horrified by the idea that citizens might try to use their right to vote to promote their own individual interests. The role of voters was to assist the magistrates in promoting true religion. Government, they believed, came from a collective covenant with God, under the terms of which all members of the church had the duty to ensure that their society refused to tolerate sinful behavior. Group pressure placed strict limits on individual dissent and debate, for the ideal was loving consensus, not compromise among competing interests. Voters exhibited remarkable deference toward a small group of established, experienced leaders.[6]

Later in American history, in the nineteenth century, the act of voting would become a deeply symbolic affirmation and assertion of manhood. But in seventeenth-century New England, it was portrayed as almost a ritual relinquishment of manhood's privileges. According to Puritan religious leaders, voting was not so much an exercise of the rational will, the faculty that was associated with manliness, as a voluntary submission to the will of God. Sermons, such as the 1671 election sermon by John Oxenbridge, explained to voters that God have given them liberty to elect their own representatives so that the people could use that freedom to show their loyalty to God.[7] The ability to "freely" choose the right ruler (the ruler God wanted) was a function of having received grace, which was an unearned gift from God and in no way favored males.

Indeed, most Massachusetts election sermons suggested that in voting, men should assume a feminine position vis-à-vis God's will by subordinating their own will to God's. Ministers often analogized the act of choosing a ruler to a woman's giving herself to her husband or, occasionally, a child's submitting to his father's will. Almost all published Puritan political sermons before 1686 compared voters to the bride of Christ or invoked the metaphor of marriage in reminding voters of their duty to make choices consistent with God's will. Ministers Thomas Walley and Samuel Danforth, for example, warned voters that God might lose interest in New England's people if they lost their spiritual ardor, just as a husband can grow cold to a wife who has lost her beauty. Others compared the people to an adulteress, an unfaithful wife, or a harlot, to warn them that the disloyal would incur God's wrath. The analogy of female submission conveyed the message that voters were supposed to act in obedience to, and be dependent on, their ministers, just as they had once been dependent on their fathers.[8] Because these sermons represent their male audience as subordinate, they are jarring and even disturbing to us now, but the feelings they aroused would have been a familiar part of the emotional experience of any man who had spent his first twenty-five to thirty years in a relationship that required him to submit to his father's will. New England men had all spent a large part of their lives occupying the role of the dependent, effeminate youth.

Yet even while voters in early New England heard messages from the pulpit about the duty to submit to governmental authority, they expected their rulers' behavior to comport with their ideals of rational manhood. Underlying men's deference for New England's political leaders was the often explicit expectation that those leaders would protect their status as independent farmers and property holders, so that they could maintain their own role as patriarch at home.[9] The expectation was not much different than a boy's expectation that his father would ultimately promote his interests and provide him with a competence. And it was a well-founded expectation, for during their first sixty years, colonial New England governments had offered settlers extraordinarily secure rights to property. Most of the colonies held their land from the king without obligations or fees other than the obligation of allegiance, and in turn they generally granted land to settlers in a form almost entirely free of tenures, rents, or other obligations. In Massachusetts, for example, the Body of Liberties of 1641 had freed landowners from virtually all feudal incidents (devices allowing certain rights over property to revert to the Crown), and had given freeholders, through their own locally elected representatives, substantial control over how much they would pay in taxes. Male settlers were "sovereign lords of their own holdings."[10] Owing no rent, having little experience with having to abase themselves to great men, the colonists in the early years grew confident that government was there to defend their property if it was threatened.

But by 1676 New England was entering a period of uncertainty and change. The long period in which New Englanders had been ignored by the English government was coming to an end, now that the Restoration of King Charles II and an increase in Atlantic trading by British merchants had provoked a new interest in tightening up imperial controls.

Agents of the Crown were now in Massachusetts, investigating the colony's compliance with the newly enacted navigation acts and other English laws. By 1676, the colonists were also reeling from the devastation caused by King Philip's War, in which various local Indian tribes had allied to try to drive them back into the sea, causing heavy casualties and even heavier property losses for the settlers. Anglo-Americans' anxiety about the security of their way of life reached a fever pitch.[11]

In 1685 the English government removed the Puritans from power in Massachusetts and imposed on the colony a new government directly answerable to the king. Worse yet, the untimely death of Charles II meant that the king was now the absolutist James II, Duke of York, who believed that citizens had no rights vis-à-vis their monarch, only privileges, which he could unilaterally take away.[12] As the new colonial governor, James appointed Sir Edmund Andros, a courtier long in his service, an autocratic and flamboyant man who seemed to New Englanders almost entirely alien. Instead of the dark, plain clothing of Puritan magistrates, he wore scarlet coats and a flowing wig. Members of his entourage got drunk and swore in public, gambled, and even danced around a May pole in Charlestown. New Englanders watched aghast as he reorganized the government, abolished established religion, and unilaterally imposed new taxes. Unlike the sober Puritan magistrates who had ruled for the past half-century, this new governor seemed to personify not manly, responsible fatherhood but the effeminate passion and vice of the very society they had hoped to leave behind. Their concern turned to outrage at Andros's most provocative act, when he declared colonists' titles to their land invalid and required them to obtain new deeds from the king, subject to quitrents.[13]

Unhappiness with Andros's policies was widespread. The charismatic minister of the town of Ipswich, John Wise, led a mass protest against the new taxes, for which he was put in jail.[14] Others complained more quietly. But apparently colonists had been discussing the idea that men had a right and an obligation to remove rulers who failed to protect the people or promote their spiritual welfare, for in April 1689, when they learned that King James had abdicated after the Glorious Revolution in England, people from the Massachusetts countryside streamed into Boston and ousted the hated Andros and his Dominion government by force. After negotiations with the new monarchs, William and Mary, Connecticut, Rhode Island, and New Hampshire were restored to their pre-Dominion status, and Massachusetts accepted a compromise government in which Puritan leaders had to share power with a royal governor, allow religious toleration, and permit non-Puritan men to vote, so long as they owned property.

Political rhetoric in Massachusetts after 1689 acquired a new emphasis on men's rights as property owners. Pamphleteers justified the rebellion against Governor Andros by explaining that the government had illegally seized their property, denying them their rights as freeholders. Defenders of the new colonial charter emphasized that it secured liberty and property rights, while its critics argued that its protection of property rights did not go far enough. Even ministers in their annual election sermons, which were now directed not to the covenanted body of the church but to the colony's rulers, took up the new rhetoric and reminded the new royal governor of his duty to protect men's property rights.[15] The assumption that government would protect property rights had always been there; now it was articulated explicitly.

But despite this new rhetoric, Massachusetts ministers' understanding of the relationship between government and the people would remain quite consistent. Ministers would continue to analogize rulers and fathers in their sermons, and to assume a hierarchical framework for government, in which subjects owed obedience to rulers. In the new, post-1689 political context, sermons about good rulers would more often stress not their authority but their obligations to their subjects—the flip side of the Puritan concept of patriarchal authority. Rulers were urged to deal "compassionately and tenderly" with their subjects, to be "careful and provident . . . as if their people were their Children," suggested Joseph Belcher in 1701. If the father of a family needed to have "a great deal of Wisdom and Prudence . . . for the right discharge of his trust in that Relation," then "how much more is requisite in a Political father, the father of a Country?" he asked. Solomon Stoddard admonished his listeners that, just "as God don't allow liberty to children to carry as they will to their Parents, so he does not allow Parents to carry as they will to their Children." And John Hancock reminded the governor that rulers held their power in trust from God, to promote the welfare of the people.[16]

Neither the hierarchical nature of authority nor the idea of manliness changed much in the half century after 1675. But the rhetorical analogy of rulers as fathers proved malleable enough to serve multiple purposes

for Puritan political writers. Good New England fathers had dual obligations to their children: to provide spiritual education and guidance, and
to provide land for their livelihood. So long as the Puritans were in
power, emphasis on the first had permitted ministers to stress citizens'
duty to be obedient and deferential. But after the crisis of the 1680s, although they could no longer expect rulers to promote true religion, the
idea that magistrates ought to behave (like fathers) as responsible pro-
tectors gave Puritan writers a way to articulate criticism of their actions.
After 1692, the metaphor of fatherhood became a way not so much to remind the people of their obligation to obey, as to remind rulers of the
limits of their power.[17]

In the task of reestablishing political stability in Massachusetts, the
trope of fatherhood played another role as well. As their own power to
choose political rulers for their colony waned, Massachusetts ministers
cast about for a new set of patriarchs who could preserve their vision of a
pious and spiritually pure society. Instead of placing this responsibility
in the hands of government, their sermons increasingly emphasized that
the task of keeping piety alive was the responsibility of individual
fathers and household heads. Published sermons about the duties of
householders to provide spiritual education for their dependents were
ubiquitous after 1690. Political sermons also became reminders that ordinary men had a special responsibility for the colony's future in their
roles as fathers and household heads. The result was a subtle mascu-
linization of householders in relation to their rulers. When Benjamin
Colman urged voters to raise their children as good Christians, exhort-
ing them, "Let us play the man for our people, and for the cities of our
God,"[18] he shifted some of government's burden of playing the man to
the shoulders of householders themselves.

The Debate about Money

If the most important political issue in seventeenth-century Massachusetts involved the limits of governmental power, the most pressing issue
in the first half of the eighteenth century was monetary policy. An increasing volume of trade between New England and the British Isles
during the eighteenth century brought New England into an international commercial system. Meanwhile, as New England families' strategies for providing for all their sons came to rely less on partitioning ex-

isting land holdings and more on the accumulation of cash, farmers began to see the value of producing extra grain or livestock for sale to foreign buyers.[19] However, despite the rapid economic expansion that overtook the New England colonies after 1720, the English government never took steps to provide the colonies with an effective supply of currency, and indeed it prohibited the export of coin and bullion to the colonies for fear of causing a currency shortage in England itself.

As New England's economy grew, the shortage of money became a persistent problem for its farmers. One difficulty was that certain kinds of obligations, like taxes or debts, could not be paid with farm produce or other in-kind payments. Another was that farmers in a cash-scarce economy had a hard time getting a fair price for their products, because they were at the mercy of buyers who offered payment in barter, and the value of that payment could vary widely.[20] Debates about how to solve these monetary problems drew increasing public attention. Printing presses, once used almost entirely for printing sermons and legal edicts to reinforce the authority of Puritan magistrates and ministers, had by the early 1720s begun to publish such debates in political pamphlets and newspapers addressed to a wide audience of male voters. Often, the debates were also part of a larger, transatlantic philosophical discussion about the implications of commercial life.[21]

One solution to the money problem that many New England farmers and their allies favored was to give local legislatures the power to issue paper money (bills of public credit backed by the promise of future taxes). Increasing the supply of paper money, it was thought, would increase trade. But paper money was also inflationary. Merchants, whose overseas trading partners would generally not accept paper money from the colonies, favored relying on only silver currency. Moreover, in their capacity as creditors, they opposed any currency whose depreciation would diminish the value of their loans.[22]

In trying to win the support of voters, both advocates and opponents of paper currency drew on images or assumptions about manhood to bolster their arguments, just as ministers writing about political theory had done. Paper money's opponents argued from a balance-of-trade point of view, saying that the region's economic problems flowed not from the lack of currency but from the unhealthy consequences of excessive consumption. According to the wealthy merchant Paul Dudley, whose argument typified the hard currency position, New Englanders spent too much on luxuries, causing an imbalance of trade and, hence, a debilitating currency shortage. Pamphleteers relied on the conventional wisdom that the consumption of luxuries was not only sinful but enervating. This assumption was directly analogous to that of medical writers who believed that male sexual health was endangered by the excessive indulgence of desire.

Although some of the pamphlet writers expressed scorn for ordinary tradesmen who had the effrontery to purchase luxury goods, most appealed to ordinary voters simply by invoking the popular and common-sense notion that household heads must balance production and consumption in order to survive.[23] A typical anonymous pamphleteer suggested that just as a household head must work hard to provide adequately for his family, he must also avoid the temptation of overspending. "Its criminal . . . if thro' Idleness we neglect to provide necessaries for our selves, or Families; it's criminal also, if we employ so much of our Labour . . . in getting things for Ornament or Delight, as to pinch or straighten our selves as to Necessaries, or render us unable to pay our Debts."[24] These anticonsumption writers suggested that the solution to the currency shortage was to restore an imagined past of frugality and virtue, and they exhorted readers to work harder, be better husbands of their household resources, and give up buying fancy things.

Paper money supporters offered a more optimistic assessment of the possibilities for economic growth. These writers also used images of manhood to convince their readers, but the men they described were neither cautious nor endangered by consumption. Instead, men were producers and fatherly providers. To these writers, currency was nothing but a medium for facilitating trade, and increasing the currency supply would encourage men to invest and improve their property. Referring to an idealized image of manly men as competent, industrious, and independent, minister John Wise, for example, assured readers that paper money was responsible for New England's prosperity, with its farms so "finely built, and fenced, with noble Stocks of Cattle feeding, and coming to a good Market." He promised more growth in the future if paper money continued to be issued.[25] And why should growth matter? Quite simply, it mattered because fathers needed to be able to provide for their sons.

The pro-paper writers spoke directly to families whose economic strategies were beginning to involve market-oriented production rather than simply dividing up an existing patrimony. They spoke directly to the most pressing concern of fathers in eighteenth-century New England: the need to provide inheritances for their sons. Credit, they argued, the ability to borrow money for the purchase and improvement of new land, would solve their problems by making economic growth possible. If the currency shortage were to continue, warned Oliver Noyes, "What then will be the consequences but Sloth and Idleness . . . [Your] Children will be viciated for want of Business, and in another Generation will Loose all that Spirit and Life, which distinguishes Free Men from Slaves." Their sons would "be brought to that sordidness and meanness of Soul, which appears in Ireland, and some other places, where the *Poor c[r]ouch like an Ass under his Burthen* at the sight of their Land-Lords, though the Man (set his Estate aside) is no better than the meanest of them." "We are but Stewards for our Children," an anonymous author admonished his readers, "and it is our duty as far as we are able to leave things so circumstanced, that they may be able to improve what by the blessing of Heaven we leave them." John Wise even framed one of his pamphlets as a fictional letter from a father to a son, claiming that a loan from the bank had enabled him to increase the family's estate and provide for both his boys.[26]

The image of manhood invoked by paper money's opponents depended on balance, conservation, avoiding excessive consumption. Paper's supporters, in contrast, tended to portray manhood in expansive terms. "Man is an Active Projecting Creature," John Colman suggested, and if there were money to be earned, "everybody almost would be Improving his talent." John Wise enthusiastically described the generative properties of paper money, actually analogizing it to male "seed." "These Bills are of a very impregnating nature," he suggested, and "they will beget and bring forth whatsoever you shall please to fancy." He even suggested that the prosperity brought by paper money could revive religion, making an extended comparison between the salutary effects of sperm on a woman's womb and infusions of money into Harvard College, which was now able to produce large classes of new ministers every year where before Harvard had brought forth nothing but "Dead Embrios or Abortions."[27]

Both sides in the paper money debate argued that their proposals were the most likely to protect freehold property rights and the ability of male householders to remain independent.[28] But the question at the center of the debate had to do with the role of money in making that stability possible. Paper money's opponents believed that money had to possess a fixed, intrinsic value, and measured a nation's wealth in the amount of gold and silver it possessed. Paper money's supporters, in contrast, saw money as a mechanism for facilitating investment and exchange, and were beginning to imagine wealth not as something fixed in time and space, but as something dynamic, measured by productivity and growth.[29]

At the same time, the debate was about more than the meaning of money, it was a debate about male identity itself. New England's development during the eighteenth century of an increasingly commercial economy presented men with new temptations and new challenges. Opportunities for consumption, while they promised pleasure, could also threaten men's economic autonomy with the possibility of debt. Perhaps they also produced anxiety in men who had been taught from infancy that their very masculinity depended on their ability to master their desires. Conservatives in the debate portrayed ideal manhood in terms of balance, stability, and good husbandry, within a context of appropriate deference to higher authority: values appropriate to a static society in which a household head's only duty to his progeny was to conserve his property for their eventual benefit.

For New England's fathers, with their commitment to pass on farms to all of their sons and not just the eldest, the emphasis on balance and conservation would have functioned reasonably well so long as they controlled an abundant supply of land. But as the shrinking land supply forced men to look outward for opportunities for growth, an ideal that emphasized for the male personality only stern discipline and cautious conservatism was becoming outdated. Other features of manhood, like the ability to forgo pleasure and work hard, more useful in an expanding economy, came to the forefront. The ideal of responsible fatherhood served as an imaginative springboard for arguments in favor of credit and increased opportunities for trade. The Puritans' equating of manhood with fatherhood was far more flexible and adaptable than some historians have acknowledged, for their high level of economic commitment to their children made them welcome market-oriented opportunities that allowed parents to provide more effectively for their dependents.

Effeminate Bureaucrats

The currency debates receded after a new war with the French in 1745 finally brought an infusion of silver currency from the British government, and Parliament prohibited any further issues of bills of credit. But the larger debate about life in a newly commercializing empire continued to simmer, especially in Massachusetts. Ever since the issuance of the 1691 charter for Massachusetts, a loose coalition of ministers, merchants, and lawyers had emerged as consistent critics of Crown policy. Their arguments about the distribution of powers between the representative assembly and its Crown-appointed governor under the provincial charter drew on the so-called Commonwealth tradition in English political thought, also referred to as classical republican political ideology.[30]

According to republican critics, the creation in England of new government institutions like the Bank of England, a funded national debt, and a standing army, as well as increasing executive patronage of members of Parliament, were all signs that English government and society in the 1700s had become hopelessly corrupt—and effeminate. English republicans rallied support for this critique by painting a nostalgic picture of an imaginary English past in which virtuous, property-owning republican citizens had possessed the independence to resist the influence of kings or lords and to protect reason and the rule of law.[31] If members of Parliament had remained virtuous and independent, they said, then the British people would be safe. But instead, the people's representatives had become placemen, economically dependent on patronage from the executive branch. The people's property was at risk.

To the middle- and upper-middle-class merchants and lawyers who had come to dominate New England politics by the 1750s, the emotional, symbolically freighted rhetoric of English republicans resonated deeply. These men had risen to positions of prominence within colonial society and many served in the colonial legislature. Yet they could never advance as far in colonial administration as they might have liked, for top positions were reserved for appointments by the Crown, and few New England men could afford to spend much time in England seeking royal favor. For these ambitious colonists, republican rhetoric provided a language for expressing grievances against a closed system of patronage that excluded them from real power. Commonwealth rhetoric allowed them to imagine political life as a conflict between courageous,

virtuous, and rational patriots "standing up for the just Rights and Privi-
ledges of their Country" and the fawning, corrupt courtiers who held
the really plum jobs in colonial administration.[32]

To men outside the colonial political elite, other issues were probably
more important during the 1750s and 1760s. The expansion of trading
networks within the British empire was continuing to draw increasing
numbers of farmers into the web of an Atlantic economy. As the level of
production for sale to distant buyers grew, so did the level of consumption of imported goods by ordinary families. Farmers' standard of living
grew, but so did their awareness of their vulnerability to fluctuations in
the market for their goods. New England's largest city, Boston, had been
beset by serious unemployment since the 1720s, as the ongoing currency shortage damaged the functioning of the local economy. The shipbuilding and distilling industries and the butchering and leather-work-
ing trades had fallen off 60 to 90 percent in the past four decades.[33] After
the Seven Years War, a postwar contraction in demand for goods transformed this economic slowdown into a serious recession. One obvious
effect of the slowing economy would have been to threaten laboring
men's ability to provide for their families—and thus to call into question
their claims to manhood.

After 1763, in its attempt to find sources of revenue to repay the colos-
sal debt left by the war, the British government began to modernize its
system for enforcing existing trade laws within the empire and raising
revenue from the rich colonial trading system that had emerged in the
Atlantic world over the past sixty years. Parliament imposed taxes on
luxury items like Madeira wine and French linens, taxes that in New
England had the greatest impact on members of the upper class, since it
was only upper-class people who traded in or consumed these luxury
goods.[34] More galling to local leaders, the parliamentary taxes threatened the customary political prerogatives of colonial assemblies by de-
priving them of control over the tax revenues needed to run their local
governments. Unwilling to abandon their taxing power, leaders in many
of the mainland North American colonies, especially in Massachusetts,
immediately raised legal objections, which they sought to explain to the
public through pamphlets and petitions to the king and the House of
Commons.[35] Notwithstanding the legal protests, Parliament pressed
ahead in 1765 with its plan to modernize imperial administration by
passing a set of stamp taxes on legal documents, licenses, and printed

matter, these for the purpose not only of raising more revenue but also to establish that it had the legal power to tax the colonies. Colonial opposition leaders appealed to the public for help in preventing the new laws from going into effect through protests against both the Stamp Act and the officials responsible for its execution. Many of their arguments invoked republican political theory, warning that political corruption could destroy the people's liberties, and so on.

Ordinary Bostonians responded enthusiastically, taking part in mass demonstrations, burning the effigies of stamp collectors, and, in some cases, tearing down their houses. It is unlikely that Boston artisans and laborers cared deeply about the financial infrastructure of the British government or the nature of political coalitions within Parliament. Rather, ordinary men in Boston had other grievances against the well-dressed, luxuriously housed men who served as agents of the Crown. The severe unemployment that had beset the town already threatened their manhood. This new challenge to men's honor by the imperial government demanded a response. As one resistance leader argued, it could not "be counted rebelling . . . for the freemen of this colony to stand for their absolute rights and defend them, as a man would his own house when insulted, for I see no difference in regard to the possession of either."[36]

Pamphlet writers opposed to the new tax laws explicitly drew on images of ideal manhood to rally popular support. Writers suggested that their opponents in Parliament, along with the men who had accepted commissions to carry out their policies in the colonies, were not real men. They were said to be corrupt, servile, base, "consult[ing] only to gratify their own pride and ambitious humour and passion."[37] They cared more for their own gain than the good of their people. They had given up their virtue to satisfy their own vanity and greed. Epithets included "vain coxcombs," along with fop, witling, tool. They were "servile," "abject," and sought office not to serve the public good but to gratify "some selfish passion."[38] They were "favourites and flatterers . . . acting in the affairs of the nation by their d[e]spotic will."[39] All of the descriptive insults suggested an absence of the moral and intellectual independence that made a man manly. As one writer suggested, they were "cringing tools" who had "cease[d] to hear, to think, or act the man" and instead had become irrational beasts, monkeys or apes.[40] The finance ministry, it was suggested, was purposely trying to make these officials dependent on its will by keeping them "in ease, idleness, or luxury, in mother Britain's lap."[41] In a word, these officials had proven themselves to be effeminate, and they were not entitled to the community's respect.

Speakers and pamphlet writers also reminded readers of the qualities that they should expect from good rulers. Good rulers were responsible, self-sacrificing, manly men, dedicated to serving the interests of the people. A good ruler was a "true friend" who cared so much for virtue that he "joyfully with all his blood would part to extricate his countrymen from woe."[42] Good rulers always put the public good before their own interests.[43] The images used to depict good rulers were often nostalgic, hearkening back to an imagined time when fathers ruled. A writer trying to encourage protests against the Stamp Act in Hartford, Connecticut, invoked the traditional Old Testament image of rulers as patriarchs. Good rulers must have "a true patriarch spirit," he suggested, like Moses, to lead their people to follow God's laws. Others explained that good rulers must be "nursing fathers," for they were trustees of the people's rights.[44]

Presumably these images resonated with ideals of manhood that were still part of New England's popular culture. Republican political thought suggested that manly virtue came from propertied independence, while in Protestant thought, the source of a man's virtue was rationality, or moral independence. But both sets of assumptions had always been part of Anglo-American New Englanders' ideas about manliness. One of New England's preeminent revolutionary writers, John Adams, invoked the Puritan intellectual tradition when he equated manhood with education and the ability to reason, and asserted that men in New England were better able to make informed and rational political decisions because of their high level of education. But he invoked the rhetoric of republicanism when he criticized Crown officials as "missionaries of ignorance, foppery, servility, and slavery" and suggested that New England men must prove their manhood by distinguishing themselves from "luxurious, effeminate, and unreasonable" placemen.[45] The critical divide in his thinking was between servile, effeminate men who were ruled by their desires, and rational, independent men who were not.[46]

Pamphlet writers' suggestion that appointed British officials were not manly was apparently effective in convincing many Bostonians that these men needed to be taught a lesson. Between August 14 and August 26, 1765, thousands of Bostonians joined in hanging and burning effigies of various royal officials and stamp commissioners. Even more striking were attacks on the property, specifically the houses, of various Crown-appointed administrators. During that twelve-day period, mobs targeted four Crown officials: the new distributor of stamps for Massachusetts, Andrew Oliver; an official of the Admiralty Court, William Story; the colony's lieutenant governor, Thomas Hutchinson; and the comptroller of customs, Benjamin Hallowell. Although the owners and occupants of the houses were sometimes personally threatened and intimidated, they were invariably allowed to escape, for the target of this mob violence was clearly the houses themselves. In the course of the attacks, mobs destroyed windows, sashes, doors, and sometimes even walls and roofs. Once inside, they went on to destroy furniture, clothing, paintings, imported wines, and books—the luxury items that were the most obvious trappings of upper-class status.

From a modern point of view, the most obvious way to interpret attacks by lower-class men on upper-class men's houses is as expressions of class-based resentment. But from the point of view of an eighteenth-century New Englander, the attacks on houses would have had another level of meaning as well. A man's house was a symbol of his authority and his manhood. In early New England, where manhood was so closely associated with property ownership and householder status, houses were metaphorically associated with men's bodies—they signified a man's ability to provide for a woman and even to perform sexually. The men who became targets of popular anger in Boston in 1765, by attempting to enforce what the people considered to be illegitimate laws, had proven themselves to be unmanly. Instead of providing for their dependents, they had been ruled by selfish passions, acquiring luxury goods that proved they were in thrall to their desires, and thus were effeminate fops no longer entitled to the people's deference. When mobs pulled down these men's houses, they demonstrated their disrespect for the men as men, defacing the most visible symbol of their manhood status. Pulling down their houses was a way of shaming them and demonstrating that the community did not consider them to be real men.[47]

Consumer Boycotts and Manly Self-Mastery

Several months of rioting in Boston, Newport, and other North American cities, along with boycotts of British goods, convinced Parliament to

withdraw its taxes. But the Finance Ministry had not given up its attempt to shift some of the England's financial burden onto the American
colonies. In 1767 Parliament passed the Townshend Acts, which imposed duties on a variety of imported consumer goods, such as glass, paper, chinaware, tea, and all kinds of imported cloth. Opposition leaders
determined that boycotts, with which they had begun to experiment
during the Stamp Act crisis, would help them to exert pressure on Parliament, since they would cut into the profits of many British merchants.
They urged the public to stop consuming British imports and to replace
them with American-made products.[48] The resistance movement now
grew to include the middling segment of the population in both cities
and towns, people who had come to depend on such commodities in
their own homes.

These protests, like the earlier ones, were rich with the symbolism of
gender. In the pamphlets published in support of the boycott movement,
a central theme was that the British government was trying to rob colonial men of their manhood, but that men could prove their manhood by
mastering their own desires for consumer products. Imports were luxuries that would drain colonial economies and reduce the colonists to
slavery. By forgoing them and using home manufactures instead, Americans would learn to be both self-denying and industrious, and would
grow in strength. In doing so they might "save [their] substance, even
[their] lands, from becoming the property of others," said one Massachusetts writer.[49]

Several historians have argued that the boycott movement, with its
advocacy of self-denial, shows eighteenth-century New Englanders to
have been hostile to modernity and commerce.[50] What they have not no-
ticed is that this narrative urging Americans to practice self-denial and
industry was also a narrative about manhood. Often writers made an explicit connection between manhood and the boycott. One argued that
men who could give up foreign luxury goods were more manly than
those who boasted of their bravery in battle. "I laugh at a man that
talks of facing cannons and redcoats, who cannot conquer his foppish
impressions of grandeur . . . How can he be a true lover of his country,
and consider himself a man of true grandeur, who would sooner be seen
strutting about the streets, clad in foreign fripperies, than be nobly independent in the russet grey! When we think of resisting the most powerful force in Europe, let us levy war against luxury, the parent of im-

becility."[51] Another, in urging New England men to give up imported consumer goods, invoked the example of their patriarchal forebears. "Never were a people so happy as our forefathers," he wrote. "They had but few wants, and luxury, extravagance, and debauchery, were known only by the names, as the things signified thereby had not then arrived from the old world."[52]

These political writers were perhaps suggesting not so much that their listeners give up their connections with the modern, commercial world as urging them to take control of their situation. By forgoing "luxuries" and showing their mastery of their own desires for consumer goods, men who participated in the boycotts would have replicated what for most of them would have been an important coming-of-age experience. Indulgence in luxury was effeminate. So long as boys were effeminate, they would remain dependent and have to submit to the authority of a superior. Rational self-mastery, however was manly. Once a man proved he was capable of it, he was entitled to respect and independence. By giving up commodities like imported sugar and cloth, New England men proved that they were men who could control their desires, and were therefore not required to submit to arbitrary authority. Essentially, participating in the boycotts gave them a sense of being in control in a political situation in which their actual control was minimal.[53]

Why should New England men have felt a need to exercise control over their government, when a century earlier their ancestors had been satisfied to leave the business of governing to their "betters"? Their increasing integration into the transatlantic market may have simply raised their consciousness of the influence of outside political and economic forces on their lives. Families in New England were increasing their level of indebtedness in order to settle their sons. Urban artisans' claims to competence or economic independence were seriously threatened by the fluctuations of a commercialized economy. The prospect of new taxes and other controls imposed by an overseas government threatened their sense of economic security, the basis for their manhood. When they expressed their displeasure by curtailing their spending, they gained a little more control over their household budget, along with a way to assert that they were men.

This concern with loss of control was reflected in another theme constantly reiterated in patriot literature, that British officials were trying to enslave colonial men and bring them under the arbitrary rule of lordships. Opposition writers' explanations of what they meant by slavery were consistent with the fears expressed by those who justified the overthrow of Governor Andros and writers in the currency debates. If Parliament prevailed, warned one, it would prove "that the Assemblies in the colonies will have no other power or authority, and the people no other freedom, estates, or privileges, than what may be called a tenancy at will; that they have exchanged, or rather lost, those privileges and rights which . . . were their birthright and inheritance, for such a disagreeable tenancy."[54] Opposition leaders feared, and sought to convince the public to fear, that Parliament was trying to change the constitution so that it could arbitrarily take away their freehold property and turn them once more into helpless dependents. Such a threat may not have been very realistic, but we can nonetheless understand its emotional impact. Both taxation and debt posed the danger of foreclosure, loss of property, and tenancy. If a man lost his land, his property, he became once again a dependent, subject to the will of another man, no longer in sufficient control of his own productivity to be able to save for his children. In effect, he lost his manhood.

Manly Revolutionaries

While to some extent the fire of opposition cooled after 1770 with the repeal of most of the Townshend Acts, Parliament's renewed attempt to collect revenue from the colonies under the Tea Act of 1773 brought it roaring back to life. Patriots argued as before that if the government were able to collect taxes on tea, it would at some point impose similar taxes on other commodities and, worse, on land. Bostonians disguised as Indians threw several shiploads of imported tea into Boston Harbor to prevent its being unloaded. To punish the province for what became known as the Boston Tea Party, Parliament passed a series of laws called the Coercive Acts, effectively vacating the province's 1691 charter, suspending all town meetings, taking away the towns' power to call juries, and expanding the powers of the Crown-appointed provincial governor. The acts also placed the city of Boston under military occupation, to be commanded by a British army general, Thomas Gage.[55]

It was only with the passage of the Coercive Acts in 1774 that Massachusetts farmers at last joined the resistance en masse, along with the merchants, lawyers, dock laborers, artisans, and other town folk who had been active since 1765.[56] The Coercive Acts (also known as the Intolerable Acts) radically changed the nature of Massachusetts men's relationship with their rulers. From 1691 to 1774 the provincial assembly had retained substantial powers, and the men who served on it were local men whose interests substantially coincided with those of the men they governed. But now the people would be forced to accept a new government imposed on them by Parliament. Not only men like Gage but also the men who would be appointed as judges in county courts seemed to be mere lackeys, interested in pleasing distant sponsors in the English court rather than citizens who shared the concerns of property owners at home. Such men would drown in luxury. They would have every incentive to increase taxes and no incentive to limit them. Meanwhile, working men would become slaves, never seeing the fruits of their labor, becoming trapped in a nightmare of tenancy, wage labor, and arbitrary taxation.[57]

In pamphlets written in 1773 and after, symbols of manhood began to figure in the articulation of a new, more activist message. No longer was it enough for the colonies to hope that good rulers would come forward in Parliament to protect them from the tyranny of the bad. Men must begin to take responsibility for protecting their liberties themselves. They would have to come forward and defend their own rights.

"Let us play the man for our God, and for the cities of our God," urged John Hancock. "Shew your zeal like men, and your lives like a free and virtuous people . . . quit yourselves like men of valour—be strong—unite hand and heart," wrote the author of a pamphlet titled *The American Alarm*. Even if we lose, argued Charles Chauncy, "we may solace ourselves with the thought, that we acted like men" and did everything possible to prevent "the greatest of all outward evils, subjection to arbitrary pleasure." "It revives my soul and rejoices my heart to find that the main body of the people . . . know that they are men, and have the spirits of men, and not an inferior species of animals, made to be beasts of burden to a lawless, corrupt administration," proclaimed Samuel Sherwood.[58]

The new militancy of opposition rhetoric after 1773 is striking. Yet it should not be read (as it sometimes is) as a sign that Americans had finally rejected a patriarchal conception of government equating paternal and political power, or abandoned a patriarchal conception of manhood in favor of the notion of men as autonomous, rights-bearing individuals. Alongside the message that men should courageously fight, if necessary, to defend their rights, there continued to appear the message that good rulers were fathers to their people. In Samuel Sherwood's 1774 sermon *To the Respectable Freemen of the English Colony of Connecticut,* for example, the idea that political communities originate in a voluntary compact appeared alongside the argument that rulers are trustees, obligated to exert their power for the good of their subjects. And when they pictured New Englanders rising up to defend their rights, revolutionary writers in New England rarely portrayed them as defending their individual interests. In fact, one of the most prominent messages in the rhetoric about the defense of rights was the idea that, as fathers, men had an obligation to protect the heritage of their children.

Men had a duty to defend their constitutional rights, because if they did not, they would leave their sons a legacy of slavery and dependence instead of propertied independence. As a petition issued by the town of Boston in 1773 asserted, "[A] virtuous and steady opposition to this ministerial plan of governing America is absolutely necessary . . . and is a duty which every freeman in America owes to his country, himself, and to his posterity." It was not only their own rights they must protect, argued a writer identified as "the British Bostonian," but also those of their sons. "Allow [the king's ministers] an influence here, and . . . your children (if you tamely submit) instead of calling you blessed, will be ready to say with the prophet Jeremiah, 'Cursed be the day wherein I was born . . . Cursed be the man that brought tidings to my father, saying, that a man child is born making him very glad.'" Stand up for your rights, he argued, "[t]hat your rights as a people, your blessings as subjects, and your children's rights as their inheritance might be inviolable, secured by the garrison of your own strength, from all invading arbitrary power, and transmitted down, as the flower of life and the beauty of blessings, to all rising generations." Your forefathers fought in wars for you, suggested Ebenezer Baldwin, but "is the death of a number of individuals in war so great a calamity to the public as a whole country's being enslaved, and the lives and the properties not only of the present, but of succeeding generations subjected to the caprice of arbitrary rulers?"[59]

Even the message that men should rise up to defend their constitutional rights included the notion that such rights were a legacy from their forefathers. "Will the Americans lose these rights? The rights their fore-fathers lived and died, fought and bled, to obtain for them?" asked the author of *The American Alarm* in 1773. "[I]f there be any of the noble spirit, life and sentiment of your progenitors, remaining in you as the hereditary inheritance of your forefathers, shew yourselves worthy of such fathers, such friends, such patrons of liberty." The people of the American colonies, Samuel Sherwood asserted, had a right to secure and defend themselves in the possession of their property regardless of any act by this king, because "[o]ur fathers acquired property in this land, and were rightfully possessed of it, previous to their obtaining a royal charter, as can easily be demonstrated."[60]

New England's rural men understood the message and were convinced. In the late summer of 1774, Massachusetts farmers began organizing for action. Towns in Berkshire, Worcester, and Middlesex Counties met in conventions to declare their commitment to upholding their rights, and to adopt plans for direct action to resist the new legislation. On September 1, General Gage ordered British Regulars to seize provincial supplies of arms and gunpowder at armories in Charlestown and Cambridge. As rumors spread through the countryside that British ships were firing on Boston, tens of thousands of armed farmers rushed off to try to defend the city against what became known as the Powder Alarm. On September 6, a mass movement of 6,000 farmers converged on Worcester to block the meetings of the newly reorganized Worcester County Court. On September 13, another mass of "Freeholders and others" closed the county court in Concord. Continuing to meet in defiance of the Coercive Acts, in October the towns sent delegates to the Massachusetts Provincial Congress, which assumed the practical responsibility for governing the province. As towns began to realize that they had been ill-prepared to fight the British army in the Powder Alarm, they started to form and drill special militia forces, to be called the Minutemen. And in April of 1775, of course, these groups of volunteer soldiers were the first Americans to take up arms to defend the rights of their country.[61]

Although some have seen the American Revolution as a struggle against patriarchal authority, the psychic reality was more complicated. New England men who wrote political pamphlets during the Revolution expressed their outrage at their tyrannical parent country without ever abandoning their idealization of the good father, or their core assumptions about patriarchal manhood. Throughout the revolutionary crisis, opponents of Crown policies drew on gender symbolism evocative of New England's father-centered culture. Early protesters invoked tradi-

tions that allowed the people to insist that rulers behave as "nursing fathers" should. Boycotts called on men to demonstrate that they were capable of self-mastery and thus entitled to the respect due to independent
men. And when the imposition of law by the British empire threatened
their collective claim to manly independence, men came out by the
thousands to defend their ground—and their manhood.

It is true that in the ninety years since the Puritans had lost control of
the government of Massachusetts, the image of rulers as powerful, angry
fathers had been replaced by the much more benign image of loving
forefathers, men who had bequeathed to New Englanders a legacy of secure property rights. The revolutionary generation's idealization of the
Puritan founding fathers of New England is deeply ironic, because, in
fact, at no time since the founding of the New England colonies had maturing sons had *less* secure expectations of inheriting a legacy of propertied independence. But the New England men who rallied to defend
their rights in 1774 and 1775 behaved in a manner consistent with their
long-held assumptions about manhood: that attacking a man's house
was a way to insult his manhood, that men with property had a right to
use force to defend it, and that real men should eschew luxury and control their desires. Rather than seeking to overthrow the notion of patriarchal privilege, they managed to channel their resentment into anger at
tyrannical governing officials who seemed to be violating the ideals their
own fathers had stood for. Images of manly restraint and responsible fatherhood remained, throughout the crisis, symbols against which to
judge the legitimacy of authority and the legality of their own actions.
Though they overthrew a system of monarchy, both leaders and backers
of the American Revolution communicated an understanding of gender
that was entirely consistent with the patriarchal manhood ideals around
which New England men had built their identities since the seventeenth
century.

Epilogue: Intimate Relationships and Autonomous Manhood in the Nineteenth Century

In modern American culture we are predisposed to think of patriarchal social arrangements as merely ways of organizing power, coercive and therefore presumptively illegitimate. This book suggests, however, that the Anglo-Americans who lived in early New England would not have seen their own social arrangements as coercive or illegitimate, nor would they have assumed that it was necessary or even desirable to change them. Their patriarchal ideal of manliness expressed what they saw as a desirable arrangement of interdependencies between human beings, one that ensured that the strong cared for the weak, that children grew to be healthy adults, and that human society was as peaceful and stable as possible. The most emotionally charged, ideologically significant social relationship, or bond of interdependence, was the one that existed between a father and his sons. The ways in which early New Englanders imagined other relationships—sexual relationships, family relationships, friendship, community—all were shaped by this intergenerational nexus. Its centrality was in part traditional and also in part an outgrowth of the Puritan attempt to reform social life, strengthen family ties and obligations, and diminish the role of all-male sociability in men's lives. It was sustained by a set of demographic conditions in the New England region that had made fathers and sons deeply dependent on each other for their own economic well-being. Because of this bond, most Anglo-American boys in New England learned to become men by learning to identify with their fathers or other adult male mentors. Young men did not become men by overthrowing their fathers, but by becoming like them.

170

To suggest that the father-son bond was central to the construction of manhood in early New England is not to suggest that relationships between youths and older men were without tension. Clearly, colonial New Englanders' unsentimental child rearing methods discouraged self-assertion. Sons could promote their own career preferences (if at all) only indirectly, by using their own unhappiness or the support of other adults as a source of pressure on their fathers. Youths who were bound out as servants or apprentices had even less leverage against their masters. However, the culture provided ways of containing the tensions produced by these imbalances. A definition of manliness that emphasized the need for rationality and self-mastery would have helped to prevent or mitigate open expressions of anger or resentment between younger and older men, allowing both to maintain reasonably peaceful working relationships for many years. When tensions bubbled over, there were mechanisms for youths to let off steam without fundamentally disturbing the assumption that older men were there to protect them. Midnight mischief and attacks on houses gave youths a way to covertly express their hostility toward the older men who held power over them while safely redirecting their anger toward symbolic targets. In times of political turmoil, portraying unpopular rulers as bad fathers allowed men to criticize them without disturbing the basic assumption that good rulers, like good fathers, were entitled to their love and deference. The writers of propaganda for the American Revolution were able to channel hostility toward tyrannical fathers into a sustained war against George III while going to great lengths to affirm that they continued to honor the legacy of their own founding fathers.

But if the ideal of patriarchal manhood was in fact coherent and meaningful to New England men, and did not connote an oppressive system of coercion to be overthrown as soon as the weakening of monarchical government made it possible for American men to express their true feelings, we are left with a puzzle. How did modern ideals of manhood and masculinity finally emerge? Under what sorts of conditions did a description of men as energetic, self-confident, competitive, autonomous individuals—rather than rational, moderate, responsible household heads—come to seem natural and normal? While there are multiple angles from which to describe the process of social change that caused this conceptual shift, the one I shall follow here tracks the main story of this book: in New England, the advent of modernity changed the meaning of human interdependence, and shifts in the organization of intimate relationships in turn changed concepts of gender.

Already by the American Revolution, some New Englanders had begun changing the parameters of their intimate relationships. Many northern Anglo-Americans were already believing personal happiness to be a more central component of marriage, and marriage was becoming more important in their thinking about the sources of social stability.[1] In the half century that followed the end of the American Revolution in 1783, the corporate economies that had sustained the patriarchal households of the seventeenth and eighteenth centuries were swept away. The economy and society of the new United States underwent dramatic expansion and change, nowhere more rapidly than in New England. Some farmers who could take advantage of expanding global demand for their grain and other farm products grew increasingly enmeshed in a commercial economy. New England merchants began to organize manufacturing ventures to produce textiles, shoes, and other products, and shipbuilding emerged as a major industry, employing many local youths.[2] Migration west also became more common, especially as western land became increasingly available for sale under the liberal public lands policies of the Jeffersonian Republicans.[3] By 1820, a transportation revolution that integrated western farms and northeastern markets diminished the viability of commercial farming in New England and hastened the emergence of a manufacturing economy there. With it came a labor market that offered employment opportunities outside of farming and encouraged young men to move away from home to find jobs.

With these changes came a transformation in the ways in which family members in much of New England worked together, and in the kinds of intimate relationships that would organize New England boys' passage to manhood. As the structure and functions of family and intimate life gradually shifted, fathers' importance in the rearing of sons declined. In the end, young men did not so much repudiate their relationships with their fathers as de-center them, shifting them from the once-pivotal place they had occupied in the experience of growing to manhood. Instead of the vertical bonds that had once tied together generations of fathers and sons, boys' relationships with their mothers and men's relationships with their wives would become the central emotional relationships in their lives.

Middling families responded to the new economic realities of the early republic by adopting different child rearing strategies that they hoped would help their children, especially their sons, achieve moral and economic success. Although parents remained deeply committed to providing a moral and economic foundation for the future of each of their children, the moral theories about rationality and control over the passions that had initially undergirded New Englanders' commitment to fatherhood were by 1790 becoming obsolete. The notion that mature, adult men were more capable of virtue than their wives and sons because of their greater rationality gave way by the end of the eighteenth century to the new ideas that virtue was displayed in love and benevolence, that women might be more capable of virtue than men because of their greater emotionality, and that children in early childhood were naturally innocent. Between 1800 and 1830, religious sects like the Baptists and the Methodists helped to popularize a new view of parenthood that placed increased emphasis on parents' duties to exert a moral influence on their children *during infancy*. Mothers were told that not only must they bear the traditional responsibility of caring for babies, but also they should serve as a child's main spiritual guide and teacher from early childhood up through early adolescence. By about 1840, women had a virtual monopoly on the education and management of young children.[4]

The reformed Protestant effort to increase parental commitment to children and to make the family more central to social life had succeeded, but not in the way that the first Protestant reformers had envisioned. The stern father who had once been at its core seemed less and less vital to the emerging middle-class family of the nineteenth century, while the loving mother who had once been feared as a corrupting influence now occupied the central place in children's lives. Older suspicions of maternal love were revised, and instead of being criticized for "coddling" their children, mothers were praised for their capacity for affection and emotional expression. Home life was increasingly differentiated from the outside world, and was celebrated as a realm of pious love and affection. Maternal-child bonding became a positive good, rather than a hazard to children's moral development. The affection with which middling northern men raised in the nineteenth century, both rural and urban, remembered their mothers attests to the depth of this bond.[5]

The encouragement of new, more intense bonds between mothers and sons produced its own set of tensions. Boys still had to find ways to differentiate from their mothers, even as the new, feminized households they lived in very likely made that process more difficult. Relationships with fathers became less central to boyhood socialization. In rural homes, boys still worked for their fathers on family farms. But even so, in the more intensely commercial economy of the early republic, fathers spent more of their time away from home, and were thus less able to supervise their boys.[6] Urban boys generally could not go to work with their fathers on a regular basis, though their fathers consciously sought to spend family time reading to or playing with their children.[7] Freed from paternal supervision, boys found the necessary distance from their sisters and mothers in the company of male age-mates. Especially if they lived in towns or cities, boys above about age six took part in a mostly unsupervised "boy culture" in which they learned to compete with each other through fighting and athletics, and learned to suppress the vulnerability and dependency they associated with their mothers. Memoirs of nineteenth-century boyhood, unlike those of earlier times, prominently feature recollections of games and play with other boys.[8]

The new primacy of motherhood did not mean that fathers suddenly abandoned their families for the marketplace; far from it. Men's social and emotional lives continued to be organized around their families, as the Puritans had envisioned. Fatherhood remained a vital component of men's experiences in nineteenth-century middle-class families. In rural northern families, fathers continued to be responsible for training boys to work, and for overseeing the way boys spent their time until age twenty-one. In urban middle-class families, fathers spent more time away from their households, but they still tried to spend substantial amounts of family time with their wives and children. They continued to work to provide patrimonies that would enable their sons to live as middling or middle-class family heads themselves, patrimonies that included craft apprenticeships and store clerkships at the beginning of the nineteenth century and were coming to include increased levels of academic education by the end of it. The basic Protestant expectation that men were responsible for "laying up for their owne," as John Winthrop had put it in 1630, remained very much alive in the northern United States, and even gained importance for northern middle-class men in the nineteenth century.[9]

But fathers' places in their sons' emotional lives changed in the nineteenth century. Though fathers generally remained responsible for overseeing older boys' occupational training and career choices, the intensity of mother-child bonding made father's role much less important to early childhood socialization. Because maternal child rearing was more focused on children as individuals, it probably also raised children's expectations that their own needs and interests would be attended to. While middle-class urban fathers became more likely to provide their sons with an extended education, rural fathers still tended to curtail educational opportunities and expected their sons to work for the family until age twenty-one or older. But rising expectations that families would support their sons' individual aspirations made visible the tension that had always surrounded the norm of deference to paternal authority. The former emotional pattern, in which young men had gone to such lengths to idealize their fathers and avoid criticizing them, appears much less often in men's personal writings from the nineteenth century. It became common for northern men to record conflict, disappointment, or estrangement when describing their relationships with their fathers, especially when they reached majority at age twenty-one. The new pattern was for men to remember instead their mothers' support in nurturing career goals and aspirations.[10]

Young men facing the uncertainties of career choice and the emotional challenges of living on their own often found reassurance and companionship in other youths, who could be more sympathetic than fathers. Young men's organizations sprang up all over, especially in northeastern cities, and promoted mutual improvement and friendship.[11] Intimate male friends often became an important source of solace for young men in this transitional period of their lives, and ideals of intimate friendship that had begun to emerge among young urban men in the eighteenth century became ubiquitous for nineteenth-century middle-class youths.[12]

The most emotionally important challenge in the life of a young man in the early republic, and often the most emotionally difficult, was to court and win a wife. Expectations of emotional intimacy in courtship, which had been rising since the 1740s, became more intense over the course of the nineteenth century. The new, emotionally intense relationships between mothers and children probably also helped to promote high expectations of courtship and marriage for both women and men, as did the greater likelihood that young people when they married would have to move away from their natal villages and be cut off from their parents and siblings. The objective of courtship became not so much the economic goal of finding a helpmeet but the emotional one of discovering a soul mate.[13]

With the influence of fathers and neighbors over young men's sexual behavior diminishing, courtship became a riskier proposition for young women. The dangers of seduction and abandonment emerged as a common theme in the fiction of the early republic, now that women could no longer count on young men to act as responsible providers.[14] In response, young women devised ways to ensure their suitors' emotional commitment. Premarital pregnancy rates suggest that Anglo-American women after 1820 commonly postponed coitus with their suitors until after they had married.[15] Courtships became long, drawn-out affairs in which women tested the depths of men's affections, and in the process created more intense romantic and sentimental ties that would help to ensure their suitors' continued commitment over the course of a marriage.[16]

The growing expectation that a man would have to win a woman's love in order to marry and attain full manhood status dramatically changed the way that middle-class men in nineteenth-century America achieved manhood. Instead of weaning themselves from maternal affection and controlling their "effeminate" desires by developing relationships with mature adult men, boys now had to earn their manhood by developing and sustaining tender feelings and emotional vulnerability in their relationships with potential mates. This was often a formidable task for young men, since the very sentiments that women wanted them to demonstrate were the ones that the boy culture of their childhood years taught them to suppress. Courtship was risky to men's self-esteem, and many expressed ambivalence toward the women who held the power to reject and wound them.[17]

Perhaps it was the emotional dissonance of this process that made nineteenth-century American men and women find so convincing a new set of concepts about gender. Nineteenth-century bourgeois culture tended to define manhood more in terms of its opposition to, or intrinsic differences from, womanhood. Although age remained a category that separated rational men from irresponsible boys, just as it separated rational men from emotional women, the ostensible differences between men and women became "more sharply etched."[18] Depictions of men as forceful, bold, and competitive were commonly juxtaposed with images of women as gentle, timid, and kind. Men's ambition and competitive drive were contrasted with women's selflessness, piety, and spiritual purity.[19]

Out of this experience of courtship came a new nineteenth-century concept of marriage as a union of opposites, idealistically conceived as based entirely on love (obscuring the ways in which it was both an arrangement of power and an economic partnership). Husbands and wives hoped for a marriage based on empathy and emotional intimacy that could provide them with a refuge in a world in which they were increasingly surrounded by strangers. The idea that men and women were opposites, however, may have made romantic intimacy difficult to sustain. In some cases nineteenth-century men expressed ambivalent feelings about their marriages, which they experienced sometimes as a comforting refuge and other times as a cage.[20]

Although we often see romantic marriage as liberating men and women from the constraints of patriarchal control and Puritan repression, in fact the nineteenth-century ideal of romantic marriage served as a new mechanism in the reformation of men's manners that the Puritans had begun. Perhaps it was even more effective than the patriarchal family, particularly in controlling male violence. Because of their presumed rationality and moderation, fathers and other older males had been responsible for controlling the passions of women, children, and young males. It was accepted that fathers would accomplish this by shaming, or at times physically chastising, their dependents. But in the nineteenth century, it was the women men loved who provided the controls. During courtship, women required men to prove their self-restraint and their devotion before they would marry. In marriage, wives pressed men, who might otherwise exhibit assertive, selfish behavior in the marketplace, to conform to their own ideals of nurturing, generosity, and virtue. Women exercised a form of social control that appeared to be noncoercive. Unlike fathers, wives could not assert their will through the use of force.

The logic of female virtue made domestic violence against women and children less tolerable. If emotionality was not a vice but a source of virtue, then there was no need for rational household heads to control it. Moreover, if virtue was manifested not in rationality but in sympathy or benevolence, then it was harder to justify cruel behavior by husbands (or fathers). Divorce on the grounds of cruelty became more common in Connecticut after the American Revolution, and in Massachusetts, too, nineteenth-century women were more likely to petition for and win divorces on grounds of cruelty by their husbands, rather than failure to provide economic support.[21]

Anglo-American men in the new republic of the United States liked to imagine themselves as autonomous, self-made men, liberated from patriarchal authority and outward control, and not embedded in relationships. It was a nineteenth-century truism that men occupied a sphere separate from home and family: men's sphere was the sphere of work, independent action, and competition in the marketplace. The fictional heroes of nineteenth-century American culture were frontiersmen like Natty Bumppo and whalers like Captain Ahab, unmarried men whose lives were attractively free of domestic commitments.[22] But a closer look at the actual lives of nineteenth-century New England men has shown that they were in fact shaped by family and intimate relationships, differently configured than those of eighteenth-century men, but just as central. The very nineteenth-century middle-class men who idealized the self-made man typically received significant help from their mothers and sisters in preparing for their careers.[23] The same middle-class men who read books about frontier heroes hoped for much more intimacy with their wives than their ancestors had and went to some lengths to spend time with their children. How can we reconcile the ideal of autonomous manhood with this reality?

Perhaps the higher expectations of intimacy between men and women, along with the ambivalent feelings these expectations engendered, help to explain why the ideal of self-sufficient and autonomous manhood emerged in the northern United States in the nineteenth century. Perhaps the idea of separate spheres was something of a fiction. Romantic marriage made men dependent and vulnerable, and these were feelings many of them found uncomfortable. Home might have been a haven in a heartless world, but it was also a place where men were reminded of their moral failings and of their dependence on women. Denominating the domestic world as feminine while escaping to a thoroughly masculine culture in the workplace allowed men to experience greater intimacy with women while simultaneously managing their own uncomfortable feelings about that intimacy, and it reassured them that they had not been irrevocably feminized.[24]

All societies have to find ways to convince boys to relinquish the sense of merger they experience with women during infancy and create mechanisms to help men negotiate the emotional risks of sexual intimacy. Puritans managed both by discouraging maternal bonding, creating idealized father figures, and strengthening the relationship between fathers and sons. But in the Protestant North in the nineteenth century, boys were raised in female-centered, emotionally intense families, with the expectation that they would experience emotionally intense relationships with their lovers and wives. They had to find different ways to manage these relationships. In some sense, men's establishment of their manhood became an intricate dance between intimacy and separation, merger and individuation. Perhaps stories of escape to the frontier were so important in nineteenth-century middle-class American culture because they offered men an outlet for the tensions associated with the emotionally intimate relationships with women that had become central to their lives. Perhaps the ideals of the manly patriarch and the rugged male individual should both be understood as cultural fantasies that allowed large numbers of American men, in different periods of the past, to deny their dependence on women. If so, the idea that the history of men and manhood in America can be told without reference to their relationships with women is a similar fantasy. It is time for us to recognize the centrality of the bonds of human intimacy as a historical force as important as any other.

Notes

Introduction

1. See, especially, Laurel Thatcher Ulrich, *Good Wives: Image and Reality in the Lives of Women in Northern New England, 1650–1750* (New York, 1980).
2. The earliest historical writing about gender in early America was done by Ruth Bloch in the 1970s. Her collected work on the subject, which has been a central influence on this book, may be found in Ruth H. Bloch, *Gender and Morality in Anglo-American Culture, 1650–1800* (Berkeley, 2002). Important recent scholarship on this history includes Kathleen Brown, *Good Wives, Nasty Wenches, and Anxious Patriarchs* (Chapel Hill, 1996); Mary Beth Norton, *Founding Mothers and Fathers: Gendered Power and the Forming of American Society* (New York, 1996); Cornelia Dayton, *Women before the Bar: Gender, Law, and Society in Connecticut, 1639–1789* (Chapel Hill, 1995); and Susan Juster, *Disorderly Women: Sexual Politics and Evangelicalism in Revolutionary New England* (Ithaca, 1994).
3. The most thorough examination to date of ideals of Anglo-American manhood in colonial New England is Lisa Wilson, *Ye Heart of a Man: The Domestic Life of Men in Colonial New England* (New Haven, 1999), which looks sympathetically at the importance of family life in defining adult men's identities.
4. On the emergence of a new set of ideas about the family in England during the sixteenth century, see Lawrence Stone, *The Family, Sex, and Marriage in England, 1500–1800* (London, 1977). On the relationship between economic and social change, the emergence of sectarian Protestantism, and changes in the family, see Christopher Hill, in *Society and Puritanism in Pre-Revolutionary England* (London, 1964), pp. 443–481; Patrick Collinson, "The Protestant Family," in Patrick Collinson, *The Birthpangs of Protestant England: Religion and Cultural Change in the Sixteenth and Seventeenth Centuries* (London, 1988). For similar developments in Germany, see Stephen Ozment, *When Fathers Ruled: Family Life in Reformation Europe* (Cambridge, Mass., 1983);
5. On social dislocation in sixteenth- and seventeenth-century England and

181

the reactions of the social groups who turned most decisively to Protestantism, see Margaret K. Spufford, *Contrasting Communities: English Villagers in the Sixteenth and Seventeenth Centuries* (Cambridge, 1974); Keith Wrightson and David Levine, *Poverty and Piety in an English Village: Terling, 1525–1700* (Oxford, 1979).

6. On the motives of migrants to New England, see Virginia deJohn Anderson, *New England's Generation: The Great Migration and the Formation of Society and Culture in the Seventeenth Century* (Cambridge, 1991), pp. 25–26.

7. For the fullest discussion of competency in the context of New England, see Daniel Vickers, "Competency and Competition: Economic Culture in Early America," *William and Mary Quarterly*, 3rd. ser., 47 (Jan. 1990): 3–29, and Vickers, *Farmers and Fishermen: Two Centuries of Work in Essex County, Massachusetts, 1630–1830* (Chapel Hill, 1994), pp. 14–23.

8. The debate about women's nature is discussed in Katherine Usher Henderson and Barbara F. McManus, eds., *Half Humankind: Contexts and Texts of the Controversy about Women in England, 1540–1640* (Urbana, 1985), and Linda Woodbridge, *Women and the English Renaissance: Literature and the Nature of Womankind, 1540–1620* (Urbana, 1984).

9. Historians who have stressed the connection between women's economic independence and misogyny include David Underdown, *Revel, Riot, and Rebellion: Popular Politics and Culture in England, 1603–1660* (Oxford, 1985), and Susan Amussen, "Gender, Family, and the Social Order, 1560–1725," in Anthony Fletcher and John Stevenson, eds., *Order and Disorder in Early Modern England* (New York, 1985). On prosecutions of unruly women, see David Underdown, "The Taming of the Scold," in Fletcher and Stevenson, *Order and Disorder*, pp. 116–136.

10. William Bradford, *Of Plymouth Plantation, 1620–1647* (New York, 1981), pp. 133–134.

11. Jenny Hale Pulsipher, *Children of the New World: King Philip's War and the Contest for Authority in New England* (Philadelphia, forthcoming); James D. Drake, *King Philip's War: Civil War in New England, 1675–1676* (Amherst, Mass., 1999); and Jill LePore, *The Name of War: King Philip's War and the Origins of American Identity* (New York, 1998).

12. Anderson, *New England's Generation*, pp. 25–26.

13. Vickers, *Farmers and Fishermen*, pp. 41–77.

14. For studies that have explored what is usually seen as a coercive model of family relations, see John Demos, *A Little Commonwealth: Family Life in Plymouth Colony* (New York, 1970); Philip J. Greven, Jr., *Four Generations: Population, Land and Family in Colonial Andover, Massachusetts* (Ithaca, N.Y., 1970); Daniel Scott Smith, "Parental Power and Marriage Patterns:

An Analysis of Historical Trends in Hingham, Massachusetts," *Journal of Marriage and the Family* 35 (1973): 406–418; and Nancy F. Cott, "Eighteenth-Century Family and Social Life Revealed in Massachusetts Divorce Records," in Nancy F. Cott and Elizabeth Pleck, eds., *A Heritage of Their Own* (New York, 1980).

15. Some historians have equated patriarchal family relationships with "traditional" values. See, e.g., Greven, *Four Generations*; Kenneth Lockridge, *A New England Town, the First Hundred Years: Dedham, Massachusetts, 1636–1736* (New York, 1970); Michael Zuckerman, *Peaceable Kingdoms: New England Towns in the Eighteenth Century* (New York, 1970); and Robert A. Gross, *The Minutemen and Their World* (New York, 1976). Others have concluded that the strength of patriarchy in New England, so unlike other Anglo-American colonial societies whose populations were dominated by young, unattached male immigrants, made it anachronistic, a throwback to a precapitalist society. See, e.g., Gary B. Nash, "Social Development," in Jack P. Greene and J. R. Pole, eds., *Colonial British America: Essays in the New History of the Early Modern Era* (Baltimore, 1984), pp. 233–261, and Jack P. Greene, *Pursuits of Happiness: The Social Development of Early Modern British Colonies and the Formation of American Culture* (Chapel Hill, 1988), pp. 36–38, 55–80.

16. The most recent findings suggest that New Englanders' reliance on family labor was entirely consistent with the growth of capitalist production. See especially Vickers, *Farmers and Fishermen*; Richard L. Bushman, "Markets and Composite Farms in Early America," *William and Mary Quarterly,* 3rd ser., 55 (July 1998): 351–374.

17. Andrew Sullivan, "The He Hormone," *New York Times Magazine,* April 2, 2000, p. 49.

18. This linguistic change did not begin to occur until the late nineteenth century. During most of the nineteenth century the term *masculine* was rarely used, and then merely as a descriptive adjective to describe the traits of men as distinct from women, without moral or emotional connotations. Only in the early twentieth century did "masculinity" begin to take on the connotations familiar to us now, such as aggressiveness, physical strength, and virility. Gail Bederman, *Manliness and Civilization: A Cultural History of Gender and Race in the United States, 1880–1917* (Chicago, 1995), pp. 18–19.

19. According to Bederman, the term *manly* was used during the nineteenth century as well. Ibid.

20. These conclusions are based on a survey of sermons about admirable men published in Massachusetts between 1674 and 1763, as well as obituaries published in the *Boston Newsletter,* the *New Hampshire Gazette,* and the

New London Summary before 1763. For the more characteristically Puritan virtues such as moderation and rationality, see, e.g., Benjamin Thompson, *A Funeral Tribute to . . . John Winthrop, Esq.* (Boston, 1676); John Cotton, *Upon the Death of That Aged, Pious, Sincere-Hearted Christian, John Alden* (Boston, 1687); obituary for John Gore, *Boston Newsletter,* Dec. 19, 1720, p. 2; obituary for the Reverend William Russell, *New London Summary,* June 19, 1761. "Courage" appeared less often, but was certainly prominently listed as one of men's virtues during wartime. See, e.g., Samuel Nowell, *Abraham in Arms* (Boston, 1678); Thomas Bridge, *The Knowledge of God . . . Strengthening to the Most Noble Exploits* (Boston, 1705); obituary for Gen. George Wolfe, *New Hampshire Gazette,* March 14, 1760; obituary for Gen. George Howe, *New London Summary,* Feb. 16, 1759, p. 3.

21. Louis Wright, *Middle-Class Culture in Elizabethan England* (Chapel Hill, 1935).

22. See, e.g., John Milton, *Samson Agonistes,* pp. 416–417, quoted in Jean H. Hagstrum, *Sex and Sensibility: Ideal and Erotic Love from Milton to Mozart* (Chicago, 1980), p. 37.

23. For a synthesis of the relevant literature, see David Gilmore, *Manhood in the Making: Cultural Concepts of Masculinity* (New Haven, 1990). Gilmore argues that in most cultures "true manhood is a precious and elusive status beyond mere maleness," a problematic status that must be tested and proved before it is socially recognized (p. 17).

24. See Phyllis Mack, *Visionary Women: Ecstatic Prophecy in Seventeenth Century England* (Berkeley, 1992), p. 6. Since manliness was understood to describe not natural, intrinsic, or even necessarily physical traits but success in fulfilling a social role, manhood could at times be uncertain or unstable. The possibility that a person could be accepted for some time as socially male despite an ambiguous set of physical characteristics is illustrated by the case of the colonial Virginia hermaphrodite Thomasine Hall, discussed in Mary Beth Norton, "Communal Definitions of Gendered Identity in Seventeenth-Century English America," in Ronald Hoffman, Mechal Sobel, and Fredrika J. Teute, eds., *Through a Glass Darkly: Reflections on Personal Identity in Early America* (Chapel Hill, 1997).

25. See, e.g., Urian Oakes, *New England Pleaded with and Pressed to Consider the Things which Concern Her Peace* (Boston, 1674), p. 15.

26. Wilson, *Ye Heart of a Man,* pp. 1–2.

27. Thomas Laqueur, *Making Sex: Body and Gender from the Greeks to Freud* (Cambridge, Mass., 1990).

28. "The Diary of Jeremiah Dummer," ed. Sheldon S. Cohen, *William and Mary Quarterly,* 3rd ser., 24 (1967): 405, entry for Dec. 1, 1709 (a Latin saying, translated by the editor); James Allin, *Evangelical Obedience the Way to Eternal Life* (Boston, 1731).

29. The manhood ideals found in seventeenth- and eighteenth-century New England evolved into the middle-class ideals of nineteenth century Anglo-American culture, which also defined manliness in terms of psychological and spiritual, as opposed to physical, traits but does not appear to have valorized the qualities of older as opposed to younger men. See, e.g., Anthony Rotundo, "Body and Soul: Changing Ideals of American Middle-Class Manhood, 1770–1920," *Journal of Social History* 16 (Summer 1983): 32–38, and Charles Rosenberg, "Sexuality, Class, and Role in Nineteenth-Century America," *American Quarterly* 25 (May 1973): 131–153.

30. The association between manhood and responsibility or rationality was consistent with the masculine ideal of competence—independence based on property ownership—which was often associated with manhood in early modern England and in its colonies. Susan Dwyer Amussen, "The Part of a Christian Man': The Cultural Politics of Manhood in Early Modern England," in Susan D. Amussen and Mark A. Kishlansky, eds., *Political Culture and Cultural Politics in Early Modern England* (Manchester, England, 1995); Brown, *Good Wives, Nasty Wenches and Anxious Patriarchs.*

31. Early modern Englishmen believed men's superior capacity for reason made them more virtuous and capable than supposedly sensual women. See, e.g., Mack, *Visionary Women,* pp. 24–34; Carol F. Karlsen, *The Devil in the Shape of a Woman: Witchcraft in Colonial New England* (New York, 1987), pp. 155–165; Joan Kelly, "Early Feminist Theory and the 'Querelle des Femmes,' 1400–1789," in Joan Kelly, ed., *Women, History, and Theory: The Essays of Joan Kelly* (Chicago, 1984), pp. 65–109; Genevieve Lloyd, *The Man of Reason: "Male" and "Female" in Western Philosophy* (Minneapolis, 1984). Scholars have not recognized that the distinction between rational and sensual was also made in comparing mature men with youths, as well as with other categories of people such as servants, Indians, and, sometimes, aristocrats or gentlemen.

32. "Diary of John Hull," in *Puritan Personal Writings: Diaries* (New York, 1982), p. 168.

33. John Saffin Notebook, 1665–1708, p. 163, American Antiquarian Society. The entries in Saffin's book are undated, but my basis for assuming his age is the fact that the entries appear to have been made chronologically. This entry was made about a decade after his wife Martha's death in 1678.

34. The clearest articulation of the idea that the state was formed through a compact of male heads of households was found in New Haven and Rhode Island. But all of the New England colonies shared patriarchalist ideas, in the form of a set of general assumptions that characterized much seventeenth-century political thought about the parallels between paternal and political rule. Norton, *Founding Mothers and Fathers,* esp. pp. 293–322. The extended seventeenth-century debate about the origins of political au-

thority that was informed by these assumptions is covered in Gordon J. Schochet, *Patriarchalism in Political Thought: The Authoritarian Family and Political Speculation and Attitudes Especially in Seventeenth-Century England* (New York, 1975).

35. Ideologies of manhood in the southern colonies are explored in Brown, *Good Wives, Nasty Wenches, and Anxious Patriarchs*; Kenneth Greenberg, *Honor and Slavery: Lies, Duels, Noses, Dressing as a Woman, Gifts, Strangers, Humanitarianism* (Princeton, 1996).

36. Anthony Fletcher, *Gender, Sex, and Subordination in England, 1500–1800* (New Haven, 1995), esp. pp. 92–93.

37. Much recent work on gender in history has been influenced by Joan Scott, whose article "Gender: A Useful Category of Historical Analysis," *American Historical Review* 91, no. 5 (Dec. 1986), suggested that gender should be thought of as related to larger historical processes because gender categories are a primary technology in struggles over power. This line of thinking has illuminated various fascinating connections. See, e.g., Karlsen, *Devil in the Shape of a Woman* (suggesting that witchcraft accusations against women in Salem in 1692 were linked to men's subconscious fear, during a period of particular economic uncertainty, that ungoverned, economically independent women might pose a threat to their status); Juster, *Disorderly Women* (spokesmen for new religious sects in the early years of the republic sometimes sought to legitimize their own social authority as religious leaders by suppressing female assertiveness within their churches); Norton, *Founding Mothers and Fathers* (early American political theory analogized men's assertion of patriarchal power over women with the state's assertion of power over subjects), and Brown, *Good Wives, Nasty Wenches, and Anxious Patriarchs* (attempts in early Virginia to redefine women and men were linguistically or symbolically linked to struggles to redefine race and class).

38. Ruth H. Bloch, "A Culturalist Critique of Trends in Feminist Theory," *Contention* 2 (Spring 1993): 98. For a fuller exploration of issues that might be raised by a relational approach to the study of gender in early Anglo-American culture, see Bloch, *Gender and Morality in Anglo-American Culture*.

39. This analysis is based in part on a psychoanalytical approach to understanding manhood that differs from the approaches of past historians, such as John Demos and Philip Greven, who have sought to use psychoanalysis to explain the emergence of particular male personality types in early New England. These past historians focused almost exclusively on the issue of filial autonomy, which they saw as being repressed through an exaggerated Oedipal antagonism between fathers and sons. But new directions in psychoanalytic theory since the 1960s point to another psychological dy-

namic in human life that is at least as central to cultural formation as the need to repress or channel Oedipal conflicts: the human need for bonding and interdependence. All human infants remain dependent on adults for a prolonged period, and they experience a sense of merger with their primary caregiver, usually their mother and invariably a woman, during the first year of life. If the most basic formative experience of all human beings is dependency and merger with another, then one of the most important functions of society must be to induce children to relinquish this early experience of merger and become responsible, productive adults, capable of caring for others—to assume not just the rights of adulthood but also its duties. This sacrifice, it is thought, is particularly difficult for boys, since they must permanently give up any sense of identification with a woman in order to become a man. Thus most cultures and societies create mechanisms to ease (or force) boys through this process. Anthropologist David Gilmore summarizes the newer psychoanalytic literature, as well as its implications for understanding the cultural organization of masculinity, in *Manhood in the Making.*

40. For the best analysis of the attempt by New England Puritans to reform popular culture, see Richard P. Gildrie, *The Profane, the Civil, and the Godly: The Reformation of Manners in Orthodox New England, 1679–1749* (University Park, Pa., 1994).

41. See Bloch, "A Culturalist Critique," p. 97.

42. For the beginnings of such an argument, see Ruth H. Bloch, "The Gendered Meanings of Virtue in Revolutionary America," *Signs* 13, no. 1 (1987): 37–58. See also the suggestion that patriarchal rhetoric remained compelling for New England farmers supporting Federalist candidates as late as 1811, in Christopher Clark, *The Roots of Rural Capitalism: Western Massachusetts, 1780–1860* (Ithaca, N.Y., 1990), pp. 51–52.

43. For an excellent study suggesting some of the ways in which the ideal of rational, moderate manhood figured in discourses about race and class in early Massachusetts, see Thomas A. Foster, "Sex and the Eighteenth-Century Man: Anglo-American Discourses of Sex and Manliness in Massachusetts, 1690–1765," Ph.D. diss., Johns Hopkins University, 2002.

1. Fathers and Sons from Infancy through Boyhood

1. Samuel Sewall, *Diary of Samuel Sewall, 1674–1729,* vol. 1 (New York, 1972), reprint from *Collections of the Massachusetts Historical Society,* ser. 5, vol. 5 (Boston, 1878), entry for April 1, 1677. Men's writings often showed fear, anxiety, and concern for their wife during childbirth. Examples can be found in Eleazer Wheelock to Stephen Williams, Aug. 18,

1737, letter 737468, Papers of Eleazer Wheelock, microfilm ed. (Hanover, N.H., 1971); Benjamin Bangs Diary, June 23, 1760, Massachusetts Historical Society.

2. William Perkins, *Works,* p. 669 (London, 1612).

3. Sewall, *Diary,* 1, April 18, 1677, p. 41.

4. For evidence that early Anglo-American fathers were more identified with the adult successes and failures of sons than mothers were, see John Demos, "The Changing Faces of Fatherhood," in John Demos, *Past, Present, and Personal: The Family and the Life Course in American History* (New York, 1986), pp. 41–67.

5. John Saffin Notebook, 1665–1708, pp. 9–10, American Antiquarian Society.

6. "Commonplace Book of Joseph Green," *Publications of the Colonial Society of Massachusetts,* vol. 34 (Boston, 1938), p. 251.

7. Ebenezer Parkman Diary, vol. 1, Jan. 29, 1749, Ebenezar Parkman Papers, Massachusetts Historical Society.

8. "Commonplace Book of Joseph Green," esp. pp. 250–253.

9. Sewall, *Diary,* 1, entries for April 2–7, 1677, p. 40. On postpartum recovery and the use of nurses, see Laurel Thatcher Ulrich, *A Midwife's Tale: The Life of Martha Ballard Based on her Diary, 1785–1812* (New York, 1990), pp. 188–191; Ross W. Beales, Jr., "Nursing and Weaning in an Eighteenth-Century New England Household," in Peter Benes et al., eds., *Families and Children: Annual Proceedings of the Dublin Seminar for New England Folklife,* vol. 10 (Cambridge, Mass., 1987), pp. 48–63, at 49–54.

10. Families in early New England rarely used wet-nurses, who were still commonly relied on in many prosperous English families but disapproved of by Puritan writers and ministers. Even babies who were cared for by wet-nurses, of course, bonded first with women, though not with their mother. John Demos, *A Little Commonwealth: Family Life in Plymouth Colony* (London, 1970), p. 133; Laurel Thatcher Ulrich, *Good Wives: Image and Reality in the Lives of Women in Northern New England, 1650–1750* (New York, 1980), pp. 138–144; Beales, "Nursing and Weaning," pp. 48–63.

11. Max Weber, *The Protestant Ethic and the Spirit of Capitalism,* trans. Talcott Parsons (New York, 1958), pp. 110–112.

12. Ruth Bloch, "American Feminine Ideals in Transition: The Rise of the Moral Mother, 1785–1815," *Feminist Studies* 4 (1978): 101–126.

13. Sewall, *Diary, passim.* See, e.g., entries for June 18, 1686; Feb. 2, 1689/90; Nov. 6, 1692.

14. Laura Thatcher Ulrich, *Good Wives: Image and Reality in the Lives of Women in Northern New England, 1650–1750* (New York, 1980), pp. 142–144; Beales, "Nursing and Weaning," pp. 56–59.

15. Karin Calvert, *Children in the House: The Material Culture of Early Childhood, 1600–1900* (Boston, 1992).

16. John Demos, *A Little Commonwealth*; Philip Greven, *The Protestant Temperament: Patterns of Child-Rearing, Religious Experience, and the Self in Early America* (Chicago, 1977).

17. Ulrich, *Good Wives*, p. 144.

18. Edmund S. Morgan, *The Puritan Family: Religion and Domestic Relations in Seventeenth-Century New England* (New York, 1966), p. 66, quoting from John Cotton, *Practical Commentary upon John*, p. 124.

19. Demos, *A Little Commonwealth*, pp. 140–141, note 18.

20. Karin Calvert has called attention to the linkage in early modern English culture between the categories of gender and age. Calvert, *Children in the House*.

21. For the Puritans' demand that godly men shun taverns and devote themselves to family life, see Richard P. Gildrie, *The Profane, the Civil, and the Godly: The Reformation of Manners in Orthodox New England, 1679–1749* (University Park, Pa., 1994).

22. Josiah Cotton Memoirs, 1726–1756, p. 47, Massachusetts Historical Society.

23. For a detailed description of family devotions, see Charles Hambrick-Stowe, *The Practice of Piety: Puritan Devotional Disciplines in Seventeenth-Century New England* (Chapel Hill, 1982), pp. 143–150.

24. The socially acknowledged role of mothers in early modern families became secondary after early childhood because traits believed by Protestant reformers to be important in child rearing, such as rationality and self-discipline, were thought to be more prevalent in the father. Fathers were also seen as best able to teach the "rational and moral self-control that raised humans above animals." Bloch, "American Feminine Ideals in Transition"; Demos, "The Changing Faces of Fatherhood"; and Stephen Ozment, *When Fathers Ruled: Family Life in Reformation Europe* (Cambridge, Mass., 1983), quotation at p. 139. For a typical exhortation to fathers to be vigilant in instructing their children, see Increase Mather, "A Call from Heaven to the Present and Succeeding Generation" (1679), in *Evans Early American Imprints 1639–1800* (New York, [1983?]–1986), no. 274, pp. 91–92 (hereinafter cited as *Evans Early American Imprints*).

25. James Axtell, *The School upon a Hill: Education and Society in Colonial New England* (New Haven, 1974), pp. 21–23.

26. Benjamin Wadsworth, *The Well-Ordered Family* (Boston, 1712), p. 60.

27. "Autobiography of the Rev. John Barnard," *Collections of the Massachusetts Historical Society*, 3rd ser., vol. 5 (Boston, 1836), pp. 178–179.

28. "Commonplace Book of Joseph Green," p. 236.

29. Of course, while fathers had the ultimate responsibility for a family's spiritual life, much of the work of parenting at this stage was still performed by mothers and other women—even if Protestant writers did not recognize that work as morally significant—and many mothers probably offered more lessons than fathers during early childhood. For the suggestion that the role of mothers in educating children expanded during the eighteenth century, see Gerald F. Moran and Maris A. Vinovskis, "The Great Care of Godly Parents: Early Childhood in Puritan New England," in Alice B. Smuts and John W. Hagen, eds., *History and Research in Child Development,* Monographs of the Society for Research in Child Development, vol. 50, nos. 4–5 (Chicago, 1986).

30. Perkins, *Works,* p. 699.

31. Samuel Sewall, *Diary,* Nov. 6, 1692.

32. Demos, *A Little Commonwealth,* pp. 134–136.

33. For typical farmers' diaries showing a pattern of remaining at home during bad weather, see John May Diary, 1708–1766, American Antiquarian Society, and *The Diary of Matthew Patten of Bedford, N.H., from 1754 to 1788* (Concord, N.H., 1903).

34. For a striking example of a fatherly expression of concern for a daughter, see the poem written by the Puritan Thomas Weld, Sr., for his daughter Hittie after she broke her shoulder in the 1670s, "A Poetical Epistle sent by my father to my sister Hitte after her shoulder bone was set, composed on Lord's day evening," Thomas Weld Commonplace Book, p. 172, Massachusetts Historical Society.

35. "Commonplace Book of Joseph Green," Jan. 16, 1712/13, p. 253.

36. "Autobiography of the Rev. John Barnard," pp. 180–181.

37. Ibid., p. 181.

38. In New Hampshire in 1740, Nicholas Gilman daily recorded the progress of his children through the measles. When his children were ill he prayed for them, administered medicine, and recorded their symptoms. Diary of Nicholas Gilman, April 1740, various entries, Connecticut Historical Society. Ebenezer Parkman took his son Billy to the doctor when he had been accidentally cut with a scythe. Ebenezer Parkman Diary, vol. 1, Aug. 3, 1749.

39. *The Diary of Matthew Patten,* pp. 13–14.

40. On paternal custody rights, see Michael Grossberg, *Governing the Hearth: Law and the Family in Nineteenth-Century America* (Chapel Hill, 1985), chap. 7. There really is no study of paternal legal responsibilities, but see Morgan, *The Puritan Family,* pp. 65–67, for a short discussion.

41. See, for examples, Jonathan Mitchel, *Nehemiah on the Wall in Troublesome*

Times (Cambridge, Mass., 1667), p. 121; William Hubbard, *The Happiness of a People in the Wisdom of Their Rulers* (Boston, 1676), p. 144.

42. Thomas Shepard, *Eye-Salve, or A Watch-word from Our Lord Jesus Christ* (Cambridge, Mass., 1672), p. 143.

43. Joseph Belcher, *The Singular Happiness of Such Heads or Rulers as Are Able to Choose Out Their People's Way* (Boston, 1701), p. 14.

44. Diary of Nicholas Gilman, Dec. 21 and 22, 1741, pp. 98–99.

45. Ibid., Jan. 12, 15, and 16, 1742, p. 101.

46. "Journal of the Rev. John Pike," Oct. 21, 1702, *Massachusetts Historical Society Proceedings,* vol. 14 (Boston, 1876): 134.

47. Ulrich, *Good Wives,* pp. 154–156.

48. Calvert, *Children in the House,* p. 46.

49. Demos, *A Little Commonwealth,* citing Otto Fenichel, *The Psychoanalytical Theory of Neurosis* (New York, 1945), at p. 141, note 20.

50. Philippe Aries, *Centuries of Childhood: A Social History of Family Life,* trans. Robert Baldick (New York, 1962), p. 58.

51. I owe this insight to Holly Brewer. It is more fully developed in her forthcoming book on conceptions of childhood and consent in eighteenth-century America, *By Birth or Consent: Children, Law, and Revolution in England and America, 1550–1820* (Chapel Hill, forthcoming).

52. See Greven, *The Protestant Temperament,* pp. 282–285, esp. p. 285 for an anecdote from the correspondence of Connecticut minister Mather Byles, Jr., that supports the inference that boys themselves understood breeching to be a significant rite of passage.

53. On the deep cultural roots of this belief, see Genevieve Lloyd, *The Man of Reason: Male and Female in Western Philosophy* (Minneapolis, 1984).

54. David Leverenz, *The Language of Puritan Feeling: An Exploration in Literature, Psychology, and Social History* (New Brunswick, N.J., 1980), p. 38.

55. My approach in this chapter has been influenced by David Gilmore's argument that while girls become women merely by growing up and assuming the domestic role of their mothers, boys must earn recognition of their manhood by going through certain kinds of culturally sanctioned tests. See David Gilmore, *Manhood in the Making: Cultural Concepts of Masculinity* (New Haven, 1990). See also Michelle Rosaldo, "Woman, Culture, and Society: A Theoretical Overview," in M. Z. Rosaldo and L. Lamphere, eds., *Woman, Culture, and Society* (Stamford, Conn., 1974).

56. Anthony Fletcher, *Gender, Sex, and Subordination in England, 1500–1800* (New Haven, 1995). See also Stephen Greenblatt, *Shakespearian Negotiations: The Circulation of Social Energy in Renaissance England* (Berkeley,

1988), esp. pp. 78–88, and Thomas Laqueur, *Making Sex: Body and Gender from the Greeks to Freud* (Cambridge, Mass., 1990).

57. Fletcher, *Gender, Sex, and Subordination.*

58. Axtell, *The School upon a Hill,* p. 60, quoting from journal of Esther Burr.

59. Ozment, *When Fathers Ruled,* p. 144.

60. Cotton Mather, "The Diary of Cotton Mather, 1681–1724," *Collections of the Massachusetts Historical Society,* 7th ser., vol. 7 (Boston, 1911), pp. 201, 239–240.

61. Diary of Nicholas Gilman, Jan. 1, 1739/40, p. 1.

62. *The Diary of Matthew Patten, passim.* See also, *Diary of Joshua Hempstead, 1711–1758* (New London, Conn., 1901), entries for Nov. 11, 1711, and Dec. 9, 1712; Ebenezer Parkman Diary, vol. 1 (1749), entry for Jan. 7, 1749. The personal papers of northern and midwestern farmers in the nineteenth century show a similar pattern of boys' work being recorded only sporadically before age ten or eleven. Shawn Johansen, "Northern Middle-Class Fatherhood in Antebellum America," Ph.D. diss., UCLA, 1994, p. 45. However, it is likely that eight- and nine-year-old boys worked for their fathers fairly often but were not mentioned in diaries and account books because their labor was not yet considered genuinely productive. Evidence from seventeenth- and eighteenth-century court records shows that younger boys did perform work for their fathers but that only at about age ten were they trusted to assume responsibilities for themselves. Daniel Vickers, *Farmers and Fishermen: Two Centuries of Work in Essex County, Massachusetts, 1630–1830* (Chapel Hill, 1994), pp. 65–66.

63. Vickers, *Farmers and Fishermen,* p. 65.

64. For relevant literature, see, e.g., Ralph Greenson, "Dis-Identifying from Mother: Its Special Importance for the Boy," *International Journal of Psycho-analysis* 49 (1968): 370–374; Robert J. Stoller, "Facts and Fancies: An Examination of Freud's Concept of Bisexuality," in Jean Strouse, ed., *Women and Analysis: Dialogues on Psychoanalytic Views of Femininity* (New York, 1974); Nancy Chodorow, *The Reproduction of Mothering: Psychoanalysis and the Sociology of Gender* (Berkeley, 1979). For the implications of this developmental theory for the cultural construction of manhood, see Gilmore, *Manhood in the Making,* pp. 26–29.

65. E. Jennifer Monaghan, "Literacy Instruction and Gender in Colonial New England," *American Quarterly* 40 (1988): 18–41. See also Kenneth A. Lockridge, *Literacy in Colonial New England: An Enquiry into the Social Context of Literacy in the Early Modern West* (New York, 1974).

66. Free schools in Boston, for example, were open only to male children until 1789. Girls were formally excluded from the Hopkins Grammar School,

which opened in New Haven in 1684. Schools in frontier settlements, however, were more likely to include a handful of girls along with the male students. Monaghan, "Literacy Instruction and Gender," pp. 30–32.

67. Peter Thacher to Jeremy Belknap, May 22, 1766, Belknap Papers, Massachusetts Historical Society.

68. I owe this observation to Lisa Wilson.

69. Morgan, *The Puritan Family,* pp. 71–75.

70. "Autobiography of the Rev. John Barnard," p. 178.

71. Josiah Cotton Memoirs, 1726–1754, p. 37.

72. William Stickney Diaries, 1766–1767, Massachusetts Historical Society.

73. For this point about age and the stages of youth in seventeenth- and eighteenth-century America, see Joseph Kett, *Rites of Passage: Adolescence in America, 1790 to the Present* (New York, 1977), chap. 1. See also John Demos, "The Rise and Fall of Adolescence," in John Demos, *Past, Present, and Personal: The Family and the Life Course in American History* (New York, 1986), pp. 92–113.

74. On the timing and process of choosing callings for boys in well-to-do Puritan families in New England, see Morgan, *The Puritan Family,* pp. 68–69, 72–75.

75. For the most detailed study of the system of "putting out" children, see Helena M. Wall, *Fierce Communion: Family and Community in Early America* (Cambridge, Mass., 1990), pp. 96–125. On Massachusetts law governing the binding out of children, see Holly Brewer, "Constructing Consent: How Children's Status in Political Theory Shaped Public Policy in Virginia, Pennsylvania, and Massachusetts before and after the American Revolution," Ph.D. diss., UCLA, 1994, pp. 382–387.

76. *Diary of Matthew Patten,* entries for Nov. 26, 1756; Nov. 2, 1757; and subsequent, through 1768.

77. *Province and Court Records of Maine,* vol. 5 (April 1711–October 1718) (Portland, 1964). For cases alleging abuse by masters, see Wall, *Fierce Communion,* pp. 115–124, and Brewer, "Constructing Consent," pp. 435–448.

78. Weber, *The Protestant Ethic,* p. 109; William Perkins, "A Treatise of the Vocations," *The Works of William Perkins* (Cambridge, 1605), pp. 903, 911, 913.

79. J. E. Crowley, *This Sheba, Self: The Conceptualization of Economic Life in Eighteenth-Century America* (Baltimore, 1974), pp. 17, 56–60.

80. Lisa Wilson, *Ye Heart of a Man: The Domestic Life of Men in Colonial New England* (New Haven, 1999).

81. Philip J. Greven, *Four Generations: Population, Land, and Family in Colonial*

Andover, Massachusetts (Ithaca, N.Y., 1970); see also Carole Shammas, "Anglo-American Government in Comparative Perspective," *William and Mary Quarterly,* 3rd ser., 52 (Jan. 1995): 104–144.

82. Vickers, *Farmers and Fishermen,* esp. pp. 72–77.

83. For the former position, see Greven, *Four Generations* and Greven, *The Protestant Temperament;* for the latter, see Vickers, *Farmers and Fishermen.*

84. For the economic and employment strategies of English youths during this period, see Ilana Ben-Amos, *Adolescence and Youth in Early Modern England* (New Haven, 1994).

85. Holly Brewer, "Entailing Aristocracy in Colonial Virginia: 'Ancient Feudal Restraints' and Revolutionary Reform," *William and Mary Quarterly,* 3rd ser., 54, no. 2 (April 1997): 307–346. On the use of partible inheritance in New England, see Greven, *Four Generations;* George Lee Haskins, *Law and Authority in Early Massachusetts: A Study in Tradition and Design* (Lanham, Md., 1960), pp. 170–172; George Lee Haskins, "The Beginning of Partible Inheritance in the American Colonies," *Yale Law Journal* 51 (1942): 1280–1315. Brewer's findings offer a major challenge to earlier assumptions about inheritance practices in the southern colonies, and may force a reassessment of conclusions that the South was moving toward modernity at a more rapid pace than colonial New England.

86. See, e.g., Stephen Innes, *Labor in a New Land: Economy and Society in Seventeenth-Century Springfield* (Princeton, N.J., 1983); Alan Taylor, *Liberty Men and Great Proprietors: The Revolutionary Settlement on the Maine Frontier, 1760–1820* (Chapel Hill, 1990), pp. 73–79; on similar tendencies in the southern backcountry, see Jack P. Greene, "Independence, Improvement, and Authority: Toward a Framework for Understanding the Histories of the Southern Backcountry during the Era of the American Revolution," in Ronald Hoffman et al., eds., *An Uncivil War: The Southern Backcountry during the American Revolution* (Charlottesville, Va., 1985).

87. Perkins, *Works,* p. 758; see also Morgan, *The Puritan Family,* chap. 3.

88. Perkins, *Works,* p. 759.

89. Sewall *Diary,* 1, entries for Oct. 5, 1694, and Jan. 14, 1694/95.

90. Ibid., entries for March 18, 1694/95; June 21, July 12, and Aug. 13, 1695.

91. See, e.g., the intervention of tutors Benjamin Colman and John Leverett in a decision about the future of Hugh Hall, described in Morgan, *The Puritan Family,* p. 73, and that of a former neighbor, Willy Nichols, in the apprenticeship between Ashley Bowen and an unscrupulous sea captain in 1741. *The Journals of Ashley Bowen of Marblehead,* ed. Philip Chadwick Foster Smith (Boston, 1973), vol. 1, at p. 11. For findings of frequent intervention by neighbors and relatives into child rearing practices, see Wall, *Fierce Communion,* pp. 87–89, 93–95.

92. Sewall, *Diary,* 1, entries for Feb. 7 and Feb. 10, 1695/96.
93. Autobiography of John Adams, in *Diary and Autobiography of John Adams,* vol. 3, ed. L. H. Butterfield (Cambridge, Mass., 1961), p. 258.
94. Ibid.
95. *Benjamin Franklin: The Autobiography and Other Writings,* ed. L. Jesse Lemisch (New York, 1961), pp. 22–35, 42.
96. Historical literature consistent with the repressive hypothesis includes Lawrence Stone, *The Family, Sex, and Marriage in England, 1500–1800,* abridged ed. (New York, 1979); Greven, *The Protestant Temperament;* Edward Shorter, *The Making of the Modern Family* (New York, 1975); Demos, *A Little Commonwealth,* pp. 134–139. These historians generally argue that the repression of ego development in children in the early modern family led to the production of a deferential society. As Lawrence Stone put it in a classic statement of this position, "the deferential behavior of the children is a defensive response to ego repression, as the only way to survive, while the authoritarian and remote behavior of the parents is an expression of the original desire for autonomy, which now at last finds an outlet in the bullying of their own children." Stone, *The Family, Sex, and Marriage,* p. 126. Other historians, in contrast, have found evidence of strong parent-child bonds. See, e.g., for England, Linda Pollock, *Forgotten Children: Parent-Child Relations from 1500 to 1800* (Cambridge, 1983); for New England, Peter Gregg Slater, *Children in the New England Mind in Death and in Life* (Hamden, Conn., 1977); Ulrich, *Good Wives;* and Wilson, *Ye Heart of a Man.*

    For connections between family and political relationships in early America, see Richard L. Bushman, *From Puritan to Yankee: Character and the Social Order in Connecticut, 1690–1765* (Cambridge, Mass., 1967); Michael Zuckerman, *Peaceable Kingdoms: New England Towns in the Eighteenth Century* (New York, 1970), esp. pp. 72–84; Melvin Yazawa, *From Colonies to Commonwealth: Familial Ideology and the Beginnings of the American Republic* (Baltimore, 1985); and Edwin G. Burrows and Michael Wallace, "The American Revolution: The Ideology and Psychology of National Liberation," *Perspectives in American History* 6 (1972): 167–306.
97. Two historians have used the repressive hypothesis to explain early New Englanders' ideas about gender and sexuality. Philip Greven argues that societywide practices like using androgynous dress, as well as evangelicals' discouragement of aggressive tendencies in boys, reflected an attempt to "feminiz[e] young children." He asserts that "since being female meant being perceived as weaker, inferior, submissive, and obedient, the clothing of children became part of the overall process of discipline by parents who sought to control and dominate the wills of their children." Greven, *The*

Protestant Temperament, pp. 46, 282. Lyle Koehler asserts: "These were anxiety-ridden, insecure, unhappy children . . . A consideration of their anguish and preoccupations can help us to understand the Puritan psyche, particularly as it affected attitudes toward the female sex." Lyle Koehler, *A Search for Power: The "Weaker Sex" in Seventeenth-Century New England* (Urbana, 1980), p. 14.

98. Ruth Bloch's work has to some extent opened up this more cultural approach to the study of child rearing. See Bloch, "American Feminine Ideals in Transition." On fatherhood in early New England, see Demos, "The Changing Faces of Fatherhood."

99. Coppelia Kahn, *Man's Estate: Masculine Identity in Shakespeare* (Berkeley, 1981), pp. 52, 63. For a synthesis of recent psychoanalytical research suggesting that connections with other males can help boys along in the process of became male-identified, see William S. Pollock, *Real Boys: Rescuing Our Sons from the Myths of Boyhood* (New York, 1998).

100. See, e.g., Judith M. Bennett, *Women in the Medieval English Countryside: Gender and Household in Brigstock before the Plague* (New York, 1987), esp. chaps. 3 and 4.

101. John Locke, *Some Thoughts concerning Education,* ed. John W. and Jean S. Yolton (Oxford, 1989), pp. 84, 105.

102. Ibid., pp. 108, 125 (a child's mind should be filled with love for parents and fear of offending them), 127 (children should be "kept as much as may be in the company of their parents").

103. Nicholas Gilman Diary, Sept. 2, 1740, p. 40.

104. One of the most important treatments of this process over the "longue duree" is Philippe Aries, *Centuries of Childhood: A Social History of Family Life* (New York, 1962).

2. Youth and the Passions

1. Diary of John Marshall, Braintree, Mass., 1689–1711, Massachusetts Historical Society, entries for March 1696/97, Sept. 28 and 29, 1697.

2. For a perceptive rendering of the "social relations of production" of seventeenth- and eighteenth-century Massachusetts farmers, see Daniel Vickers, *Farmers and Fishermen: Two Centuries of Work in Essex County, Massachusetts, 1630–1850* (Chapel Hill, 1994).

3. On the centrality of male kin relationships in structuring New England communities during the seventeenth and early eighteenth centuries, see John J. Waters, "Family, Inheritance, and Migration in Colonial New England: The Evidence from Guilford, Connecticut," *William and Mary Quar-*

terly, 3rd ser., 39, no. 1 (Jan. 1982): 64–86; John J. Waters, "The Traditional World of the New England Peasants: A View from Seventeenth-Century Barnstable," *New England Historic Genealogical Register* 130 (Jan. 1976): 3–21.

4. *Diary of Joshua Hempstead . . . from September, 1711 to November 1758* (New London, Conn., 1901).

5. On the ethic of neighborliness among New England women, see Laurel Thatcher Ulrich, *Good Wives: Image and Reality in the Lives of Women in Northern New England, 1650–1750* (New York, 1980), pp. 51–67. On the role of interdependent credit relationships in encouraging social integration in early New England communities, see Bruce H. Mann, *Neighbors and Strangers: Law and Community in Early Connecticut* (Chapel Hill, 1987). On the human costs of neighborliness, see Helena Wall, *Fierce Communion: Family and Community in Early America* (Cambridge, Mass., 1990).

6. On the goals of labor exchanges in Essex County farm communities, see Vickers, *Farmers and Fishermen*, pp. 60–62, 237–247.

7. For tavern licensing practices, see David W. Conroy, *In Public Houses: Drink and the Revolution of Authority in Colonial Massachusetts* (Chapel Hill, 1995).

8. On Puritan antipathy to traditional festivals in England, see David Underdown, *Revel, Riot, and Rebellion: Popular Politics and Culture in England, 1630–1660* (Oxford, 1985).

9. William Bradford, *Of Plymouth Plantation, 1620–1647*, ed. S. E. Morison (New York, 1981), p. 363; Anne Bradstreet, "To the Memory of My Dear and Ever Honored Father Thomas Dudley, Esq. Who Deceased, July 31, 1653, and of His Age 77," in Joseph R. McElrath, Jr., and Allan P. Robb, eds., *The Complete Works of Anne Bradstreet* (Boston, 1981); see also Thomas Prince, ed., *Memoirs of Roger Clap* (1731; repr. Seattle, 1929), p. 7.

10. On the Puritan movement's attempt to reform manners and transform popular culture in Anglo-America, see Richard P. Gildrie, *The Profane, the Civil, and the Godly: The Reformation of Manners in Orthodox New England, 1679–1749* (University Park, Pa., 1994).

11. William Perkins, *Works* (London, 1612), pp. 61, 447.

12. For typical Puritan admonitions about speech, see Cotton Mather, "Optanda, Good Men Described and Good Things propounded . . ." (Boston, 1692), *Evans Early American Imprints*, no. 623, pp. 16–17.

13. Edmund Quincy (1628–98), "The Christian Dayly Walk," in Compositions and Memoranda Book, July 1665–Sept. 1697, Quincy Family Papers, Q.P.8, Massachusetts Historical Society.

14. Bradford, *Of Plymouth Plantation*, p. 363; Bradstreet, "To the Memory."

15. Relations within the church were supposed to be analogous to the relationships of brothers and sisters: free from contention, thoughtful of each other, and united in their mutual pursuit of each others' welfare. John Winthrop, "A Modell of Christian Charity," *Collections of the Massachusetts Historical Society*, 3rd ser., vol. 7 (Boston, 1838), pp. 45–46.

16. Diary of John Marshall, miscellaneous entries from February through September 1697.

17. Wall, *Fierce Communion*, pp. 87–89, 93–95.

18. See discussion and cases cited in Wall, *Fierce Communion*, pp. 53–57, 74–80. Wall's cases suggest that colonists outside New England shared similar assumptions about neighborly intervention in marriages.

19. Suffolk Files, vol. 50, p. 115 (last will and testament of Peter Oliver of Boston, April 8, 1670), Massachusetts Archives.

20. "Commonplace Book of Joseph Green," *Publications of the Colonial Society of Massachusetts*, vol. 34 (Boston, 1938), p. 230.

21. Josiah Cotton Memoir, 1726–1756, p. 94, Massachusetts Historical Society.

22. John May Diary, entries for Dec. 15, 1711, to Dec. 21, 1712, American Antiquarian Society.

23. For classical ideals of friendship in early modern English literature, see Lauren J. Mills, *One Soul in Bodies Twain: Friendship in Tudor Literature and Stuart Drama* (Bloomington, Ind., 1937), esp. chaps. 4 and 5. Friendship was a rational commitment, based on admiration for the friend's virtue, and superior to the passion of sexual love for women. The ideal of noble male friendship was assumed to be accessible only to gentlemen, since only they possessed the independence needed for virtue. Christian friendship was based on grace, and was thus theoretically accessible to a broader group.

24. On Reformation-era disparagement of the medieval and Renaissance ideal of true friendship, see Benjamin Nelson, *The Idea of Usury: From Tribal Brotherhood to Universal Otherhood* (Princeton, 1949). But for the argument that the English Reformation's ideal of Christian friendship could form the basis for a relationship of deep personal affinity between two men, see Francis Bremer, *Congregational Communion: Clerical Friendship in the Anglo-American Puritan Community, 1610–1692* (Boston, 1994).

25. John Winthrop to Sir William Springe, Feb. 8, 1629/30, *Winthrop Papers* (Boston, 1929), vol. 2, pp. 203–206.

26. On the juxtaposition of images of the male friend and the sodomite in Puritan New England, see Michael Warner, "New English Sodom," in Jonathan Goldberg, ed., *Queering the Renaissance* (Durham, N.C., London, 1994), pp. 330–358; on homosexuality in Elizabethan culture generally, see Alan Bray, "Homosexuality and the Signs of Male Friendship in Eliza-

bethan England," ibid., pp. 40–61. On nineteenth-century Christian friendship and intense emotional bonds between men, see Donald Yacovone, "Abolitionists and the 'Language of Fraternal Love,'" in Mark C. Carnes and Clyde Griffen, eds., *Meanings for Manhood: Constructions of Masculinity in Victorian America* (Chicago, 1990).

27. Ebenezer Pemberton, *Advice to a Son . . .* (London, 1705), pp. 13, 21. On the circumstances of this sermon, see Michael C. Batinski, *Jonathan Belcher, Colonial Governor* (Lexington, Ky., 1996), pp. 10–11.

28. Cotton Mather, "Directions for a Son Going to the Colledge," *Bulletin of the American Congregational Association* 3, no. 2 (Jan. 1952): 16–17.

29. The purpose of Josiah Cotton's memoir, he said, was "[t]hat my Posterity should know from whence they are descended . . . that they may not be un-acquainted with their collateral Relations; but may as opportunity & occa-sion do allow, manifest that Friendship & natural Affection to those of the same Blood, which Nature & Religion do require." Josiah Cotton Memoir, introduction.

30. Harvard graduate Joseph Green kept a record of letters he wrote as a young man in the 1690s that he felt to have been especially significant in his secu-lar and spiritual life. Ten of these were written to family members; only one was to a college friend. Letters to family members all expressed con-cern about their recipients' spiritual as well as temporal welfare, but his letter to his friend, along with a list of his former classmates and what they were doing, expressed interest only in their worldly, temporal affairs—to him, less important than spiritual matters. "Commonplace Book of Joseph Green," p. 230.

31. Wigglesworth's diary recorded the spiritual relations of various male pa-rishioners during the early 1650s. Among them, a Mr. Collins, John Green, and an unnamed male all credited their fathers with having brought them to Christ, while Joseph Champney emphasized the role played by his pas-tor. Edmund S. Morgan, ed., "The Diary of Michael Wigglesworth, 1653–1657," *Publications of the Colonial Society of Massachusetts*, vol. 55 (Boston, 1951), pp. 426–442.

   Puritan Roger Clap emphasized his relationship with his pastor, John Warham. Roger Clap, *Memoirs of Captain Clap* (Seattle, 1929), pp. 6–7.

32. *Memoirs of Captain Clap*, pp. 9–10.

33. Michael Wigglesworth, "Autobiography," in *New England Historical and Genealogical Register*, vol. 17 (Albany, 1863), pp. 137–139. Wigglesworth attended college in the early 1650s.

34. "Diary of Michael Wigglesworth," pp. 426–427.

35. "Autobiography of the Rev. John Barnard," *Collections of the Massachusetts Historical Society*, 3rd ser., vol. 5 (Boston, 1836).

36. Josiah Cotton Memoirs, *passim*.

37. Ilana Ben-Amos, *Adolescence and Youth in Early Modern England* (New Haven, 1994), pp. 175–182. In other parts of Europe during this period, horizontal bonding among young men received more formal, institutional support through journeymen's associations. See John R. Gillis, *Youth and History: Tradition and Change in European Age Relations, 1770–Present* (New York, 1981), pp. 22–23.

38. See Gildrie, *The Profane, The Civil, and the Godly,* pp. 106–107.

39. See, e.g., Samuel Nowell, *Abraham in Arms* (Boston, 1678), p. 15; Solomon Stoddard, *Dangers of a Speedy Degeneracy* (Boston, 1705), p. 20.

40. For examples, see Joseph H. Smith, ed., *Colonial Justice in Western Massachusetts, 1639–1702: The Pynchon Court Record* (Cambridge, Mass., 1961), entries for March 9, 1692, p. 331; Nov. 4, 1695, p. 343.

41. Worthington C. Ford, ed., *The Diary of Cotton Mather* (New York, 1912), vol. 2, pp. 216–217.

42. *Colonial Justice in Western Massachusetts,* entry for March 20, 1677/78, p. 289.

43. Deposition of John Brown, Dec. 10, 1681, *Colson v. Wilson,* Middlesex Folio 96, Middlesex Folio Collection, Massachusetts Archives. The Middlesex Folio Collection is a set of folios in which all known court papers filed in connection with cases brought in the county courts of Middlesex County, Massachusetts, between 1649 and approximately 1730, as well as miscellaneous papers thereafter, have been filed. The Middlesex Folio Collection and two related collections, the Records of the Court of General Sessions for Middlesex County and the Middlesex County File Papers, are housed in the Judicial Archives of the Massachusetts State Archives, Boston.

44. On youthful misbehavior in New England, see Roger Thompson, *Sex in Middlesex: Popular Mores in a Massachusetts County, 1649–1699* (Amherst, 1986). On groups of unmarried men in Europe participating charivari, see Natalie Zemon Davis, "The Reasons of Misrule," *Society and Culture in Early Modern France* (Stanford, Calif., 1975), pp. 97–123.

45. For the argument that in England there existed a "youth culture where manhood was learnt by drinking, fighting, and sex," see Anthony Fletcher, *Gender, Sex, and Subordination in England, 1500–1800* (New Haven, 1995), pp. 88–95. See also Gillis, *Youth and History,* esp. pp. 22–38. More qualified conclusions are found in Ben-Amos, *Adolescence and Youth in Early Modern England,* pp. 183–207.

    On Puritans' attempts to control adolescent rebelliousness, see David Leverenz, *The Language of Puritan Feeling: An Exploration in Literature, Psychology, and Social History* (New Brunswick, N.J., 1980), pp. 71–85.

46. On the Puritans' abolition of sports in England, see Underdown, *Revel, Riot, and Rebellion.* On sports in early New England, see Bruce Daniels, *Pu-*

ritans at Play: Leisure and Recreation in Colonial New England (New York, 1995), pp. 165–176.

47. John Brock, "The Autobiographical Memoranda of John Brock," ed. Clifford K. Shipton, *Proceedings of the American Antiquarian Society,* n.s. 54 (1949): 5–6.

48. Ibid.

49. Ibid.

50. L. Jesse Lemisch, ed., *Benjamin Franklin: The Autobiography and Other Writings* (New York, 1961), pp. 27–28, 35, 45–47.

51. The basics of the two positions are articulated in Kathleen Verduin, "'Our Cursed Natures': Sexuality and the Puritan Conscience," *New England Quarterly* 56 (June 1983), and Edmund S. Morgan, "The Puritans and Sex," *New England Quarterly* 15 (Dec. 1942).

52. Placing children out into families other than their family of birth was not uncommon. Sometimes young people age fourteen to nineteen were placed out so that they could be supervised while avoiding typical emotional conflicts with their own parents. Edmund S. Morgan, *The Puritan Family: Religion and Domestic Relations in Seventeenth-Century New England,* 2nd ed. (New York, 1966), pp. 74–79. See, however, John Demos, *A Little Commonwealth: Family Life in Plymouth Colony* (London, 1970), pp. 70–75, for queries about the typicality of such placements, and Wall, *Fierce Communion,* pp. 96–125, for the finding that parents usually placed out children for financial reasons.

53. See, e.g., "Indenture of Elon Harris, 15, to Samuel White of Boston, Marriner" (dated Aug. 11, 1702), Suffolk Files, vol. 55, p. 72, Massachusetts Archives; "Indenture of Wizeman Muzovin to John Goffe, Cordwainer" (dated July 22, 1701), Suffolk Files, vol. 52, p. 145, Massachusetts Archives; "Indenture of Thomas Deer to Benjamin Girdler, Marriner, by Overseers of the Poor for Marblehead" (dated March 1, 1706/7), Middlesex Folio Collection, folio 64x.

54. Samuel Sewall, *Diary of Samuel Sewall, 1674–1729,* vol. 1 (New York, 1972), entry for Aug. 12, 1676, pp. 15–16.

55. John Leverett, president of Harvard College, to Rev. Timothy Woodbridge, Cambridge, Feb. 1709, Wyllys Family Papers, Connecticut Historical Society.

56. Nicholas Venette, *Conjugal Love; or, the Pleasures of the Marriage Bed Considered in Several Lectures on Human Generation,* 20th ed.(London, 1750), p. 46. This belief persisted well into the nineteenth century. In an earlier edition, Venette had suggested that in order for generation to occur, "the Male ought to be of a middle Age . . . have the Genital Parts well formed . . . be vigourous, full of Blood & Spirits, and possess all what is requisite for

the Caressing of a Woman amorously." Venette, *The Mysteries of Conjugal Love Reveal'd,* 3rd ed. (London, 1712), p. 334.

57. John Armstrong, *The Oeconomy of Love: A Poetical Essay* (London, 1736), p. 7. Armstrong's guide also warns of the dangers of masturbation, as does the ubiquitous *Onania,* first published in London in 1710. The popularity of such guides suggests an increased concern during the eighteenth century about sexual indulgence by young men, especially masturbation. Older sex guides, such as *Aristotle's Masterpiece* and Venette's *Conjugal Love,* do not mention masturbation as dangerous, but *Onania,* which went through dozens of editions in the eighteenth century, is devoted entirely to the subject. *Onania* also warned men against marrying too young, which would exhaust them, stunt their growth, and leave them "for ever after weak and enfeebled." *Onania; or, the Heinous Sin of Self-Pollution,* 10th ed. (Boston, 1724, repr. of London ed.), p. 48.

58. For an application of this insight to the characterization of male relationships in Shakespeare's plays, see Coppelia Kahn, *Man's Estate: Masculine Identity in Shakespeare* (Berkeley, 1981).

59. See, e.g., Noadiah Russell, "Diary of Noadiah Russell, Tutor at Harvard College, Beginning Anno. Dom. 1682," *New England Historical and Genealogical Register,* vol. 7 (Boston, 1853), Oct. 27, 1682; Feb. 13, 1683; May 23, 1683, pp. 58–59. "Diary of Michael Wigglesworth," entries for Feb. 15 and Feb. 25, 1652, pp. 324–325. For other examples, see Daniel B. Shea, Jr., *Spiritual Autobiography in Early America* (Princeton, 1968), p. 78.

60. On the historical specificity of such assumptions, see Rotundo, *American Manhood,* esp. chaps. 10 and 11.

61. "Diary of Michael Wigglesworth," entries for Feb. 15 and Feb. 25, 1652, pp. 324–325.

62. Alan Bray, "To Be a Man in Early Modern Society: The Curious Case of Michael Wigglesworth," *History Workshop Journal* 41 (1996): 155–165, esp. 156 and 159.

63. It is likely that the "sin" to which Wigglesworth was referring was not sexual contact with a potential disease transmitter, but masturbation. Some medical authorities during this period suggested that a type of gonorrhea, whose chief symptom was involuntary seminal emission, could be caused by masturbation. See, e.g., citation of medical authorities in *Onania* (Boston, 1724), p. 16.

64. "Diary of Michael Wigglesworth," Feb. 15, 1654/55, p. 398.

65. Jean H. Hagstrum, *Sex and Sensibility: Ideal and Erotic Love from Milton to Mozart* (Chicago, 1980), pp. 336–337.

66. For similar conclusions, see Bray, "To Be a Man in Early Modern Society."

67. Quoted in Thomas Laqueur, *Making Sex: Body and Gender from the Greeks to Freud* (Cambridge, Mass., 1990), p. 123.

68. The ideal was not always achieved, even by the most devout. Michael Wigglesworth, for one, struggled with his passions throughout his life, scandalizing friends and fellow ministers after the death of his first wife when he fell in love with his twenty-year-old serving maid and married her. Morgan, *The Puritan Family,* pp. 55–56, citing *Collections of the Massachusetts Historical Society,* ser. 4, vol. 8, pp. 94–95. It was only his third marriage that he approached with the calm, rational deliberation that signified a manly readiness in his society. "Rev. Michael Wigglesworth, Memoir, Autobiography, Letters and Library," *New England Historical and Genealogical Register,* vol. 17 (Albany, 1863), p. 140.

69. Morgan, *The Puritan Family,* esp. pp. 48–52.

70. See e.g., Morgan, *The Puritan Family,* pp. 79–86; Ulrich, *Good Wives,* pp. 119–125.

71. Jonathan Hopkinson deposition, dated Jan. 30, 1675, *Acie v. Pickard, Essex County Quarterly Courts File Papers,* W.P.A. transcript, vol. 23.

72. Solomon Stoddard, letter dated July 19, 1701, published as part of "An Answer to Some Cases of Conscience" (1722), reprinted in Perry Miller and Thomas H. Johnson, eds., *The Puritans* (New York, 1938), pp. 456–457. For Puritan associations between wigs and effeminacy, see "Nicholas Noyes on Wigs," *Publications of the Colonial Society of Massachusetts,* 20 (1920): 120–128; Michael Wigglesworth, extracts from sermons, "On the Wearing of the Hair, *New England Historical and Genealogical Register,* vol. 1 (Boston, 1847), pp. 368–371.

73. *Oxford English Dictionary,* 2nd ed. (Oxford, 1989).

74. Sewall, *Diary,* vol. 3, entries for Oct. 10 and 12, 1720, p. 266.

75. For men's increasing awareness of the risk of rejection in courtship in the eighteenth century, see Lisa Wilson, *Ye Heart of a Man: The Domestic Life of Men in Colonial New England* (New Haven, 1999), pp. 38, 56–57.

76. See, e.g., the suggestion that a soldier in love would put on "his fine knotted Scarf and powdered Periwig [to] go to show himself to that adorable Babe, his Lady Venus, Leaving oftentimes a desperate siege and important State affairs." [A. B.,] *The Ten Pleasures of Matrimony* (London, 1683; repr. London, 1922), pp. 6–7.

77. Sewall, *Diary,* vol. 3, entries for Oct. 19, 20, and 24, 1720, pp. 267–272.

78. *Boston Weekly News Letter,* March 13, 1735, p. 2.

79. See Cornelia Dayton, *Women before the Bar: Gender, Law, and Society in Connecticut, 1639–1789* (Chapel Hill, 1995), pp. 173–187, indicating that especially before 1670 in Connecticut (including New Haven), male fornicators were pursued even more vigorously than female ones. See also Thompson, *Sex in Middlesex,* pp. 29–30, for findings of increasing tolerance of premarital sex for men in Middlesex County, Massachusetts, after 1670. In Hingham, Massachusetts, to take one town for which data have

been analyzed, before 1680 somewhere between 8 and 11.1 percent of first babies were born within eight months of their parents' marriage. The premarital pregnancy rate rose steadily to over 30 percent by the late eighteenth century, eventually falling again to around 10 percent between 1840 and 1860. Daniel Scott Smith and Michael S. Hindus, "Premarital Pregnancy in America, 1640–1971: An Overview and Interpretation," *Journal of Interdisciplinary History* 5, no. 4 (Spring 1975): 537–570, Appendix I at p. 561.

80. Samuel Sewall, *Diary*, 1, entry for Feb. 1, 1695/96, p. 420.

81. *Beale v. Row*, cited in Thompson, *Sex in Middlesex*, pp. 61–64.

82. *Crouch v. Grant*, 1668, cited in Thompson, *Sex in Middlesex*, p. 42.

83. *Aris v. Blanchard*, Middlesex Folio Collection, Folio 157, 1691.

84. "Diary of Michael Wigglesworth," Feb. 15, 1652; Feb. 15, 1654/55; and April 17, 1655, pp. 323, 398–399, 404–406.

85. For background on early modern European beliefs about sexuality and the body, see Paul-Gabriel Bouce, "Some Sexual Beliefs and Myths in Eighteenth-Century Britain," in Bouce, ed., *Sexuality in Eighteenth Century Britain* (Totowa, N.J., 1982), pp. 28–46; Anthony Fletcher, "The Protestant Idea of Marriage in Early Modern England," in Fletcher, ed., *Religion, Culture, and Society in Early Modern Britain: Essays in Honour of Patrick Collinson* (Cambridge, 1994); Angus McClaren, *Reproductive Rituals: The Perception of Fertility in England from the Sixteenth to the Nineteenth Century* (London, 1984); and Laqueur, *Making Sex*. Laqueur argues that early modern Europeans described gender differences as hierarchical rather than oppositional.

86. For a general discussion of Galenist physiological principles, see Everett Mendelsohn, *Heat and Life: The Development of the Theory of Animal Heat* (Cambridge, 1964).

87. See, e.g., *Aristotle's Masterpiece* (London, 1698), p. 4: "Force and heat of Procreating Matter, constantly increases till Forty-five, Fifty-five, and Sixty-Five, then begins to flag, the Seed by degrees becoming unfruitful."

88. Laqueur, *Making Sex*.

89. Venette, *Conjugal Love*, p. 80. As Anthony Fletcher argues, there was no dispute in seventeenth-century England that regular orgasm was good for the health of both men and women, since the build-up of excessive humors caused by unfulfilled lust could produce illness, including "green-sickness," an unnatural weakness and pallor seen in young women. Fletcher, *Gender, Sex, and Subordination in England*, pp. 46–55. For a New England example of this idea, see *Crouch v. Grant*, Middlesex Folio Collection, Folio 52, deposition of Sarah Crouch (1669). See also Fletcher, "The Protestant Idea of Marriage in Early Modern England."

90. *Aristotle's Masterpiece* (1698), pp. 92–93. On emotions, see Ruth Harvey, *The Inward Wits: Psychological Theory in the Middle Ages and the Renaissance* (London, 1975), p. 26. Although they emphasized that balance would produce health, some writers discussed excessive heat, which was thought to be particularly male, in admiring terms. See, e.g., Venette, *The Mysteries of Conjugal Love Reveal'd,* 3rd ed. (London, 1712), pp. 90–91.

91. Joyce Oldham Appleby, *Economic Thought and Ideology in Seventeenth-Century England* (Princeton, 1978).

92. *Aristotle's Masterpiece* (1698), p. 92; *Aristotle's Masterpiece* (1755), p. 39.

93. Venette, *Conjugal Love,* pp. 109–110.

94. On traditional European beliefs that women had lower rational and moral capacities than men, see Carol Karlsen, *The Devil in the Shape of a Woman: Witchcraft in Colonial New England* (New York, 1987), esp. pp. 153–161.

95. See *Aristotle's Masterpiece* (1698), pp. 5, 17–18; *Aristotle's Masterpiece* (1755), pp. 28–29; see also Phyllis Mack, *Visionary Women: Ecstatic Prophesy in Seventeenth-Century England* (Berkeley, 1992), pp. 25–28.

96. *Aristotle's Masterpiece* (1698), p. 45.

97. Ibid., p. 46. For a good example of the association between women and consumer desire, see also *The Ten Pleasures of Matrimony.* Commonplace book entries made between 1721 and 1726 by William Byrd, a Virginian, reflect the same understanding in a non-Puritan culture of female insatiability as a threat to male sexual capacity. See Kenneth A. Lockridge, *On the Sources of Patriarchal Rage: The Commonplace Books of William Byrd and Thomas Jefferson and the Gendering of Power in the Eighteenth Century* (New York, 1992). Byrd copied many of his entries from Venette's *Conjugal Love* (personal communication with Kenneth Lockridge).

98. A classic Freudian psychological explanation would suggest that early modern ideas about sexuality encouraged young men to repudiate desire in order to resolve the Oedipal conflict, whereby the boy sacrifices his desire for the woman in favor of a mature identification with the father. Following feminist object-relations theory, I would emphasize instead that urging men to control sexual desire expressed a common male fear of merger or regression, and offered a way to buttress the stability of masculine selfhood that was consistent with the patriarchal family structure. Other features of early modern thought, including overt misogyny and the emphasis on women's sexual voraciousness, are also consistent with a fear of merger. For historians who have made use of object-relations theory to explain the history of masculinity, see Fletcher, *Gender, Sex and Subordination,* and John Tosh, "What Should Historians Do with Masculinity? Reflections on Nineteenth-Century Britain," *History Workshop Journal* 38 (1994): 179–202.

3. Youth and the Challenge of the Eighteenth Century

1. Philip J. Greven, Jr., *Four Generations: Population, Land, and Family in Co- lonial Andover, Massachusetts* (Ithaca, N.Y., 1970); Kenneth A. Lockridge, "Land, Population, and the Evolution of New England Society, 1630–1790, and an Afterthought," in Stanley N. Katz, ed., *Colonial America: Essays in Politics and Social Development* (Boston, 1971), pp. 466–491; and Robert A. Gross, *The Minutemen and Their World* (New York, 1976).

2. This summary is drawn from the following sources: Daniel Vickers, *Farmers and Fishermen: Two Centuries of Work in Essex County, Massachu- setts, 1630–1850* (Chapel Hill, 1994); Christopher M. Jedrey, *The World of John Cleaveland: Family and Community in Eighteenth-Century New England* (New York, 1979); Greven, *Four Generations*; Fred Anderson, *A People's Army: Massachusetts Soldiers and Society in the Seven Years War* (New York, 1985), pp. 32–39; and Richard L. Bushman, "Markets and Composite Farms in Early America," *William and Mary Quarterly*, 3rd ser., 55, no. 3 (July 1998): esp. 364–367.

3. Jonathan Burnham, *The Life of Jonathan Burnham* (Portsmouth, N.H., 1814), Peabody Essex Museum imprints collection, Salem, Mass.

4. John Cleaveland autobiography, Cleaveland Family Papers, Peabody Essex Museum.

5. Philip Chadwick Foster Smith, ed., "The Journals of Ashley Bowen," *Publi- cations of the Colonial Society of Massachusetts*, vol. 44 (Boston, 1973), pp. 6–24.

6. The best chronicle of these changes is Bernard Bailyn, *The New England Merchants in the Seventeenth Century* (Cambridge, Mass., 1955). On the cultural style of this emerging merchant class, see Richard Bushman, *The Refinement of America: Persons, Houses, Cities* (New York, 1992).

7. "Diary of Jeremiah Dummer," ed. Sheldon S. Cohen, *William and Mary Quarterly*, 3rd ser., 24 (1967): p. 409 (entry for March 18, 1709/10).

8. Ibid., p. 421, note 48, quoting Jeremy Belknap.

9. For a witty and perceptive discussion of genteel social life and social inter- action, see David Shields, *Civil Tongues and Polite Letters in British America* (Charlottesville, 1997), especially his commentaries on heterosexual friendship in early eighteenth-century genteel culture, pp. 40–46.

  For the thoroughly libertine subculture among white Englishmen in the West Indian slaveholding colonies, see Trevor Burnard, "The Sexual Life of an Eighteenth-Century Jamaican Slave Overseer," unpublished paper in possession of the author. Kenneth Lockridge finds young men in eigh- teenth-century Virginia aspiring to gentility who also assumed the "poses of the libertine sublime" because of their anger toward women who blocked their access to marriage and wealth. Lockridge, "That Tuneful Rage: The Short Happy Life of Robert Bolling, 1738–1775," unpublished paper in possession of the author. For the sexual culture of eighteenth-century London, see Roy Porter, "Mixed Feelings: the Enlightenment and Sexuality in Eighteenth-Century Britain," in Paul-Gabriel Bouce, ed., *Sexuality in Eighteenth-Century Britain* (Manchester, England, 1982).

10. The extent to which Anglo-American merchants relied on kinship as opposed to other social ties is debated in Bailyn, *New England Merchants in the Seventeenth Century,* pp. 34–36, 79–82, 87–91; Alfred D. Chandler, *The Visible Hand: The Managerial Revolution in American Business* (Cambridge, Mass., 1977), pp. 17–19; and Thomas Doerflinger, *A Vigorous Spirit of Enterprise: Merchants and Economic Development in Revolutionary Philadelphia* (Chapel Hill, 1986).

11. See Steven C. Bullock, *Revolutionary Brotherhood: Freemasonry and the Transformation of the American Social Order, 1730–1840* (Chapel Hill, 1996).

12. Obituary of Nathaniel Leonard, *Boston News Letter,* June 25, 1761, p. 3; Obituary of John Jones, ibid., Sept. 17, 1772, p. 3. Seventeenth- and early eighteenth-century obituaries and funeral sermons might describe men as amiable, as noted earlier, but were more likely to emphasize their usefulness to society. Public virtue did not disappear from the list of virtues expected of eighteenth-century men, but the importance of the private virtues was enhanced.

13. See, e.g., list of vessels owned by T. Orne, 1740–1758, *Essex Institute Historical Collections* (Salem, Mass., 1901), vol. 37, pp. 77–80.

14. See Isaac Watts, "To Mr. William Nokes. Friendship," "The Afflictions of a Friend," and "The Reverse: Or, the Comforts of a Friend," in *Lyric Poems,* book 2 (London, 1740?); "On Friendship," *Boston Evening Post,* Feb. 21, 1763.

15. Edmund Quincy (1703–1788), minutes of meetings of the Wednesday Night Club, Oct. 2 and Nov. 30, 1722, Miscellaneous Bound, Massachusetts Historical Society.

16. For the commitments of Franklin's Junto, see L. Jesse Lemisch, ed., *Benjamin Franklin: The Autobiography and Other Writings* (New York, 1961), pp. 197–204.

17. Stephen Foster, *The Long Argument: English Puritanism and the Shaping of New England Culture, 1570–1700* (Chapel Hill, 1991).

18. "Autobiography of the Rev. John Barnard," *Collections of the Massachusetts Historical Society,* 3rd ser., vol. 5 (Boston, 1836), pp. 186–187.

19. See Mary McManus Ramsbottom, "Religious Society and the Family in Charlestown, Massachusetts, 1630–1740," Ph.D. diss., Yale University,

1987, pp. 208–209 and accompanying citations. It is likely that urban men began earlier to experience the changes that made these kinds of groups desirable to them.

20. For two societies started by different students within a few years of each other, see "A Religious Society at Harvard College, 1719," *Publications of the Colonial Society of Massachusetts*, vol. 24 (Boston, 1923); Quincy (1703–1788), minutes of meetings of the Wednesday Night Club, beginning Sept. 24, 1722. See also Ebenezer Turell, "An Account of a Society in Harvard College, 1722," in *Publications of the Colonial Society of Massachusetts*, vol. 12 (Boston, 1909), pp. 220, 227–231.

21. "The Orders of the Young Men's Meeting," in "Ebenezer Parkman's Book for Sundry Collections, 1718," Ebenezer Parkman Papers, Box 2, Folder 4, American Antiquarian Society. See also Ramsbottom, "Religious Society and the Family in Charlestown," p. 213.

22. Ebenezer Parkman, untitled manuscript booklet, dated Aug. 24, 1719, Ebenezer Parkman Papers, Box 2, Folder 4, American Antiquarian Society.

23. On declining numbers of male entries into church covenants, see Cedric Cowing, "Sex and Preaching in the Great Awakening," *American Quarterly* 20 (Fall 1968): 624–644; Richard D. Shiels, "The Feminization of American Congregationalism, 1730–1835," *American Quarterly* 33 (1981): 46–62.

24. Ramsbottom, "Religious Society and the Family in Charlestown," pp. 215–219.

25. See, e.g., Edmund Quincy to Ebenzer Parkman, June 15, 1722, and Edmund Quincy to Ebenezer Parkman, April 1, 1723, Quincy Family Papers, Massachusetts Historical Society.

26. Albert Hirshmann, *The Passions and the Interests* (Princeton, 1977); Allan Silver, "Friendship in Commercial Society: Eighteenth-Century Social Theory and Modern Sociology," *American Journal of Sociology* 95, no. 6 (May 1990): 1474–1504.

27. For numbers of taverns in various parts of Massachusetts, see David W. Conroy, *In Public Houses: Drink and the Revolution of Authority in Colonial Massachusetts* (Chapel Hill, 1995), pp. 141–142, 147–152.

28. Increase Mather, *Necessity of Reformation* (Boston, 1679), p. 6.

29. On the growing popularity of dances and parties given after weddings in rural New England during the eighteenth century, see Bruce C. Daniels, *Puritans at Play: Leisure and Recreation in Colonial New England* (New York, 1995), pp. 112–120.

30. Shields, *Civil Tongues*, p. 45. For examples of a gentleman's attendance at tea and dinner parties, see Carl Bridenbaugh, ed., *Gentleman's Progress: The Itinerarium of Dr. Alexander Hamilton, 1744* (Chapel Hill, 1948), pp. 109–

110, 129, 133–134, 138–139. Hamilton assiduously recorded his assessments of the ladies he met during these visits, commenting particularly on their looks, clothes, and conversational ability, and he also made a point of writing down the compliments that he had paid them.

31. Shields, *Civil Tongues,* pp. 108–109, citing "Sisyphus," *New England Courant,* April 2, 1722; notice to ladies who flirt during church, *New England Courant,* Sept. 25, 1721. For more evidence of the increasingly sexual representation of elite white women in portraiture, see Laurel Thatcher Ulrich, *Good Wives: Image and Reality in the Lives of Women in Northern New England, 1650–1750* (New York, 1980), pp. 115–117.

32. For examples of men's literary productions celebrating beautiful women, see "To the Ladies at Boston in New England," *Boston Gazette,* Nov. 19, 1731; W. S., *The Antigonian and Bostonian Beauties: A Poem* (Boston? 1751?). For a discussion of the social dynamics of balls and examples from other Anglo-American colonies, see Shields, *Civil Tongues,* pp. 145–156.

33. For a New England example of sophisticated gentlemen looking at, commenting on, and flirting with women in shops, see *Itinerarium of Dr. Alexander Hamilton,* p. 102; for a mid-eighteenth-century English counterpart, see Laurence Sterne, *A Sentimental Journey through France and Italy,* ed. Ian Jack (Oxford, 1984).

34. See, for illustrations, [James Forrester,] *The Polite Philosopher* (London; repr. New York, 1758) (a Boston edition was also printed in 1762, but no copies survive); R. L. [Richard Lingard], *A Letter of Advice to a Young Gentleman Leaving the University concerning his Behavior and Conversation in the World* (New York, 1696); "The True Original Receipt for Composing a Modern Love-Letter," *Boston Evening Post,* no. 9, Oct. 13, 1735, p. 3; "The Form of a Modern Love-Letter, Drawn Up By a Set of Pretty Fellows . . .," *American Magazine,* Aug. 1744, p. 510.

35. Daniel Scott Smith, "The Dating of the American Sexual Revolution," in Michael Gordon, ed., *The American Family in Social-Historical Perspective* (New York, 1973); Daniel Scott Smith and Michael Hindus, "Premarital Pregnancy in America, 1640–1971: An Overview and Interpretation," *Journal of Interdisciplinary History* 5 (1975): 537–545; Robert V. Wells, "Illegitimacy and Bridal Pregnancy in Colonial America," in Peter Laslett, Karla Osterveen, and Richard M. Smith, eds., *Bastardy and Its Comparative History* (London, 1980).

36. Cornelia Dayton, *Women before the Bar: Gender, Law, and Society in Connecticut, 1639–1789* (Chapel Hill, 1995), pp. 187–200, esp. 187–188.

37. Wells, "Illegitimacy and Bridal Pregnancy," pp. 354–355; Daniel Scott Smith, "American Illegitimacy and Prenuptial Pregnancy," in Laslett, Osterveen, and Smith, eds., *Bastardy and Its Comparative History,* esp.

Table 17.5 at p. 372. Smith shows that the rate of illegitimate births in Middlesex County, Massachusetts, in 1764 was only 10 per 1,000 total births. The comparable rate in Massachusetts in the 1880s was 19 per 1,000, and in England and Wales in the 1880s was 47 per 1,000. Thus the bastardy rate for late eighteenth-century Massachusetts seems to have been quite low, even though it was rising slightly.

38. This conclusion is consistent with the earlier discussion about legal procedures for dealing with bastardy.

39. The decriminalization of bastardy actions does not necessarily show that New Englanders were becoming morally lax and tolerant of sexual promiscuity. Dayton's research shows that prosecutions for fornication in Connecticut after 1740 tended to exempt wealthier and middle-ranked women and men. As Dayton suggests, this selective pattern of prosecution may show not so much that New Englanders cared less about sexual promiscuity as that they began to believe middle-class families should be allowed to deal with it privately, with minimal exposure to public shame. Dayton, *Women before the Bar,* pp. 207–223.

40. In New Haven, unwed mothers were allowed to pursue men for child support in private civil actions without first confessing to fornication. Dayton, *Women before the Bar,* pp. 206–207, 217–223; and cf. Laurel Thatcher Ulrich, *A Midwife's Tale, The Life of Martha Ballard Based on Her Diary, 1785–1812* (New York:, 1990), for discussion of late-eighteenth-century bastardy proceedings before justices of the peace.

41. See, e.g., the following diary entry by Matthew Patten on April 5, 1757: "was at James Walkers on John Pattens being apprehended by Margret Holms for his Getting her with child for which he agreed with her for 300 L old Tenor and he pd Charges." *The Diary of Matthew Patten of Bedford, N.H.* (Concord, N.H., 1903), p. 35.

42. *Gill Belcher v. Mary Belcher,* petition for annulment of marriage dated Dec. 28, 1738, Suffolk File #129726, vol. 793, Massachusetts Archives.

43. See Roger Thompson, *Sex in Middlesex: Popular Mores in a Massachusetts County, 1649–1699* (Amherst, Mass., 1986), pp. 27–31. In addition to cases cited by Thompson for the period before 1700, see *Proctor v. Choat,* Essex County Court of General Sessions, July 1705, file papers (agreement not to name Choat as the father); *Perry v. Dix,* Middlesex County Court of General Sessions, 1710/11, Folio 41x, Middlesex Folio Collection (offer to conceal the name of the father for a small sum of money); *Pickworth v. Smith,* Essex County Court of General Sessions, March 1718/19, file papers (agreement to conceal name of father); *Farmer v. Richardson,* Middlesex County Court of General Sessions, 1725/26, Folio 86x, Middlesex Folio Collection (agreement to conceal name of father).

44. *Wyman v. Thompson,* Middlesex County Court of General Sessions, deposi-

tions of Samuel and Sarah Wyman and Samuel Parker, 1726, Folio 150x, Middlesex Folio Collection.

45. Ibid.

46. Evidence of such settlements becomes less visible in Massachusetts court records after around 1730, when criminal bastardy proceedings against men stopped being heard in the Court of General Sessions. Of course, there is no way of knowing in any period what percentage of unwed mothers were paid private settlements by their lovers, since most of those settlements were never a matter of public record.

47. For an example of a father who tried to insist that his daughter's lover behave in a "manly" way by marrying her, see *Rex. v. Daniel Francis* (1724), cited in Dayton, *Women before the Bar*, p. 203.

48. Smith and Hindus, "Premarital Pregnancy in America, 1640–1971"; on England, see Lawrence Stone, *The Family, Sex and Marriage in England, 1500–1800* (New York, 1977); John Gillis, *For Better, for Worse: British Marriage, 1600 to the Present* (New York, 1985).

49. Benjamin Bangs Diary, various entries in December 1747 and June 1748, Massachusetts Historical Society.

50. On bundling, see Henry Stiles, *Bundling: Its Origins, Progress and Decline in America* (repr. Detroit, 1973). See also Laurel Thatcher Ulrich and Lois K. Stabler, "'Girling of It' in Eighteenth-Century New Hampshire," in Peter Benes et al., eds., *Families and Children: The Dublin Seminar for New England Folklife: Annual Proceedings* (Cambridge, Mass., 1985), pp. 24–36, which finds that young men and women in eighteenth-century New Hampshire practiced bundling, or "staying with" each other overnight as a way to get to know each other.

51. For example, John Adams's father, warning him about his reputation in 1758, pointed out that it mattered not at all to the relatives that he had not formally declared his intentions for Hannah Quincy: "He says I have waited on H. Q. two Journeys, and have called and made Visits there so often, that her Relations among others have said I am courting of her." John Adams, *The Diary and Autobiography of John Adams*, ed. L. H. Butterfield (Cambridge, Mass., 1961), vol. 1, p. 119.

52. *Huldah Reed vs. Samuel Stone*, deposition of Lydia Reed, Jan. 24, 1750, Middlesex County Court of General Sessions, File Papers, Box 2, Massachusetts Archives.

53. Ulrich and Stabler, "'Girling of It.'" While the evidence of premarital pregnancy suggests that parents were becoming increasingly willing to tolerate premarital intercourse, that willingness was not particularly innovative or modern: English villagers had long condoned sexual intercourse after an engagement, within a context of community oversight.

54. Dayton, *Women before the Bar*, pp. 194–198; Thompson, *Sex in Middlesex*.

55. *Huldah Reed v. Samuel Stone,* deposition of E—— Rice and Thomas Skilton, Jr., March 8, 1750, Middlesex County Court of General Sessions, File Papers, Box 2. This case probably involved a false accusation by the woman, and it came into the Court of General Sessions because the man found evidence that would allow him to prove that another man had fathered the child. Women as well as men became more selective about their marital choices during the eighteenth century, which sometimes meant that a woman had more than one lover before she married.

56. Letters from Robert Treat Paine to Ephraim Keith, Sr., May 28, 1763, and Ephraim Keith, Jr., to Robert Treat Paine, June 2, 1763, *The Papers of Robert Treat Paine,* ed. Stephen Riley and Edward Hanson (Boston, 1992), vol. 2 (hereinafter, *Papers of R. T. Paine*), pp. 251–255.

57. Ephraim Keith, Jr., to R. T. Paine, June 2, 1763, *Papers of R. T. Paine,* 2, p. 254.

58. An example of the extreme lengths to which a young man could go to avoid marrying his lover is found in the case of Amasa Sessions of Pomfret, Connecticut, in 1742. After getting his lover, Sarah Grosvenor, pregnant, he convinced her to obtain an abortion, which caused her death. Cornelia Hughes Dayton, "Taking the Trade: Abortion and Gender Relations in an Eighteenth-Century New England Village," *William and Mary Quarterly,* 3rd ser., 48 (Jan. 1991): 19–49.

59. I am indebted to conversations with Ruth Bloch for the pre-Revolutionary periodization of this development. See also Ruth H. Bloch, "Changing Conceptions of Sexuality and Romance in Eighteenth-Century America," *William and Mary Quarterly,* 3rd ser. 60 (Jan. 2003); Bloch, "The Gendered Meanings of Virtue in Revolutionary America," *Signs: Journal of Women in Culture and Society* 11 (Fall 1987): 37–58; Bloch, "Religion, Literary Sentimentalism, and Popular Revolutionary Ideology," in Ronald Hoffman and Peter J. Albert, eds., *Religion in a Revolutionary Age* (Charlottesville, 1994); Bloch, "Women, Love, and Virtue in the Thought of Edwards and Franklin," in Barbara Oberg and Harry S. Stout, eds., *Benjamin Franklin, Jonathan Edwards, and the Representation of American Culture* (New York, 1993).

60. "In Praise of Marriage," *American Magazine,* Aug. 1744, p. 510. For other examples, see "Virtuous Love and Lust," *American Magazine,* Feb. 1744, pp. 245–247; "Observations on Love and Marriage," *American Magazine,* May 1745, pp. 200–201; "Reflections of a Batchelor . . .," *New Hampshire Gazette,* Jan. 9, 1761, p. 4; answer to "Reflections", *New Hampshire Gazette,* Jan. 30, 1761.

61. Robert Dodsley, *The Oeconomy of Human Life,* 7th ed. (London; repr. Boston, 1752), p. 26. This book was widely available in New England be-

fore the Revolution; see, e.g., advertisements for its sale in the Connecticut *Courant,* Sept. 15, 1766, as well as issues dated Sept. 22 (p. 5) and Oct. 13, 1766, (p. 4), and Jan. 5, 1767 (p. 1).

62. G. J. Barker-Benfield, *The Culture of Sensibility: Sex and Society in Eighteenth-Century Britain* (Chicago, 1992).

63. Bloch, "Changing Conceptions of Sexuality in Eighteenth-Century America"; see also Bloch, "Women, Love, and Virtue"; Bloch, "The Gendered Meanings of Virtue in Revolutionary America."

64. Samuel Quincy to R. T. Paine, May 1755, *Papers of R. T. Paine,* 1, pp. 266–267.

65. Notebook, 1754–1758, Nathan Fiske Papers (passage notes "copied from the American Magazine, vol. 1, p. 27"), American Antiquarian Society.

66. Adams, *Diary and Autobiography,* 1, p. 74.

67. See, esp., Notebook, 1754–1758, Nathan Fiske Papers, American Antiquarian Society; Thomas Collins Notebook, 1759, American Antiquarian Society; and Jeremy Belknap, Memoranda Book, 1760–1764, and Poems, 1757 (e.g., love poem to Sally), in Misc. Volumes, 1744–1791, Belknap Papers, Massachusetts Historical Society. These New England men's entries usually celebrated romantic love. Compare the misogynist writings of William Byrd and Thomas Jefferson, cited in Kenneth A. Lockridge, *On the Sources of Patriarchal Rage: The Commonplace Books of William Byrd and Thomas Jefferson and the Gendering of Power in the Eighteenth Century* (New York, 1992).

68. For a summary of the literature, see David Gilmore, *Manhood in the Making: Cultural Concepts of* Masculinity (New Haven, 1990).

69. On the impact of romantic courtship on men's sense of self in eighteenth-century New England, see Lisa Wilson, *Ye Heart of a Man: The Domestic Life of Men in Colonial New England* (New Haven, 1999), chap. 2.

70. Dodsley, *Oeconomy of Human Life,* pp. 25, 28.

71. John Barnard, *A Present for an Apprentice* (Boston, 1747), pp. 76–77.

72. Adams, *Diary and Autobiography,* 1, p. 119.

73. Ibid., p. 67.

74. Robert Treat Paine to Ellen Hobart, Aug. 3, 1763, *Papers of R. T. Paine,* 2, p. 259.

75. *American Magazine,* Sept. 1744, pp. 546–548.

76. "The Choice of a Husband in a Letter to a Friend," *New Hampshire Gazette,* Feb. 29, 1760, p. 2.

77. "Lavinia" to Robert Treat Paine (Oct. 1757?), *Papers of R. T. Paine,* 2, p. 57; Robert Treat Paine to Ellen Hobart, Aug. 3, 1763; Robert Treat Paine to Ellen Hobart (after Aug. 3, 1763), *Papers of R. T. Paine,* 2, pp. 260, 266.

78. This mid-eighteenth-century notion lasted throughout the early republi-

can period following the American Revolution. Jan Lewis, "The Republican Wife: Virtue and Seduction in the Early Republic," *William and Mary Quarterly,* 3rd ser., 44 (Oct. 1987): 689–721.

79. On the late-eighteenth-century American ideal of the "man of feeling," see Andrew Burstein, *Sentimental Democracy: The Evolution of America's Romantic Self-Image* (New York, 1999).

80. John Cleaveland to Mary Dodge, Feb. 13, 1746/47, Cleaveland Papers, Box 2, "Correspondence with Wives," Phillips Library, Peabody Essex Museum, Salem.

81. Mary Dodge to Ezekiel Dodge, February 12, 1746/47, Cleaveland Family Papers, Box 2, "Correspondence with Wives."

82. Mary Dodge to John Cleaveland, March 23, 1746/47, Cleaveland Family Papers, Box 2, "Correspondence with Wives."

83. For example, John Adams's friend William Crawford wrote to him in 1760: "I lodge at Mrs. Eager's, and enjoy there the Conversation of a young Lady, of distinguished merit, who in old Times was known by the name of the fair Jilt. Give my Compliment to the young Ladies where you think it proper." William Crawford to John Adams, Jan. 13, 1760, in L. H. Butterfield, ed., *Papers of John Adams,* vol. 1 (Cambridge, Mass., 1977), p. 38.

84. R. T. Paine to Ephraim Keith, May 28, 1763, reproduced in part in Edward W. Hanson, "'A Sense of Honor and Duty': Robert Treat Paine of Massachusetts and the New Nation," Ph.D. diss., Boston College, 1992, p. 97.

85. *Wyman v. Thompson,* Middlesex County Court of General Sessions, 1726, depositions in Folio 150x, Middlesex Folio Collection.

86. For the sources of this cultural development, see Bloch, "The Gendered Meanings of Virtue in Revolutionary America"; Jay Fliegelman, *Prodigals and Pilgrims: The American Revolution against Patriarchal Authority, 1750–1800* (Cambridge, 1982); and Kenneth Silverman, *A Cultural History of the Revolution: Painting, Music, Literature in the Colonies and the United States . . . 1763–1789* (New York, 1976).

87. See, e.g., letters to unidentified male friends on friendship, Jeremy Belknap commonplace books, 1758–1764, Belknap Papers, Massachusetts Historical Society; letters of Joseph Brigham and Ephraim Wheelock, 1780s, Brigham Family Papers, American Antiquarian Society; letters of William Livingston to Noah Welles, 1742–1759 (totaling seventy-nine letters during this period alone), Johnson Family Papers, Yale University Library. Most evidence of the popularity of these sentimental ideas about friendship comes from well-educated youths. It is hard to know whether similar ideas had percolated into popular culture by this time, since men who did not go to college tended not to write letters to friends.

Intimate epistolary friendships between men (and also between women) became more common during the early nineteenth century. See E. Anthony Rotundo, *American Manhood: Transformations in Masculinity from the Revolution to the Modern Era* (New York, 1993), esp. 75–91, and Donald Yacovone, "Abolitionists and the 'Language of Fraternal Love,'" in Mark E. Carnes and Clyde Griffen, eds., *Meanings for Manhood: Constructions of Masculinity in Victorian America* (Chicago, 1990).

88. Letter from Ezekiel Dodge to R. T. Paine, May 5, 1747, *Papers of R. T. Paine,* 1, pp. 12–13.

89. Ibid.

90. Such language also became conventional in courtship letters at around this time, and marital love was also described as friendship. It is sometimes difficult to distinguish letters of friendship from the highly stylized essays on loving friendship that men sent to the women they were courting. See, e.g., Jeremy Belknap to "Dear Friend," Aug. 16, 1762, in Memorandum Book, 1760–1764, Belknap Papers, Massachusetts Historical Society.

91. Samuel Haven to R. T. Paine, May 9, 1747, *Papers of R. T. Paine,* 1, p. 13; see also Jeremy Belknap "To my much honored Friend XXXXXX," Jan. 9, 1762, in Memorandum Book, 1760–1764, Belknap Papers, Massachusetts Historical Society.

92. Israel Cheever to Robert Treat Paine, July 27, 1749, *Papers of R. T. Paine,* 1, p. 58.

93. Dodge to R. T. Paine, May 5, 1747; Dodge to R. T. Paine, June 8, 1747; Dodge to R. T. Paine, Jan. 15, 1748/49, *Papers of R. T. Paine,* 1, pp. 12–13, 15, 40–41.

94. Rotundo, *American Manhood.*

4. Manhood and Marriage

1. "Diary of Cotton Mather, 1681–1708," *Collections of the Massachusetts Historical Society,* (Boston, 1911), p. 125.

2. On the duties of husbands generally, see John Demos, *A Little Commonwealth: Family Life in Plymouth Colony* (New York, 1970), pp. 91–96; Steven Ozment, *When Fathers Ruled: Family Life in Reformation Europe* (Cambridge, Mass., 1983), pp. 50–57. On the meanings that seventeenth- and eighteenth-century men and women accorded to productive work within the household economy, see Laurel Thatcher Ulrich, *Good Wives: Image and Reality in the Lives of Women in Northern New England, 1650–1750* (New York, 1980); Daniel Vickers, *Farmers and Fishermen: Two Centuries of Work in Essex County, Massachusetts, 1630–1850* (Chapel Hill, 1994); and J. E. Crowley, *This Sheba, Self: The Conceptualization of Economic Life in Eighteenth-Century America* (Baltimore, 1974). p. 6.

3. Because it was difficult for men to support themselves without a wife, most married. On the typical eighteenth-century pattern of work, accumulation of capital, and preparation for marriage, see Fred Anderson, *A People's Army: Massachusetts Soldiers and Society in the Seven Years' War* (New York, 1984), pp. 32–36, and Vickers, *Farmers and Fishermen*, pp. 219–259. Historians have little information at this point on men who remained unmarried.

4. See, e.g., Philip J. Greven, Jr., *Four Generations: Population, Land, and Family in Colonial Andover, Massachusetts* (Ithaca, N.Y., 1970), pp. 72–89. The definition of husband is found in the *Oxford Universal Dictionary on Historical Principles*, 3rd ed. (Oxford, 1955).

5. John May Diary, 1708–1766, entries for 1711, *passim,* American Antiquarian Society.

6. James Freeman to Robert Treat Paine, Aug. 26, 1751, and March 9, 1752, *The Papers of Robert Treat Paine,* ed. Stephen Riley and Edward Hanson (Boston, 1992), vol. 2. For data on age at marriage, see Douglas Lamar Jones, *Village and Seaport: Migration and Society in Eighteenth-Century Massachusetts* (Hanover, N.H., 1981), pp. 72–73.

7. John May Diary, Dec. 11 to Dec. 18, 1711.

8. James Freeman to Robert Paine, Aug. 26, 1751, *Papers of R. T. Paine,* 2. In, Halifax, Freeman's new home, communal controls on sexual morality were less stringent than in New England. His letters to Paine refer to "a dear native of Ireland," possibly a mistress, with whom he was spending time, and whom he apparently married a year or two later.

9. Nancy Cott, "Divorce and the Changing Status of Women in Eighteenth-Century Massachusetts," *William and Mary Quarterly,* 3rd ser., 33 (1976): 612; Marylynn Salmon, *Women and the Law of Property in Early America* (Chapel Hill, 1986), pp. 73–74; Lyle Koehler, *A Search for Power: The Weaker Sex in Seventeenth-Century New England* (Urbana, 1980), pp. 48–49.

10. Benjamin Wadsworth, *The Well-Ordered Family* (Boston, 1712), pp. 23, 35, 29.

11. Samuel Man, "Advice to His Children Who Were Soon to Enter the Married State, Written in 1704," *New England Historical and Genealogical Register,* vol. 6 (Boston, 1852), pp. 39–41; see also Edmund S. Morgan, *The Puritan Family: Religion and Domestic Relations in Seventeenth-Century New England,* rev. ed. (New York, 1966), pp. 47–48.

12. "In Praise of Marriage," *American Magazine* (Aug. 1744), pp. 509–510; "The Reflections of a Batchelor," *New Hampshire Gazette,* Jan. 9, 1761, p. 4; untitled, *New Hampshire Gazette,* Feb. 20, 1761, p. 2.

13. "Observations on Love and Marriage," *American Magazine* (May 1745), p. 201.

14. Nancy Cott, "Eighteenth-Century Family and Social Life Revealed in Massachusetts Divorce Records," *Journal of Social History* 10 (1976–77): pp. 20–43, at p. 30.

15. John Winthrop, "A Modell of Christian Charity" (1630), quoted in Vickers, *Farmers and Fishermen*, pp. 219–220.

16. *Poor Richard's Almanac* (1734); for similar sentiments, see Job Shepard, pseud., *Poor Job, 1750* (Newport: J. Franklin).

17. Samuel Sewall, *Diary of Samuel Sewall, 1674–1729*, vol. 2 (New York, 1972), pp. 125–126.

18. *Hannah Medberry v. Ebenezer Medberry*, Suffolk File #129746, vol. 793, (Hannah Medberry petition for divorce *a mensa et thoro*, Feb. 2, 1767), (Silvanus Martin deposition, May 15, 1767), Massachusetts Archives.

19. Ibid., Silvanus Martin deposition.

20. *Lufkin v. How*, Suffolk File #129735, vol. 793, (deposition of Thomas Jacques, Feb. 1761).

21. On the social value of work, see Crowley, *This Sheba, Self*. It was the familial context that gave productive work its meaning. Vickers, *Farmers and Fishermen*, pp. 219–220.

22. "Rev. Michael Wigglesworth, Memoir, Autobiography, Letters and Library," *New England Historic Genealogical Register*, vol. 17 (Albany, 1863), p. 140. On Puritan ideas about marriage, see Morgan, *The Puritan Family*, pp. 35–64.

23. Josiah Cotton Memoirs, 1726–1756, Massachusetts Historical Society.

24. Hendrik Hartog, *Man and Wife in America: A History* (Cambridge, Mass., 2000).

25. On New England divorce law and practices, see Cornelia Dayton, *Women before the Bar: Gender, Law, and Society in Connecticut, 1639–1789* (Chapel Hill, 1995), chap. 3; Cott, "Divorce and the Changing Status of Women." For divorce statistics, see also Koehler, *A Search for Power*; Sheldon S. Cohen, "The Broken Bond: Divorce in Providence County, 1749–1809," *Rhode Island History* 44 (1985): 67–79; and Sheldon S. Cohen, "What Man Hath Put Asunder: Divorce in New Hampshire, 1681–1784," *Historical New Hampshire* 41 (1986): 118–141.

26. Laurence Stone, *Road to Divorce: England, 1530–1987* (New York, 1990).

27. My conclusions here draw on Dayton, *Women before the Bar*, pp. 108–122, Cott, "Divorce and the Changing Status of Women," and Cott, "Eighteenth-Century Family and Social Life Revealed." For statistics, see Koehler, *Search for Power*, Appendix 1 (seventeenth-century New England, all colonies), and Dayton, *Women before the Bar*, p. 135, Table 6, and Appendices 1 and 2 (seventeenth-century New Haven and seventeenth- and eighteenth-century Connecticut). Statistics provided by Koehler and Dayton, which make it possible to identify the grounds for petitions before

1770, reveal that 60 to 72 percent of female petitions for which the grievance is known were founded on a complaint of desertion, sometimes in combination with other causes. While Cott's (eighteenth-century Massachusetts) findings do not show grounds for petitions by decade, they do suggest that 65 percent of female petitions in Massachusetts between 1692 and 1786 contained allegations of desertion or nonsupport. Cott, "Eighteenth Century Family and Social Life Revealed," p. 30. She also indicates, however, that eighteenth-century women alleging desertion were unlikely to be granted a divorce without the added grounds of cruelty or adultery. Cott, "Divorce and the Changing Status of Women," pp. 607–608.

28. By way of comparison, women did not commonly seek divorces based on their husbands' cruelty or infidelity, even though courts in seventeenth-century Massachusetts and Connecticut did occasionally grant divorces to women on those grounds. See Dayton, *Women before the Bar,* pp. 108–117, and Koehler, *Search for Power,* Appendix 1. In contrast, men who sought to end their marriages often alleged adultery on the part of their wives, suggesting that sexual fidelity, rather than productivity, was seen as more central to the marital obligations of wives. Cott, "Divorce and the Changing Status of Women," p. 601. After 1700, female divorce petitioners alleging adultery alone became increasingly rare in Massachusetts, possibly reflecting changes in legal practice following the Puritans' loss of control over the provincial government, rather than changes in popular beliefs about marital and gender roles.

29. *Catherine (or Katherine) v. Elijah Cobb,* Suffolk File #129748, vol. 793 (depositions of Joseph Cobb, Oct. 8, 1767, and John Cooper, Sept. 5, 1767). In the end, the issue in the Cobb case was her madness.

30. *Russell v. Mary Knight,* Suffolk Files, vol. 793 (Hannah Meriam deposition, Aug. 21, 1766); quotation reordered. A man could obtain a divorce from his wife solely on the basis of her adultery, but the same was not necessarily true for a woman, depending on the jurisdiction and of the case. For discussions of the availability of divorce based on adultery, see Dayton, *Women before the Bar,* pp. 110–112, and Cott, "Divorce and the Changing Status of Women," pp. 599–608. What is interesting about these cases is the parties' own insistence on making their economic contributions to the marriage an issue, even though this was not legally relevant because proof of the wife's adultery alone would have excused the husband from his obligation to support her.

31. Stephen Lufkin submitted two petitions in the case, presumably on the basis of legal advice, the first seeking a divorce on the grounds of her adultery, and the second, in the alternative, a divorce from bed and board (to be excused from having to pay for her support) on the grounds that she had

kept "a secret & unlawful communion with other Men" and had run him into debt as well. *Lufkin v. Lufkin,* Suffolk File #129735, vol. 793 (Stephen Lufkin complaint dated Dec. 17, 1760, and Stephen Lufkin complaint dated Dec. 23, 1760).

32. Ibid., Petition of Tabitha Lufkin, Feb. 11, 1761.

33. See, e.g., Carl N. Degler, *At Odds: Women and the Family in America from the Revolution to the Present* (New York, 1980); John Demos, "The American Family in Past Time," *American Scholar* 43 (1974): 42.

34. Conclusions about the origin of the stereotype of husbands as producers and women as conservers/spenders remain necessarily speculative. Some historians of early modern England and its colonies suggest that sixteenth- and seventeenth-century idealizations of women's domesticity and frugality were a direct response to women's increasing opportunities to earn and spend their own money through participation in commercial activities and trade. See, e.g., David Underdown, "The Taming of the Scold," in Anthony Fletcher and John Stevenson, eds., *Order and Disorder in Early Modern England* (New York, 1985), pp. 116–136; Susan Dwyer Amussen, *An Ordered Society: Gender and Class in Early Modern England* (New York, 1988); Kathleen M. Brown, *Good Wives, Nasty Wenches, and Anxious Patriarchs: Gender, Race, and Power in Colonial Virginia* (Chapel Hill, 1996), pp. 22–32.

35. Definition of husband in the *Oxford Universal Dictionary on Historical Principles*, 3rd ed. (Oxford, 1955).

36. T. H.Breen, "'Baubles of Britain': The American and Consumer Revolutions of the Eighteenth Century," *Past and Present* 119 (May 1988): pp. 73–104, at p. 78.

37. Commercial life and the growing consumer marketplace were central issues of debate before and during the American Revolution. While most historians suggest that Americans during the Revolution were demonstrating their resistance to commerce and commercialism, it has been recently argued that the debate about consumption was an attempt to make sense of and accommodate it into American life. See J. G. A. Pocock, "Virtue and Commerce in the Eighteenth Century," *Journal of Interdisciplinary History* 3 (1972): 119–134; Gordon Wood, *The Creation of the American Republic, 1776–1787* (Chapel Hill, 1969); and Edmund S. Morgan, "The Puritan Ethic and the American Revolution," *William and Mary Quarterly,* 3rd ser., 24 (Jan. 1967): 3–43, for the anticommercial position, and T. H. Breen, "Narrative of Commercial Life: Consumption, Ideology, and Community on the Eve of the American Revolution," *William and Mary Quarterly,* 3rd ser., 50 (July 1993): 471–501, for the newer argument.

38. During the American Revolution, elite or upper-middle-class women who

took the lead in organizing boycotts of tea and wearing homespun clothing were not only protesting British trade policies but also challenging gender stereotypes that portrayed them as greedy spenders incapable of controlling their own desires. On women's consumer boycotts, see Linda Kerber, *Women of the Republic: Intellect and Ideology in Revolutionary America* (Chapel Hill, 1980), pp. 35–45.

39. On women's participation in trade in seventeenth- and eighteenth-century New England, see Ulrich, *Good Wives,* pp. 43–48; and Laurel Thatcher Ulrich, "'A Friendly Neighbor': Social Dimensions of Daily Work in Northern Colonial New England," *Feminist Studies* 6 (1980): pp. 392–405. On women's credit and trade networks, see Dayton, *Women before the Bar,* chap. 2.

40. *Lufkin v. Lufkin,* Suffolk File #129735, vol. 793 (petition of Tabitha Lufkin, Feb. 11, 1761).

41. *Benjamin Green v. Jemimah Chadwick,* Suffolk File #129731, vol. 793 (petition of Benjamin Green, decree dated Feb. 20, 1753).

42. For a similar juxtaposition of accusations of adultery and allegations that a wife had wasted her husband's estate, see the petitions of Stephen Lufkin, note 31.

43. John Armstrong, *The Oeconomy of Love: A Poetical Essay* (London, 1736), p. 38.

44. *Aristotle's Masterpiece* (London, 1755), p. 29; *Aristotle's Masterpiece* (London, 1698), p. 8.

45. Nicholas Venette, *Conjugal Love; or, the Pleasures of the Marriage Bed . . . ,* 20th ed. (London, 1750), p. 147.

46. *Aristotle's Masterpiece* (1755 ed.), pp. 39, 29.

47. For the argument that Puritans were accepting of sexuality in the context of marriage, see Edmund S. Morgan, "The Puritans and Sex," *New England Quarterly* 15 (1942): 591–607. For an analysis of the ways in which Puritan teachings about love and marriage sanctified the authority of male household heads, see Carol F. Karlsen, *The Devil in the Shape of a Woman: Witchcraft in Colonial New England* (New York, 1987), pp. 160–173.

48. John Saffin Notebook, 1665–1708, pp. 83–84, American Antiquarian Society.

49. Venette, *Conjugal Love,* p. 80.

50. *New London Summary,* May 15, 1761, p. 2.

51. On distinct attitudes toward marital and premarital sexuality in the colonial period, see John D'Emilio and Estelle B. Freedman, *Intimate Matters: A History of Sexuality in America* (New York, 1988), pp. 17–27.

52. Vickers, *Farmers and Fishermen,* p. 226.

53. Edmund S. Morgan, *The Puritan Family: Religion and Domestic Relations in Seventeenth-Century New England,* 2nd ed. (New York, 1966), pp. 48–53.

54. John Saffin Notebook, 1665–1708, p. 39.
55. For these aspects of Puritan teachings on marriage, see Morgan, *The Puritan Family*, pp. 48–51, 59–64. For evidence of popular beliefs about marriage in seventeenth-century New England, see Ulrich, *Good Wives*, pp. 107–113. On similarities between Protestant and medical ideas about sexuality, see Anthony Fletcher, "The Protestant Idea of Marriage in Early Modern England," in Fletcher, ed., *Religion, Culture, and Society* (Cambridge, England, 1994).
56. For eighteenth-century explanations of the difference between lust and virtuous love, see "Virtuous Love and Lust," *American Magazine* (Feb. 1744): 245–247; "A Letter from a Jew Traveller at Paris," *American Magazine* (Sept. 1743): 25–28; "Rules and Maxims for Promoting Matrimonial Happiness," *New Hampshire Gazette,* Dec. 19, 1760, p. 2.
57. See my argument about fears of sexual excess in Chapter 2.
58. Venette, *Conjugal Love,* pp. 101–102.
59. Demos, *A Little Commonwealth,* pp. 92–96; see also Thomas Foster, "Deficient Husbands: Manhood, Sexual Incapacity, and Male Marital Sexuality in Seventeenth Century New England," *William and Mary Quarterly,* 3rd ser., 56 (Oct. 1999): 723–744.
60. *Russell v. Mary Knight,* Suffolk Files, vol. 793 (deposition of Jonathan Knight, Aug. 26, 1766). According to Mary, the reason he did not "lodge" with her was that he went to prostitutes instead.
61. Male impotence was not automatic grounds for divorce. In Massachusetts and Connecticut in the seventeenth century, only four out of eight divorce petitions on grounds of impotence were granted. Koehler, *A Search for Power,* pp. 78–79. In Massachusetts in the eighteenth century, only one divorce was granted out of four such petitions. Cott, "Divorce and the Changing Status of Women in Eighteenth-Century Massachusetts," p. 598.
62. *Aristotle's Masterpiece* (1755 ed.), pp. 52–53.
63. *Elizabeth v. Joseph Bredeen,* Suffolk File #129728, vol. 793, (petition of Elizabeth Bredeen, April 1744).
64. According to *Aristotle's Masterpiece,* a woman who "do not use Copulation, to eject her seed, she often times falls into strange Diseases, as appears by young Women and Virgins" (1698 ed., p. 18).
65. The confidence with which she asserted her claim to the court may have been somewhat misplaced, as her petition was never decided on. Possibly the court simply expected her to be patient with her husband and wait to see whether his infirmity would resolve itself.
66. *Judith Walker v. Simeon Walker,* Suffolk File #129777, vol. 794, (depositions of Thomas Temple and Levi Walker, dated Jan. 19, 1773).
67. Ibid., deposition of Silent Wild.
68. Ibid., deposition of Dinah Temple.

69. Ibid., answer of Simeon Walker.

70. Angus McLaren, *Reproductive Rituals: The Perception of Fertility in England from the Sixteenth to the Nineteenth Century* (London, 1984); *Aristotle's Masterpiece* (1698 ed.), p. 18.

71. On causes of barrenness, see *Aristotle's Complete Masterpiece,* 26th ed. (1755), pp. 49–50; on male remedies, p. 51; for an earlier English source suggesting remedies to "cause standing of the Yard" or "augment Sperme and natural Seed," see [Leonard Sowerby], *The Ladies Dispensatory* (London: R. Ibbitson, 1652), p. 139.

72. [A. B.,] *The Ten Pleasures of Matrimony* (London, 1683), pp. 5l, 68.

73. Notice from New Haven, April 28, 1759, in *Boston Evening Post,* no. 1236, May 7, 1759.

74. On the authority of Anglo-American household heads over their wives, see Carole Shammas, "Anglo-American Household Government in Comparative Perspective," *William and Mary Quarterly,* 3rd ser., vol. 52, no. 1 (Jan. 1995): 104–144; Norma Basch, *In the Eyes of the Law: Women, Marriage, and Property in Nineteenth-Century New York* (Ithaca, N.Y., 1982); Salmon, *Women and the Law of Property.*

75. Joyce O. Appleby, *Economic Thought in Seventeenth-Century England* (Princeton, 1978); William James Booth, *Households: On the Moral Architecture of the Economy* (Ithaca, N.Y.: 1993).

76. For discussions of early modern English and Anglo-American views of women as sensual, lustful, and natural, and men as rational, virtuous, and civilized, see Ruth H. Bloch, "The Gendered Meanings of Virtue in Revolutionary America," *Signs: Journal of Women in Culture and Society* 13, no. 1 (1987): 37–58; Phyllis Mack, *Visionary Women: Ecstatic Prophecy in Seventeenth-Century England* (Berkeley, 1992), pp. 24–34; Karlsen, *The Devil in the Shape of a Woman,* pp. 155–165; Joan Kelly, "Early Feminist Theory and the 'Querelle des Femmes,' 1400–1789," in Joan Kelly, ed., *Women, History, and Theory: The Essays of Joan Kelly* (Chicago, 1984), pp. 65–109; Audrey Eccles, *Obstetrics and Gynaecology in Tudor and Stuart England* (Kent, Ohio, 1982); Genevieve Lloyd, *The Man of Reason: "Male" and "Female" in Western Philosophy* (Minneapolis, 1984).

77. Case of Jacob Chamberlain, Middlesex Folio Collection, Folio 22x, 1704/05.

78. Wadsworth, "The Well-Ordered Family," p. 37.

79. Morgan, *The Puritan Family,* p. 38, note 33, citing photostat collection of the Massachusetts Historical Society, March 5, 1684/85.

80. The basic rationale for the Puritans' liberalization of divorce *a vinculo,* which allowed the wronged party to remarry, was their commitment to removing unfit husbands from householder status to ensure that women

came under the sway of more rational, more moral household governors. See D. Kelly Weisberg, "'Under Greet Temptations Heer': Women and Divorce in Puritan Massachusetts," *Feminist Studies* 2 (1975).

81. *Mary v. Michael Homer,* Middlesex Folio Collection, Folios 160 and 161, deposition of John Foster, October 1694.

82. Ibid., deposition of Mary Homer.

83. Case of Dr. Henry Smith, Suffolk Files 4668 to 4738, vol. 49, Supreme Judicial Court papers, April 1700.

84. See discussion of peace bonds in wife-abuse cases in Connecticut, Dayton, *Women before the Bar,* pp. 136–138.

85. *Russell v. Mary Knight,* Suffolk Files, vol. 793, (deposition of Jonathan Knight, Aug. 26, 1766).

86. *Katherine v. Elijah Cobb,* Suffolk Files, vol. 793 (deposition of John Cooper, Sept. 5, 1767).

87. *Maj. James Richardson, Esq., v. Hannah Richardson,* Suffolk File #129769, vol. 794 (deposition of Phinehas Butler, Dec. 1772). My thanks to Cornelia Dayton for bringing this case to my attention.

88. Ibid., deposition of Nathan Rugg, Dec. 7, 1772.

89. Ibid., deposition of Jotham White of Townsend, Middlesex Co., Dec. 7, 1772.

5. Manliness and the Use of Force

1. *Blanchard v. Shepard,* Middlesex Folio Collection, folios 183–185, Sept. 1679, Massachusetts State Archives, Boston.

2. On the success of early New England communities at achieving social cohesion, see Timothy H. Breen and Stephen Foster, "The Puritans' Greatest Achievement: A Study of Social Cohesion in Seventeenth-Century Massachusetts," *Journal of American History* 60 (1973): 5–22; Kenneth Lockridge, *A New England Town: The First Hundred Years* (New York, 1970). David Flaherty's work on the incidence of crimes of violence in eighteenth-century Massachusetts confirms that the rate of assault was relatively low. David H. Flaherty, "Crime and Social Control in Provincial Massachusetts," *Historical Journal* 24 (1981): 339–360. Puritan insistence on the strict control of aggression has been a consistent theme in the literature on early New England. For classic examples, see Richard Bushman, *From Puritan to Yankee: Character and the Social Order in Connecticut, 1690 to 1765* (Cambridge, Mass., 1967); Michael Zuckerman, *Peaceable Kingdoms: New England Towns in the Eighteenth Century* (New York, 1970); John Demos, *A Little Commonwealth: Family Life in Plymouth Colony* (London, 1970); and Philip Greven, *The Protestant Temperament: Patterns of Child-Rearing, Reli-*

gious Experience, and the Self in Early America (Chicago, 1977), esp. pp. 109–123.

3. Definitions and word usages are from the *Oxford Universal Dictionary on Historical Principles,* 3rd ed. (Oxford, 1955).

4. The general argument connecting the rise of Protestantism with changes in personality is of course Max Weber's. On New Englanders' campaign before 1750 to reform manners, see Richard P. Gildrie, *The Profane, the Civil, and the Godly: The Reformation of Manners in Orthodox New England, 1679–1749* (University Park, Pa., 1994). Further broad links between the disciplining of human impulses and the rise of a modern state are suggested by Norbert Elias, *The Civilizing Process,* 2 vols., trans. Edmund Jephcott (Oxford, 1978, 1982; first published 1939), and Michel Foucault, *Discipline and Punish: The Birth of the Prison,* trans. Alan Sheridan (New York, 1977).

5. Shepard's local reputation for hotheadedness had also won him an invitation to join a mob in attacking praying Indians on Deer Island during King Philip's War in 1675. Sources for information on the Blanchards and the Shepards are Deloraine Pendre Corey, *The History of Malden, 1633–1785* (Malden, 1899), pp. 122, 487, and Thomas Bellows Wyman, *The Genealogies and Estates of Charlestown, . . . 1629–1818* (Boston, 1879).

6. *Shepard v. Blanchard,* Middlesex Folio 193, Shepard complaint dated Sept. 20, 1700; Blanchard answer dated Sept. 20, 1700.

7. Middlesex Folio 27x, James Converse deposition, July 1703.

8. Middlesex Folio 27x, Peter Edes and Joshua Converse depositions, n.d. (1707); John Dexter deposition, n.d. (1707).

9. Ibid., Joanna Sheppard deposition, March 9, 1707.

10. Ibid., Samuel Wade deposition, Dec. 8, 1707; Abigail Shepard deposition, Dec. 8, 1707.

11. Middlesex Folio 29x, statement and court order, April 16, 1708.

12. It has been suggested that the exaggerated insults and self-inflation so typical of early New Englanders' verbal fights were the product of a child-rearing style that heightened concerns about shame, reputation, and disgrace. John Demos, "Shame and Guilt in Early New England," in Carol Z. Stearns and Peter N. Stearns, eds., *Emotion and Social Change: Toward a New Psychohistory* (New York, 1988), pp. 69–85.

13. The main body of evidence for this analysis comes from the Records of the Court of General Sessions for Middlesex County and the Middlesex Folio Collection. The cases are from Folios 82—232, 1x–96x, and 1A–73A, which provided comprehensive information on disputes occurring between 1680 and 1730. Court papers for cases dated 1736 to 1763, if available, were found in the Middlesex County File Papers, 1737–1828, boxes 1–4. These sources yielded a sample of 103 separate disputes between

males that resulted in prosecutions for violent incidents. Of these, 72 were reported in considerable detail.

The County Court of General Sessions' broad jurisdiction over misdemeanors meant that it adjudicated cases involving the most ordinary and routine kinds of aggressive behavior by and between males. The very ubiquitousness of these acts can tell us more about the role of violence in the enactment of manly identity than can crimes of exceptional violence or unusual seriousness, which cases were heard in the province's Superior Court of Judicature.

14. The basis for this conclusion was biographical data on the age and marital status of parties to assault cases involving at least one male plaintiff and at least one male defendant, in Middlesex County, between 1680 and 1740. The sample consisted of all males involved in assault cases during these years for whom demographic data was available in town histories or genealogical records—that is, about 80 percent of all males involved in assault cases (not including wife abuse cases). After 1740, demographic data were not available in a sufficient number of cases to justify further conclusions.

15. This average represents the median age and marital status out of a sample of all males for whom complete demographic data could be obtained.

16. These thirty cases represent all cases between 1680 and 1710 for which detailed information about the underlying dispute could be determined from the available records.

17. For an analysis that has influenced my understanding of male violence in early New England, see Susan Dwyer Amussen, "Punishment, Discipline, and Power: The Social Meanings of Violence in Early Modern England," *Journal of British Studies* 34 (Jan. 1995): 1–34.

18. *Crosby v. Richardson*, Middlesex Folios 102 and 103, deposition of Simon Crosby, Jr., June 19, 1683.

19. *Edmund Goffe v. Amos Marrett*, Middlesex Folio 31x, Amos Marrett deposition, June 18, 1707, and Edmund Goffe deposition, n.d.

20. *Spaulding v. Chamberlain*, Middlesex Folio 167, Joseph Spaulding, Sr., deposition, May 12, 1698.

21. *Francis Chope v. Solomon Green*, Middlesex Folio 183, depositions of Francis Chope and John and Joseph Drinker, Aug. 5, 1685.

22. *John How v. John Eames, Sr.*, Middlesex Folio 59x, depositions of John Eames, Jr., and Caleb Drury, Dec. 1715, deposition of John Eames, Sr., n.d.

23. *Blanchard v. Shepard*, Middlesex Folios 183–185, depositions of Samuel Blanchard, Joseph Blanchard, and statement by Samuel Blanchard, Sept. 1679.

24. *Nathaniel Hudson v. Philip Goss*, Middlesex Folio 196, deposition of Nathaniel Sawyer, Dec. 10, 1695.

25. See Philippa Maddern, *Violence and Social Order: East Anglia, 1422–1442* (Oxford, 1992).
26. *Samuel Morrow v. Daniel Morrow and wife,* Middlesex Folio 24x, deposition of Joshua Sawyer, n.d., and deposition of Edward Farmer, John Burnett, John Vinton, Thomas Grover, dated April 22, 1706.
27. See, e.g., *Hugh Mackling v. John Harrington,* Middlesex Folio 86x, 1721, and cases cited in Holly Brewer, "Constructing Consent: How Children's Status in Political Theory Shaped Public Policy in Virginia, Pennsylvania, and Massachusetts before and after the American Revolution," Ph.D. diss., UCLA, 1994.
28. Signed statement of John Shine, John Griffin, and William See, Oct. 27, 1701, Suffolk Files, vol. 53, p. 86.
29. *Crosby v. Richardson,* Middlesex Folio 102, deposition of Thomas and Joseph Crosby, June 19, 1683.
30. *Ehrlich's Blackstone,* ed. J. W. Ehrlich (New York, 1959), pp. 240–241. Violent disputes over property, and the acquisition of property through force, were of course a way of life in medieval England. On the origins of the common-law concept of divided, nonunitary interests in land, which implied that ownership of rights to land could be acquired through possession, see Harold W. Berman, *Law and Revolution: The Formation of the Western Legal Tradition* (Cambridge, Mass., 1983), pp. 453–457. It is still possible in modern American legal systems to acquire title to property through adverse possession—that is, long use of property in opposition to the interests of the titleholder. See, adverse possession defined and cases cited in Henry Campbell Black, ed., *Black's Law Dictionary,* 5th ed. (St. Paul, 1979).
31. Such rights as commons of pasture and rights of way are technically described as incorporeal hereditaments, to which title could be acquired through prescription under English common law. See *Ehrlich's Blackstone,* pp. 127–130 and 280–282. See also definition of "common" rights and "prescription" in *Black's Law Dictionary,* pp. 249, 1064–1065.
32. Alice Morse Earle, *Child Life in Colonial Days* (New York, 1899; repr. Stockbridge, Mass., 1993), pp. 312–314, reports that some seventeenth-century Anglo-American communities in North America still followed the English custom of "beating the bounds," whereby once a year the men and boys of a community walked around boundaries, commons, and public highways to keep their locations alive in the minds of the young, restored landmarks, and collectively resolved boundary disputes.
33. Eventually, the development of a recording system in New England would make these demonstrations unnecessary, by creating a written record to replace the community's collective memory. For discussions of the develop-

ment of a recording system, see David T. Konig, "Community Custom and the Common Law: Social Change and the Development of Land Law in Seventeenth-Century Massachusetts," *American Journal of Legal History* 18 (1974): 137–177, and George L. Haskins, "The Beginnings of the Recording System in Massachusetts," *Boston University Law Review* 21 (1941): 281–304.

34. *John Bigelow v. Jacob Bullard,* Middlesex Folio 91, deposition of Christopher Hall, Oct. 5, 1680.

35. *Powers v. Law,* Middlesex Folio 3x, deposition of Daniel Shepard and Ebenezer Davis, Aug. 18, 1702. The pun on the defendant's name, Law, was almost certainly intended, although it is likely that the pun also referred to other understandings, both religious and customary, of what it meant for a man to have "a law within himself."

36. The best description of the dual character of early New England men is Richard Bushman, *From Puritan to Yankee: Character and Social Order in Connecticut, 1690–1765* (Cambridge, Mass., 1967), esp. pp. 19–21 and 286–287. See also Demos, "Shame and Guilt in Early New England," on the curiously self-aggrandizing tone that men assumed when involved in disputes.

37. *Blood v. Wheeler,* Middlesex Folio 108, deposition of Josiah Blood, June 17, 1684.

38. Ibid., deposition of John Howard, June 16, 1685.

39. *Allen v. Waite,* Middlesex Folio 34x, complaint of Joseph Allen, Jr., March 8, 1707.

40. See also Eli Faber, "Puritan Criminals: The Economic, Social and Intellectual Background to Crime in Seventeenth-Century Massachusetts," *Perspectives in American History* 11 (1977–78): 81–144, at 103, for data consistent with this hypothesis from a slightly earlier period. Faber finds that for all persons tried for all crimes in Middlesex County between 1650 and 1686, 80 percent were freemen, and the majority came "from the county's middle and upper ranks."

41. As Alan Taylor has pointed out, public demonstrations of possessory rights on the Maine frontier had potential evidentiary significance in legal disputes over title to land. "'A Kind of Warr': The Contest for Land on the Northeastern Frontier, 1750 to 1820," *William and Mary Quarterly,* 3rd ser., 46, no. 1 (Jan. 1989): 3–26. For discussion of the role played by these legal concepts in rural violence before 1820, see Alan Taylor, *Liberty Men and Great Proprietors: The Revolutionary Settlement on the Maine Frontier, 1760–1820* (Chapel Hill, 1990), and Michael A. Bellisles, "The Establishment of Legal Structures on the Frontier: The Case of Revolutionary Vermont," *Journal of American History* 73, no. 4 (March 1987): 895–915.

42. See, e.g., Edward Countryman, "Out of the Bounds of the Law: Northern Land Rioters in the Eighteenth Century," in Alfred F. Young, ed., *The American Revolution: Explorations in the History of American Radicalism* (De Kalb, Ill., 1976), pp. 37–69.
43. The younger Simon was apparently not tried.
44. Entry of judgment in *Jonathan Fosdick v. Samuel Everton,* Charlestown, Nov. 1696, *Middlesex County Court of General Sessions Records, 1686–1723.*
45. *Shattuck v. Perry,* Concord, 1702, and presentment of Shattuck, Traino, and Holding, Charlestown 1704, in *Middlesex County Court of General Sessions Records, 1686–1723.* For a fuller description of the adolescent "subculture" in seventeenth-century Middlesex County, see Roger Thompson, *Sex in Middlesex: Popular Mores in a Massachusetts County, 1649–1699* (Amherst, 1986).
46. *Colson v. Wilson,* Middlesex Folio 96, statement of Frances Wilson, Dec. 20, 1681.
47. This man is identified nowhere by name, and in three depositions is referred to simply as "Adam Colson's negro."
48. *Colson v. Wilson,* Middlesex Folio 96, depositions of Mary Colson and Adam Colson, Dec. 20, 1681, and undated.
49. Ibid., statement of Frances Wilson, Dec. 20, 1681.
50. Ibid., deposition of Adam and Mary Colson and Sarah Daston, n.d.
51. Ibid., deposition of John Brown, Dec. 10, 1681.
52. Ibid., statement of Frances Wilson, Dec. 20, 1681.
53. Ibid., statement of Aaron Thomas Parker; John Webster, Jr.; et al., Dec. 10, 1681.
54. Ibid., deposition of John Wilson, Dec. 10, 1681. See also deposition of Jonathan Dunton.
55. Ibid., deposition of David Barheller, n.d.
56. *Samuel Parry v. William Shattuck,* Middlesex Folio 4x, deposition of Joseph Sanderson, May 4, 1702.
57. For the suggestion that such attacks on houses were a way to shame the men who owned them and insult their manhood, see Robert St. George, *Conversing by Signs: Poetics of Implication in Colonial New England Culture* (Chapel Hill, 1998), esp. chap. 3.
58. Examples of violence by seamen from the Middlesex county Court records include an incident involving an attack by at least twenty officers and crew members of HMS *Weymouth* on Charlestown residents in 1711, described in the grand jury presentment of Dalby Thomas, esq., et al., and related depositions in *Sprague v. Thomas* and *Miller v. Thomas,* April 1711, Middlesex Folio 49x. For the argument that seamen inhabited a uniquely violent and

antiauthoritarian culture, see Marcus Rediker, *Between the Devil and the Deep Blue Sea: Merchant Seamen, Pirates, and the Anglo-American Maritime World, 1700–1750* (Cambridge, 1987).

59. On aristocratic concepts of honor, see Mervyn James, "English Politics and the Concept of Honour, 1485–1642," *Past and Present,* supplement 3, 1978.

60. After the beginning of the Andros occupation of Boston, Sewall described several processions announcing that duels were to be fought between military men. See, e.g., *Diary of Samuel Sewall,* vol. 1 (New York, 1972), entry for Feb. 22, 1686/87, p. 173.

61. Complaint by Joseph Jacobs, Sept. 30, 1713, and deposition of William Gedney, sheriff, Oct. 1, 1713, Essex County Court files, Peabody Essex Library, Salem.

62. Thirteen disputes concerned land and livestock, twelve involved resisting constables, and thirty-three concerned other grievances that cannot be placed in a single category.

63. For this argument, see David Konig, *Law and Society in Puritan Massachusetts: Essex County, 1629–1692* (Chapel Hill, 1979); William E. Nelson, *Dispute and Conflict Resolution in Plymouth County, Massachusetts, 1725–1825* (Chapel Hill, 1981); Bruce Mann, *Neighbors and Strangers: Law and Community in Early Connecticut* (Chapel Hill, 1987); and Cornelia Dayton, *Women before the Bar: Gender, Law, and Society in Connecticut, 1639–1789* (Chapel Hill, 1995).

64. David Flaherty's findings show that the rate of prosecution for serious violent crimes actually declined from about 21.3 per 100,000 in the population per year in the 1690s to 12.5 per 100,000 in the 1720s, and 9.2 per 100,000 in the 1740s, before beginning to rise slightly to 11.8 per 100,000 per year in the 1760s. David Flaherty, "Crime and Social Control in Provincial Massachusetts," *The Historical Journal* 24 (1981): 339–360.

65. See presentment of Jos. Crofts, Jn. Phillis, Joseph Strode, and Thomas Loden for abuse to Col. Edmund Goffe, Charlestown, March 1720/21; indictment of Isaac Stearns, Joseph Crosby, Samuel Fassett, and Enoch Kidder for assaulting Jonathan Haskett, Esq., Charlestown, March 1722/23; indictments against Col. Edmund Goffe, Esq., and Amos Marrett, gent., and John Dixson, Jr., and Ephraim Cook for attacking each other, Charlestown, Dec. 1726; and presentment of Robert Poor and William Cross for assault on Daniel Goffe, merchant, Cambridge, May 1730. *Middlesex County, Court of General Sessions Records,* 1686–1723 and 1723–1735.

66. David Conroy, *In Public Houses: Drink and the Revolution of Public Authority in Colonial Massachusetts* (Chapel Hill, 1995), pp. 147–148.

67. Deposition of George Oake, Boston, Jan. 10, 1689, sworn in Court of Assistants (in case of *Rex v. John Newell*), manuscript collections, ms. no. Ch.F.10.20, Boston Public Library.

68. Transcript of proceedings dated Aug. 5, 1719, *Joseph Spaulding v. John Chamberlain et al.*, Middlesex Folio 69x. In a separate incident in Essex County, when blacksmith Thomas Manning leaned out of a chamber window in an Ipswich tavern, some men upstairs in the garret poured liquor down onto his hat. Both Manning and witnesses considered the gesture to be "saucie" and an incitement to a fight. See deposition of Nathaniel Perkins, Sept. 25, 1705, in *Burbank v. Manning*, Essex County, Court of General Sessions Papers.

69. See, e.g., *Leathe v. Richardson*, Middlesex Folio 73x, depositions of Henry Tottingham and Josiah Wyman, Jan. 10, 1720/21; *Sprague v. Goold*, Middlesex Folio 23A, deposition of Joseph Lampson, Samuel Nichols, John Knower, Jacob Winslow, and Thomas Knower, dated Dec. 31, 1728.

70. *Middlesex County Court of General Sessions Records*, vol. 4 (1748–1761).

71. Ibid.

72. On the leveling, democratizing possibilities of tavern culture, see Conroy, *In Public Houses*.

73. *Timothy Richardson v. Francis Leathe*, Middlesex Folio 73x, deposition of Henry Tottingham, Jan. 10, 1720/21.

74. Ibid.

75. *Rex v. Robert Wheeler et al.*, Stow, 1755, *Middlesex County Court of General Sessions Records*, 1748–1761; court order dated Oct. 1756, Middlesex County General Sessions, file papers, 1756 session.

76. *Joshua Parker v. Henry Allen, Job Carlisle, and James Maynard*, Middlesex Folio Collection, 1723.

77. The other two cases were similar. Richard Does, William Symms, and Benjamin Hale (identified as a worsted comber, mariner, and mariner, respectively, in their early to midtwenties) stole apples from the orchard of Elias Stone, broke into the house, and harassed Elias' wife, Abigail, and two guests. See *Rex v. Does, Symms, and Hale*, Charlestown, Dec. 1733, *Middlesex County Court of General Sessions Records*, 1723–1735. Robert Wheeler, in company with an unidentified group of youths, was accused of acting "in a riotous manner [at night] with prodigious hallowing and shouting and making a rout" and shooting a gun at the house of Nathan Whitney while his wife was inside. See *Rex v. Robert Wheeler et al.*, Stow, 1755, *Middlesex County Court of General Sessions Records*, 1748–1761.

Patterns of violent behavior by young men in other parts of Massachusetts show a similar development during this period. In November 1762, for example, Essex County youths Barnabas Dodge and Nathaniel Fairfield were presented, along with two other young men, for "riotously breaking the dwelling house" of William Vanncent and assaulting his wife. Presentment of Dodge, Dodge, Fairfield, and Snow, Nov. 1762, *Essex County Court of General Sessions Records*. In a separate incident, Barnabas Dodge, Nathan Fairfield, and three other youths pleaded guilty in April 1763 to "beating upon the dwelling of John Cogswell with stones, clubs, and poles," breaking the windows, and "putting him and his family in great terror." Entry of judgment against Brown, Quarles, White Fairfield, and Dodge, April 2, 1763, *Essex County Court of General Sessions Records*.

6. Manhood and Politics

1. George Lee Haskins, *Law and Authority in Early Massachusetts: A Study in Tradition and Design* (New York, 1960), pp. 73–74. After 1647, in Massachusetts male household heads over age twenty-four were also given a limited right to vote for local officials even if they were not church members. For Connecticut, see Richard Bushman, *From Puritan to Yankee: Character and the Social Order in Connecticut, 1690–1765* (Cambridge, Mass., 1967), esp. pp. 3–21.
2. Jonathan Mitchel, *Nehemiah on the Wall in Troublesome Times* (Cambridge, Mass., 1667), p. 7.
3. Peter Laslett, ed., *Patriarcha and Other Political Works of Sir Robert Filmer* (Oxford, 1949); Gordon Scochet, *Patriarchalism in Political Thought: The Authoritarian Family and Political Speculation and Attitudes, Especially in Seventeenth-Century England* (Oxford, 1975).
4. Locke's *First Treatise* was an extended denial of Filmer's *Patriarcha* and the idea that fatherhood and divine right could be the basis of sovereignty. Peter Laslett, ed., *Locke's "Two Treatises of Government" 1690: Two States* (Cambridge, 1952). Because early Americans (in New England and in the Chesapeake region) also employed the analogy between fatherhood and politics, Mary Beth Norton describes them as Filmerian. The general point is apt, but (perhaps because her book does not extend into the eighteenth century) Norton does not develop the differences between Puritan and non-Puritan political thought, which were important. Mary Beth Norton, *Founding Mothers and Fathers: Gendered Power and the Forming of American Society* (New York, 1996).
5. Mitchel, *Nehemiah on the Wall in Troublesome Times*, pp. 7–8, 20–21; William Hubbard, *The Happiness of a People in the Wisdom of Their Rulers* (Boston, 1676), pp. 2–9, 19–23; Thomas Shepard, *Eye-Salve, or a Watchword from Our Lord Jesus Christ* (May 1672), p. 40.
6. On the role of the covenant in organizing political and social relationships

in seventeenth-century New England, see Edmund S. Morgan, *The Puritan Family: Religion and Domestic Relations in Seventeenth-Century New England*, 2nd ed. (New York, 1966), chap. 1, and T. H. Breen, *The Character of a Good Ruler: A Study of Puritan Political Ideas in New England, 1630–1730* (New Haven, 1970). On the pressure to avoid dissent, see Haskins, *Law and Authority*, pp. 73–79, and Michael Zuckerman, *Peaceable Kingdoms: New England Towns in the Eighteenth Century* (New York, 1970). See also Edward M. Cook, Jr., *The Fathers of the Towns: Leadership and Community Structure in Eighteenth-Century New England* (Baltimore, 1976), arguing that town leaders did not simply inherit their positions as selectmen or deputies but worked their way into those positions through years of service in lesser jobs. The achievement of political status, it could be argued, was analogous to the achievement of manhood status, for males were not born into it but worked their way up in progressive stages.

7. John Oxenbridge, *New England Freemen Warned* (Cambridge, Mass., 1673); Breen, *The Character of a Good Ruler*, pp. 47–53.

8. Samuel Torrey, *An Exhortation unto Reformation* (Boston, 1674); Thomas Walley, *Sermon* (New Plymouth, 1670), p. 10; Samuel Danforth, *A Brief Recognition* (Cambridge, Mass., 1670), p. 13; John Higginson, *The Cause of God* (Cambridge, Mass., 1663), p. 1; Increase Mather, *A Discourse* (Boston, 1677), p. 56.

9. This argument is more fully developed in Richard Bushman, "Massachusetts Farmers and the Revolution," in Richard M. Jellison, ed., *Society, Freedom, and Conscience: The Coming of the Revolution in Virginia, Massachusetts, and New York* (New York, 1976), pp. 77–124.

10. Ibid., p. 101.

11. For statistics on casualties and property losses, see James Drake, *King Philip's War: Civil War in New England, 1675–1676* (Amherst, 1999), p. 168. See also Jill Lepore, *The Name of War: King Philip's War and the Origins of American Identity* (New York, 1998), who suggests that for ordinary colonists, "the loss of habitations became the central crisis of the war" (p. 77).

12. Breen, *The Character of a Good Ruler*, pp. 89–90, 137–139.

13. The most detailed description of these events can be found in Viola Barnes, *The Dominion of New England* (New York, 1960), pp. 174–211; see also Breen, *The Character of a Good Ruler*, pp. 138–147.

14. See, generally, Breen, *The Character of a Good Ruler*.

15. See, for example, Benjamin Wadsworth, *Rulers Feeding and Guiding Their People* (Boston, 1716), pp. 10–20; John Hancock, *Rulers Should Be Benefactors* (Boston, 1722), p. 9; John Barnard, *The Throne Established* (Boston, 1734), p. 20.

16. Joseph Belcher, *The Singular Happiness of Such Heads or Rulers as Are Able to Choose Out Their People's Way* (Boston, 1701), pp. 14, 23; Solomon Stoddard, *The Way for a People to Live Long in the Land That God hath Given Them* (Boston, 1703), p. 3; Hancock, *Rulers Should Be Benefactors,* pp. 14–15.

17. These different uses of the image of manhood were rooted in the same psychic experiences. As Richard Bushman has suggested, the experience of having had powerful fathers conditioned men to defer to government authority, but it may also have made them especially wary of fathers who overreached their power. Bushman, *From Puritan to Yankee,* pp. 20–21.

18. Benjamin Colman, *David's Dying Charge to the Rulers and People of Israel* (Boston, 1723), p. 26.

19. See Daniel Vickers, *Farmers and Fishermen: Two Centuries of Work in Essex County, Massachusetts* (Chapel Hill, 1994), pp. 245–246.

20. For the most thorough discussion of the currency issue in New England politics, see Margaret Ellen Newell, *From Dependency to Independence: Economic Revolution in Colonial New England* (Ithaca, N.Y., 1998).

21. For a discussion of these debates prior to the American Revolution, see J. E. Crowley, *This Sheba, Self: The Conceptualization of Economic Life in Eighteenth-Century America* (Baltimore, 1974); for the debates that followed the Revolution, see Drew R. McCoy, *The Elusive Republic: Political Economy in Jeffersonian America* (New York, 1980).

22. Newell, *From Dependency to Independence,* pp. 181–235.

23. One such elitist was the merchant Thomas Paine, whose son Robert would later have such a glittering social life, and who ridiculed the pretenses of ordinary tradesmen who wore silk stockings and allowed their wives to wear silks and satins for everyday social calls.

24. Paul Dudley, "Objections to the Bank of Credit Lately Projected at Boston" (1714), in Andrew McFarland Davis, ed., *Colonial Currency Reprints* (hereafter, *CCR*), vol. 1 (New York, 1910), pp. 239–261; Thomas Paine, "A Discourse Shewing the First Cause of the Streits of This Province . . . Is Its Extravagancy" (1721), *CCR,* vol. 2, p. 284; Anon., "An Addition to the Present Melancholy Circumstances of the Province Considered . . ." (1719), *CCR,* vol. 1, p. 373.

25. John Wise, "A Word of Comfort to a Melancholy Country" (1721), *CCR,* vol. 2, p. 177.

26. Oliver Noyes, "A Letter From a Gentleman, Containing some Remarks upon the Several Answers Given unto Mr. Colman . . ." (1720), *CCR,* vol. 2, p. 12; Anon., "Money the Sinews of Trade" (1731), *CCR,* vol. 2, pp. 443–444; and John Wise, "A Letter from Amicus Patriae to His Son" (1720), *CCR,* vol. 2, pp. 248–249.

27. John Colman, "The Distressed State of the Town of Boston, &c., Considered" (1720), *CCR*, vol. 1, p. 406; Wise, "A Word of Comfort," pp. 172, 173.

28. Elisha Cooke, "New News from Robinson Cruso's Island" (1720), *CCR*, vol. 2, p. 132; Edward Wigglesworth, "A Letter from One in the Country to His Friend in Boston" (1720), *CCR*, vol. 1, p. 430.

29. Newell, *From Dependency to Independence*, passim.

30. For the history of the Massachusetts opposition during the colonial period, see Bernard Bailyn, *The Origins of American Politics* (New York, 1968).

31. On the origins of radical Whig ideology, see J. G. A. Pocock, *The Machiavellian Moment: Florentine Political Thought and the Atlantic Republican Tradition* (Princeton, 1975), pp. 406–422. The narrative about the republic in past times was best expressed in James Harrington, "The Common Wealth of Oceana," in Charles Blitzer, ed., *Political Writings of James Harrington* (New York, 1955), pp. 43–54.

32. Quotations from John Trenchard and Thomas Gordon, *Cato's Letters* (1724), pp. 116–118, 178–181. For discussion, see Bailyn, *The Origins of American Politics*.

33. On the economic crisis in Boston during this period, see Gary Nash, *The Urban Crucible: Social Change, Political Consciousness, and the Origins of the American Revolution* (Cambridge, Mass., 1979) and G. B. Warden, "Inequality and Instability in Eighteenth-Century Boston: A Reappraisal," *Journal of Interdisciplinary History* 6, no. 4 (Spring 1976).

34. Edmund S. Morgan and Helen M. Morgan, *The Stamp Act Crisis: Prologue to Revolution*, rev. ed. (Chapel Hill, 1995), pp. 27–33.

35. Ibid., pp. 35–40.

36. Benjamin Church, *Liberty and Property Vindicated*, (Hartford, 1765), p. 596.

37. Samuel Sherwood, *To the Respectable Freemen of the English Colony of Connecticut* (New Haven, 1774), pp. viii, ix, 21.

38. Nathan Fiske, *The Importance of Righteousness to the Happiness and the Tendency of Oppression to the Misery of a People* (Boston, 1774), p. 18.

39. [The British Bostonian,] *The American Alarm* (Boston, 1773), p. 9

40. *Oppression: A Poem by an American* (London, 1765; repr. Boston, 1765), p. 4.

41. *Boston Gazette and Country Journal*, Aug. 12, 1765, quoted in Richard Bushman, *King and People in Provincial Massachusetts* (Chapel Hill, 1992), p. 195.

42. *A New Collection of Verses* (New Haven, 1765), pp. 3, 13.

43. Fiske, *The Importance of Righteousness*, p. 15.

44. Eliphalet Huntington, *The Freeman's Directory* (Hartford, 1768), pp. 4–14.

45. John Adams, "A Dissertation on the Canon and Feudal Law" (1765), in George Peek, Jr., ed., *The Political Writings of John Adams* (New York, 1954), pp. 12, 18, 16, 18.

46. For quotations, see Trenchard and Gordon, *Cato's Letters*, p. 88, 114. On the gender symbolism in radical Whig political thought, see J. G. A. Pocock, "The Mobility of Property and the Rise of Eighteenth-Century Sociology," in his *Virtue, Commerce, and History* (Cambridge, 1985), pp. 114–115; Ruth H. Bloch, "The Gendered Meanings of Virtue in Revolutionary America," *Signs* 13, no. 1 (1987): 37–58.

47. The analysis of house attacks as symbolic attacks on bodies is suggested by Robert St. George, *Conversing by Signs: Poetics of Implication in Colonial New England Culture* (Chapel Hill, 1998), chap. 3, esp. pp. 263–295.

48. Edmund S. Morgan and Helen M. Morgan, *The Stamp Act Crisis: Prologue to Revolution*, 3rd ed. (Chapel Hill, 1995); Crowley, *This Sheba, Self.*

49. *Boston Evening Post,* Nov. 16, 1767.

50. Edmund Morgan, "The Puritan Ethic and the American Revolution," *William and Mary Quarterly*, 3rd ser., 14 (Jan. 1967): 3–43, argues that the revolutionary boycott movement expressed an anticommercial suspicion of luxury and prosperity that were deeply embedded in the Puritan ethic. For the view that republicanism was also opposed to commerce, see Pocock, *The Machiavellian Moment;* McCoy, *The Elusive Republic.* Recent work by economic historians has cast doubt on the assumption that early New England's settlers were ever really anticommercial. See, e.g., Vickers, *Farmers and Fishermen,* as well as Richard Lyman Bushman, "Markets and Composite Farms in Early America," *William and Mary Quarterly*, 3rd ser., 55 (July 1998): 351–374.

51. *Boston Evening Post,* Dec. 7, 1767.

52. *A Discourse Delivered at the Dedication of the Tree of Liberty, July 25, 1768* (Providence, 1768), p. 4.

53. For a suggestive reinterpretation of the meaning of revolutionary boycotts, see T. H. Breen, "Narrative of Commercial Life: Consumption, Ideology, and Community on the Eve of the American Revolution," *William and Mary Quarterly*, 3rd ser., 50 (July 1993): 471–501.

54. Quotation from [Thomas Fitch et al.,] "Reasons Why the British Colonies . . . Should Not be Charged with Internal Taxes" (New Haven, 1764), in Bernard Bailyn, *Pamphlets of the American Revolution, 1750–1776,* vol. 1 (Cambridge, Mass., 1965), p. 393; for other examples of warnings about slavery, see Stephen Hopkins, "The Rights of the Colonies Examined" (Providence, 1765), ibid., p. 522; Oxenbridge Thacher, "The Sentiments of a British American" (Boston, 1764), ibid., p. 490; James Otis, "The Rights of the Colonies Asserted and Proved" (Boston, 1764), ibid., p. 434.

55. Richard D. Brown, *Revolutionary Politics in Massachusetts: The Boston Com-*

mittee of Correspondence and the Towns, 1772–1774 (Cambridge, Mass., 1970), pp. 178–200.

56. Ibid., pp. 23–27; Robert Gross, *The Minutemen and Their World* (New York, 1976), pp. 40–41.

57. Bushman, *King and People,* pp. 196–197.

58. John Hancock, *An Oration* (Boston, 1774), p. 20; [The British Bostonian,] *The American Alarm* (Boston, 1773), p. 24; [Charles Chauncy,] *A Letter to a Friend* (Boston, 1774), p. 25; Samuel Sherwood, *To the Respectable Freemen of the English Colony of Connecticut,* (New Haven, 1774), p. vi.

59. *The Votes and Proceedings of the Freeholders . . . of the Town of Boston . . . the 5th and 18th days of November, 1773* (Boston, 1773), p. 5; *The American Alarm,* pp. 11, 16; Ebenezer Baldwin, "Appendix, Stating the Heavy Grievances the Colonies Labour Under," in Samuel Sherwood, *A Sermon, Containing Scriptural Instructions to Civil Rulers,* (New Haven, 1774), p. 78.

60. *The American Alarm,* p. 16, 17; Sherwood, *A Sermon, Containing Scriptural Instructions to Civil Rulers,* p. 31.

61. For discussions of these events, see Gross, *The Minutemen and Their World,* pp. 53–57; Brown, *Revolutionary Politics in Massachusetts,* pp. 212–219; and John Brooke, *The Heart of the Commonwealth: Society and Political Culture in Worcester County, Massachusetts, 1713–1861* (Cambridge, 1989), pp. 144–148.

Epilogue

1. Nancy Cott, "Divorce and the Changing Status of Women in Eighteenth-Century Massachusetts," *William and Mary Quarterly* 3rd ser. 33 (1976); Jan Lewis, "The Republican Wife: Virtue and Seduction in the Early Republic," *William and Mary Quarterly* 3rd ser., 44 (1987): 691–721; Jay Fliegelman, *Prodigals and Pilgrims: The American Revolution against Patriarchal Authority, 1750–1800* (Cambridge, 1982), pp. 123–131.

2. Winifred Barr Rothenberg, *From Market-Places to a Market Economy: The Transformation of Rural Massachusetts, 1750–1850* (Chicago, 1992); see also Daniel Vickers, *Farmers and Fishermen, Two Centuries of Work in Essex County, Massachusetts* (Chapel Hill, 1994), pp. 290–297, 309–323.

3. Joyce Appleby, *Inheriting the Revolution: The First Generation of Americans* (Cambridge, Mass., 2000), p. 64 and accompanying citations.

4. Ruth Bloch, "American Feminine Ideals in Transition: The Rise of the Moral Mother, 1785–1815," *Feminist Studies* 4 (1978): 101–126; Mary P. Ryan, *Cradle of the Middle Class: The Family in Oneida County, New York, 1790–1865* (Cambridge, England, 1981), pp. 66–69; Stephen M. Frank, *Life with Father: Parenthood and Masculinity in the Nineteenth-Century American North* (Baltimore, 1998), p. 33.

5. For the ideology of domesticity and the idea that home and family were a separate sphere, see Nancy F. Cott, *The Bonds of Womanhood: "Women's Sphere" in New England, 1780–1835* (New Haven, 1977). On maternal ideals, see Bloch, "American Feminine Ideals in Transition." On nineteenth-century men's recollections of their mothers, see Frank, *Life with Father,* pp. 133, 142.

6. Frank, *Life with Father,* pp. 58–60.

7. Ibid., pp. 67–72.

8. E. Anthony Rotundo, *American Manhood: Transformations in Masculinity from the Revolution to the Modern Era* (New York, 1993), pp. 31–55.

9. This discussion draws primarily on Frank, *Life with Father,* pp. 58–64, 67–82, and 148.

10. Ibid., pp. 144–147.

11. Rotundo, *American Manhood,* pp. 62–63.

12. Ibid., pp. 75–91.

13. Ibid., pp. 109–128. For Anglo-American courtship ideals in the nineteenth century, see Ellen Rothman, *Hands and Hearts: A History of Courtship in America* (New York, 1984), and Karen Lystra, *Searching the Heart: Women, Men, and Romantic Love in Nineteenth-Century America* (New York, 1989).

14. See for discussion, Lewis, "The Republican Wife," and Cathy Davidson, *Revolution and the Word: The Rise of the Novel in America* (New York, 1986).

15. Daniel Scott Smith and Michael S. Hindus, "Premarital Pregnancy in America, 1640–1971: An Overview and Interpretation," *Journal of Interdisciplinary History* 5 (Spring 1975): 537–570; Daniel Scott Smith, "The Dating of the American Sexual Revolution: Evidence and Interpretation," in Michael Gordon, ed., *The American Family in Socio-Historical Perspective,* 2nd ed. (New York, 1978), pp. 426–438.

16. Lystra, *Searching the Heart,* pp. 166–185.

17. Rotundo, *American Manhood,* pp. 111–116.

18. Ibid., p. 22.

19. Ibid., pp. 105–108.

20. Ibid., pp. 129–146, 176–177.

21. Cornelia Dayton, *Women before the Bar: Gender, Law, and Society in Connecticut, 1639–1789* (Chapel Hill, 1995), pp. 107–108; Cott, "Divorce and the Changing Status of Women," pp. 592–603.

22. G. J. Barker-Benfield, *The Horrors of the Half-Known Life: Male Attitudes toward Women and Sexuality in Nineteenth-Century America* (New York, 1976), pp. 8–18.

23. Ryan, *Cradle of the Middle Class,* pp. 165–179, 183–185.

24. See Rotundo, *American Manhood,* pp. 174–178.

Index

Adams, John, 40–41, 91, 161
Africans, as non-manly, 17, 129, 136–137
age, as component in defining manhood, 12–13
Allen, Joseph, 133
Andros, Edmund, 147, 151, 165
assaults, male-on-male: measuring incidence of, 125; pattern of prosecutions for, 125, 132, 140–141; justifications for, by mature males, 125–134; against constables, 132–134; justifications for, by youths, 134–138, 144; attacks on houses, 135–138, 144; in taverns, 141–144
autonomous manhood: in early New England, 9–10; ideal of, in 19th century, 171, 176–179

babies: birth of, 18, 19; fathers' and mothers' relationships with, 19–21
bachelors, 97
Baldwin, Ebenezer, 167
Bangs, Benjamin, 86–87
Barnard, John, 23, 24, 25, 33, 53, 80
bastardy, 85
Belcher, Gill, 85
Belcher, Joseph, 25, 152
Belcher family: Andrew, 52; Jonathan, 52
Belknap, Jeremy, 32
Berry, Thomas, 60, 61
Bigelow, John, 132
Blanchard family: Abraham, 122–123, 130; George, 122; Joshua, 122–123, 130; Samuel, 120, 121–124, 127, 130
Blessington, Charles, 139
Blood, Robert, 132–133
Boston Tea Party, 165

Bowen, Ashley, 75–76
boycotts, 162–165, 169, 219n38
boyhood: vs. manhood, 10; as new stage of childhood, 27–35
boys: as non-men, 13, 14, 17; fathers' roles in rearing, 14, 30–31; after toddler stage, 22–24; clothing, 27–29; socialization by fathers or male mentors, 29–32, 33–36, 42–45; education, 32–33
Bradford, William, 5
Bredeen, Elizabeth, 113
breeching, 27–29
Brock, John, 56
Bullard, Jacob, 132
bundling, 87
bureaucrats, as effeminate, 158, 160–162
Burnham, Jonathan, 74–75

Chamberlain, John, 142
Chamberlain, Thomas, 126
Chamberlin family: Experience, 115–116, 118; Jacob, 116
Charles II, 150, 151
Chauncy, Charles, 166
Cheever, Israel, 96
child care: during infancy, 19–20; during illnesses, 24–26
childhood, as dependent, emotional, and unproductive, 21–22, 26, 28–29, 30–31, 32, 42, 43, 44
child rearing: in 17th and 18th centuries, 20–24, 27–35, 37–44; in 19th century, 172–173
children's clothing, 22, 27–29
Chope, Francis, 126–127
Clap, Roger, 53

239